The *Collected* Poetry of
Nikki Giovanni

Also by Nikki Giovanni

Chronology and notes by Virginia C. Fowler

WILLIAM MORROW

An Imprint of HarperCollinsPublishers

The *Collected* Poetry of
Nikki Giovanni

1968–1998

Contents ▪

Black Feeling Black Talk

Black Judgement

Re: Creation

My House

The Women and the Men

Cotton Candy on a Rainy Day

Those Who Ride the Night Winds

Occasional Poems

The *Collected* Poetry of
Nikki Giovanni

Introduction

"We cannot possibly leave it to history as a discipline," Nikki Giovanni writes in an essay, "nor to sociology nor science nor economics to tell the story of our people."[1] Instead, she continues, that story must be told by writers. To read through this volume of Giovanni's poetry is indeed to read "the story" of the last thirty years of American life, as that life has been lived, observed, and reflected about by a racially conscious Black woman. The "Black is beautiful" slogan of the 1960s is given joyous and vivid embodiment in a poem like "Beautiful Black Men," for example, which celebrates the arrogant new strut of Black men "walking down the street." At the same time, we are reminded by a work like "Woman Poem" that the new racial pride was not always as liberating for Black women as it was for Black men because "it's a sex object if you're pretty/and no love/ or love and no sex if you're fat/get back fat black woman be a mother/grandmother strong thing but not woman."

The rage felt by so many Black Americans at America's persistent and destructive racism is registered in poems like the fine "Great Pax Whitie," which includes allusions to the assassinations of John F. Kennedy and Malcolm X. The topicality of many of Giovanni's poems grounds them in the historical moment in which they were written, even as the emotional and intellectual responses to specific events transcend the particular and become universal. Although such topicality is frequently disparaged by literary critics, it is central to Giovanni's conception of poetry and the poet. "Poetry," she has written, "is but a reflection of the moment. The universal comes from the particular" (*Sacred Cows*, p. 57). Further, she has stated that "I have even gone so far as to think one of the duties of this profession is to be topical, to try to say something about the times in which we are living and how we both view and evaluate them"

[1]*Sacred Cows . . . and Other Edibles* (New York: William Morrow, 1988), p. 61; hereafter cited in text.

(*Sacred Cows* pp. 32–33). This conception of the poet and poetry is consistent with the aesthetic theories of the Black Arts Movement, from which Giovanni was one of the most popular and controversial young writers to emerge; these writers sought to create, in the words of Amiri Baraka, "an art that would actually reflect black life and its history and legacy of resistance and struggle!"[2]

Giovanni herself connects the importance of topicality in poetry to the tradition of the African *griot*; like the *griots*, she writes, Black American poets "have traveled the length and breadth of the planet singing our song of the news of the day, trying to bring people closer to the truth" (*Sacred Cows*, pp. 33–34). Her poems thus often speak directly about specific events or people, giving expression to the emotions they provoke and disclosing the realities and truths that underlie them—as she sees them. Giovanni does not believe, however, that the poet is a "god," or that the poet has visionary powers beyond those of people who are not poets or writers. She also denies the power of poetry to change the world; as she has stated, "I don't think that writers ever changed the mind of anybody. I think we always preach to the saved."[3] What, then, is poetry? And why does she write it?

The answers to those questions are inextricably tied to Giovanni's consciousness of her identity as a Black American and to her recognition of the struggle of Black Americans to find a voice that would express themselves and their realities: "The African slave bereft of his gods, his language, his drums searched his heart for a new voice. Under sun and lash the African sought meaning in life on earth and the possibility of life hereafter. They shuffled their feet, clapped their hands, gathered a collective audible breath to release the rhythms of the heart. We affirmed in those dark days of chattel through the White Knights of Emancipation

[2] Amiri Baraka, "Foreword: The Wailer," in *Visions of a Liberated Future: Black Arts Movement Writings by Larry Neal*, ed. Michael Schwartz (New York: Thunder's Mouth Press, 1989), p. x.

[3] Arlene Elder, "A MELUS Interview: Nikki Giovanni," *MELUS* 9 (Winter 1982): 61–75; reprinted in *Conversations with Nikki Giovanni*, ed. Virginia C. Fowler (Jackson: University Press of Mississippi, 1992), p. 126.

that all we had was a human voice to guide us and a human voice to answer the call" (*Sacred Cows*, p. 52.) Giovanni's poetry (as well as her prose) represents her own efforts to give voice to her vision of truth and reality as honestly as she can because, she has said, "the only thing you bring . . . is your honesty."[4] The "truth" her poetry speaks, then, is always the truth as she honestly sees it, and this honesty of expression is what, for her, determines that her poetry is, in fact, art: "I like to think that if truth has any bearing on art, my poetry and prose is art because it's truthful." (*Sacred Cows*, p. 66). Articulating through poetry her vision of reality is the equivalent of the slaves' recognition that their survival depended on their finding "a human voice to guide us and a human voice to answer the call." The loneliness inherent in the human condition is, Giovanni has said, assuaged by art, for "we are less lonely when we connect," and "Art is a connection. I like being a link. I hope the chain will hold" (*Sacred Cows*, p. 58).

The development of a unique and distinctive *voice* has been perhaps the single most important achievement of Giovanni's career. Although even the most superficial perusal of this volume will reveal many changes in tone, in ideas, and in subjects throughout Giovanni's writing career, what remains consistent— even while we watch it grow in maturity and confidence—is the voice speaking to us from the page. Many readers of Giovanni's poetry actually come to her written work after having heard her read from it. And in part because Giovanni has literally taken her poetry "to the people" through hundreds of public lectures and readings over the last thirty-five years, her spoken voice is immediately recognizable by countless people. Seeking to simulate spoken language, the poetry itself possesses distinctive oral qualities. Because it is always intended to be read aloud, its full impact can frequently be felt only through hearing it. In her poetry Giovanni attempts to continue African and African-American oral traditions, and she seems in many ways to have less reverence for the written word than for the spoken.

[4]Ibid., p. 128.

Often, for example, Giovanni's poetry draws our attention to the limitations and artificiality of language and of language shaped into what we call "art." In "My House," for example, the speaker repeatedly asks us "does this really sound/like a silly poem?" until she finally and explicitly asserts that "english isn't a good language/to express emotion through/mostly i imagine because people/try to speak english instead/of trying to speak through it." Written language, the poem suggests, becomes a barrier to expression and understanding when we treat it as an end in itself rather than as a means to an end. The aesthetic assumption underlying this conception of language is obviously far removed from notions of "art for art's sake." Unless it is connected to the realities of life, art, for Giovanni, lacks both meaning and value.

One of Giovanni's most explicit, though lighthearted, treatments of the subject of language and poetry is found, appropriately, in "A Poem for Langston Hughes." This playful love poem represents one of the few instances in her poetry in which Giovanni consciously attempts to employ the style of another writer. The poem's rhythms, rhyme, and images collectively evoke the essence of Langston Hughes, whose poetry and career have significantly influenced Giovanni's own. Drawing almost nonsensically on many of the formal elements of poetry, the speaker of the poem states:

> metaphor has its point of view
> allusions and illusion . . . too
>
> meter . . . verse . . . classical . . . free
> poems are what you do to me

Poetry, Giovanni here suggests, cannot be reduced to its component parts or rhetorical devices, for poetry is not removed from life but expressive and experiential.

Giovanni's desire, as she states it metaphorically at the end of "Cotton Candy On A Rainy Day," is "To put a three-dimensional picture / On a one-dimensional surface." As a poet who equates the survival of her people with their ability to use the only thing left them, their "human voice," Giovanni must rely on language to create written poems with the immediacy and impact of the spoken word, poems that, like such Black musical forms as the spirituals, the blues, and jazz, communicate directly to a reader/listener. Thus, she has said that she does not polish or revise the individual words or lines of a poem, but instead will rework the entire poem, for "a poem is a way of capturing a moment. . . . A poem's got to be a single stroke, and I make it the best I can because it's going to live. I feel if only one thing of mine is to survive, it's at least got to be an accurate picture of what I saw. I want my camera and film to record what my eye and my heart saw."[5] The poem is, in many ways, a kind of *gestalt*.

Giovanni frequently writes as though she wishes to distinguish her own poems from the artifice we might normally associate with poetry. Because she sees poetry as "the culture of a people,"[6] she seems to believe that it has an urgency and significance we are not accustomed to expecting from it. A recent poem in praise of Black women provides a good example of Giovanni's strategy of insisting that we see the "single stroke" of meaning. Her strategy in "Stardate Number 18628.190," a poem written for the twenty-fifth anniversary issue of *Essence* magazine, is to repeat, in three of the poem's five stanzas, that what we are reading is not art, but something else. The poem opens and closes, in fact, with the assertion that "This is not a poem." What, then, is it? The entire piece endeavors to identify and represent itself as the Black women whom it in fact celebrates. It accumulates images evocative of the many everyday activities, extraordinary accomplishments, and modes of being of Black women, "the Daughters of the Diaspora." These Daughters have given not a "poem" but "a summer quilt," a metaphor used by Giovanni elsewhere, as well as by numerous contemporary women writers. In "Stardate," Giovanni employs the

[5]Claudia Tate, *Black Women Writers At Work* (New York: Continuum, 1983); reprinted in Fowler, *Conversations with Nikki Giovanni*, p. 146.
[6]Nikki Giovanni, *Gemini: An Extended Autobiographical Statement on My First Twenty-Five Years of Being a Black Poet* (1971; reprint, New York: Penguin, 1985), p. 95.

quilt as a metaphor of family history and family love; the pieces of the quilt are scraps of cloth, each of which reminds the speaker of an event and a person in her family's history, including "grandmother's wedding dress," "grandpappa's favorite Sunday tie," "the baby who died," and Mommy's pneumonia. An appropriate symbol of the transformative powers by which Black Americans have resisted the oppression enacted upon them, the quilt represents the Black woman's creation of beauty out of discarded, worthless bits of material. Even more, however, the history evoked by the quilt and the love and human connection found in that history are what distinguish the quilt from "art": "This does not hang from museum walls . . . nor will it sell for thousands . . . This is here to keep me warm." Unlike the "art" collected in museums, which may have great monetary value but is, the lines imply, cold and sterile, the quilt's value is based on its warming, life-sustaining, and life-nurturing powers.

The opening words of the third stanza offer a variation on the assertion that "This is not a poem." Beginning with the claim that "This is not a sonnet," the third stanza delineates the music created and sung by Black women, from the spirituals to rap. Significantly, the stanza ends with the reiterated denial that it is a sonnet and the counterclaim that it is instead "the truth of the beauty that the only authentic voice of Planet Earth comes from the black soil . . . tilled and mined . . . by the Daughters of the Diaspora." Perhaps because the sonnet is frequently regarded in Western literary tradition as one of the most elegant poetic forms, mastery of which is often expected of aspiring writers, Giovanni seizes on it in order to juxtapose its artifice to the authenticity of the Black woman's voice. What constitute the "authenticity" of that voice, the poem suggests, are the comfort, support, celebration, encouragement, unselfishness, and prayerfulness that it has lifted itself to speak and sing. In other words, authenticity is a function of human conduct, of ethical behavior. The Black woman's voice is authentic because, as the poem concludes, the Black woman has made "the world a hopeful . . . loving place." Such authenticity of voice is for Giovanni clearly superior to the aesthetic form in which that voice might cast its words. Further, while the sonnet may be a poetic form prized in Western literary traditions, it is not a form capable of expressing Black realities; the Black woman's "authentic" voice has created its own forms through which to sing and speak.

Giovanni's insistence that aesthetic value emerges from and is dependent upon moral value surfaces not only in this poem from the 1990s, but in the poems throughout this volume. It is a corollary to her equally consistent belief that the poet writes not from experience but from empathy: "You try as a writer to put yourself into the other person's position. Empathy. Empathy is everything because we can't experience everything. Experience is important, but empathy is the key."[7] Many of Giovanni's poems, both early and more recent, make obvious use of empathy, including such pieces as "Poem For Aretha," "Poem For A Lady Whose Voice I Like," "Poem For Angela Yvonne Davis," and "Linkage." But for Giovanni, empathy is not simply a tool for poetically appropriating lives and experiences removed from the world inhabited by the poet; on the contrary, empathy is key to human life and understanding because it is key to human connection (one of the primary purposes of art as she sees it). Empathy enables us to collapse the dualistic structures that polarize our world into "us" and "them." Not surprisingly, many of Giovanni's poems attribute a powerful capacity for empathy to Black women, who "wipe away our own grief . . . to give comfort to those beyond comfort" ("Hands: For Mother's Day"). The Black woman's unselfish willingness to empathize with others constitutes one of the sources of her authenticity of voice.

As one reads through the poems in this volume, one cannot avoid recognizing that race and gender are inextricably intertwined constituents of Giovanni's thematic concerns. The significance of individual women in the poet's life is evident from the outset of her career—teachers, friends, her mother, and her grandmother are represented in her poems as crucial to her sense of self and well-being. In her mature poems, especially in those from *My House* for-

---

[7]Virginia C. Fowler, "An Interview with Nikki Giovanni" in Fowler, *Conversations with Nikki Giovanni*, p. 202.

ward, Giovanni demonstrates increasing awareness of the extent to which gender is a problematic component of identity for women. As she says in "A Poem Off Center," "maybe i shouldn't feel sorry / for myself / but the more i understand women / the more i do." Even Giovanni's early militant poems remark the subordinate role women were expected to play in the "revolution." Other early poems take note of the sexist treatment to which the successful Black woman is apt to be subjected by the Black man. In "Poem For A Lady Whose Voice I Like," for example, the male speaker attributes Lena Horne's success to her physical attractiveness and the attention bestowed on her by white people, rather than to her abilities and talent as a singer; his final exasperated charge is that "you pretty full of yourself ain't chu," to which she replies, "show me someone not full of herself / and i'll show you an empty person."

Countless poems play variations on this theme, reiterating the idea that the position women are expected to occupy—solely because of their gender—leaves them "empty" in one way or another. Expected to "sit and wait / cause i'm a woman" ("All I Gotta Do"), women live in a world.

made up of baby clothes	to be washed
food	to be cooked
lullabies	to be sung
smiles	to be glowed
hair	to be plaited
ribbons	to be bowed
coffee	to be drunk
books	to be read
tears	to be cried
loneliness	to be borne
	"[Untitled]"

Expected to devote their lives to the needs of others, women do not necessarily receive any gratitude for such devotion, but may actually be punished for it. As Giovanni says in "Boxes,"

everybody says how strong
i am

only black women
and white men
are truly free
they say

it's not difficult to see
how stupid they are

i would not reject
my strength
though its source
is not choice
but responsibility

Variations on the idea expressed in the final stanza may be found frequently in Giovanni's poetry.

While many of Giovanni's poems explore and describe women's lives, others celebrate women—Black women in particular—as a way of providing an antidote to the slurs so often cast upon them. None offers a more audacious celebration than the enormously popular "Ego Tripping (there may be a reason why)." Without question one of the most powerful celebrations of the Black woman ever written, the poem attributes to her the creation of all the great civilizations of the world. Far from being bound to a narrow and confined existence, the speaker asserts, in the poem's famous concluding words, that "I . . . can fly / like a bird in the sky. . . ." Although "Ego Tripping" accumulates outrageous claims to power ("the filings from my fingernails are / semiprecious jewels," "The hair from my head thinned and gold was laid / across three continents"), it also accurately reflects Giovanni's frankly chauvinistic belief that whatever good we find in our world is attributable to the Black woman. Characteristically, in this poem and many others (as well as in her prose), Giovanni urges that we not be ashamed of an aspect of identity over which we have no control—in this case, gender—just because the world in which we live uses it as a basis for oppression. Although she does not deny the reality of the oppression, she rejects the notion that the victim is responsible for her own oppression. Instead, in what is a frequent gesture, she embraces her gender and her race, and, in poems like "Ego Tripping," offers her own definition and description of the Black woman. She once commented, in fact, that "Ego Tripping" was written in opposition to the gender roles typically taught to little girls; it "was really written for little girls. . . . I really got tired of hearing all of the little girls' games, such as Little Sally Walker."[8]

The speaker in "Poem (For Nina)" similarly emphasizes the importance of embracing her racial identity. If the white world cannot see beyond the color of her skin, and tries to oppress her because of it, then she will embrace in order to celebrate that component of her identity:

> if i am imprisoned in my skin let it be a dark world
> with a deep bass walking a witch doctor to me for
> spiritual consultation
> let my world be defined by my skin and the color of
>   my people
> for we   spirit to spirit   will embrace
> this world

The centrality of race and gender in Giovanni's poetry is evident throughout this volume, which brings together all of the poetry she published between 1968 and 1999. Especially in her later poetry, African American history becomes an important focus. A notable example is the powerful "But Since You Finally Asked," which was written to commemorate the tenth anniversary of the slave memorial at Mount Vernon. The initial public reading

[8]Barbara Reynolds, *And Still We Rise: Interviews with 50 Black Role Models* (Washington: Gannet New Media Services, 1988), p. 94.

of this poem at the Mount Vernon ceremony was accompanied by a deluge of rain, and to the participants gathered on the slope overlooking the Potomac River nature itself seemed to join in mourning the "many thousand gone." Giovanni's poem recounts the history of African people brought to America in chains, who were never "asked . . . what we thought of Jamestown," never told "'Welcome' . . . 'You're Home'." The poem juxtaposes the ideals expressed in the Declaration of Independence and the Constitution to the realities of life for Black Americans, the only Americans, the poem suggests, who have actually believed in and tried to practice those ideals—which were never intended to include them. Brutally enslaved, denied their humanity, erased from history, Black Americans "didn't write a constitution . . . we live one." Echoing words from the Negro National Anthem ("Lift Every Voice and Sing"), Giovanni concludes the poem with a celebration of the courage, integrity, and generosity of her people.

This poem makes clear why Nikki Giovanni continues to be so well loved: she is the definitive "poet of the people." The significant body of work collected here will allow readers to follow her development as a poet and a thinker. More than anything, this collection dramatizes Giovanni's dynamism, her refusal to continue journeying down familiar poetic paths, her commitment to growth and change. To borrow from her own words in "Stardate," we might well say that this is not just a collection of poems but "a celebration of the road we have traveled . . . [and] a prayer . . . for the roads yet to come!"

—VIRGINIA C. FOWLER
July 1995

Chronology

1943 ▩ Born Yolande Cornelia Giovanni, Jr., on June 7 in
Knoxville General Hospital, Knoxville, Tennessee, the daughter of
Yolande Cornelia (1919–) and Jones "Gus" Giovanni (1914–82),
and the sister of Gary Ann (1940–), aged two years, nine
months. Knoxville is the home of Giovanni's maternal
grandparents, John Brown (1887–1962) and Emma Louvenia
Watson (1898–1967). In August the family of four moves to
Cincinnati, Ohio, home of her father, where her parents take jobs
as houseparents at Glenview School, a home for Black boys. The
children and their mother make frequent visits to their
grandparents' home in Knoxville throughout their childhood. At
some point during Giovanni's first three years, her sister—for
reasons no one really understands—begins calling her Nikki.

1947 ▩ The family leaves Glenview and moves briefly to
Woodlawn, a suburb of Cincinnati. Giovanni's father teaches at
South Woodlawn School and works evenings and weekends at the
YMCA. Because Woodlawn has no elementary school for Black
children, Gary lives with her father's half brother and his wife,
Bill and Gladys Atkinson, in Columbus, Ohio, where she attends
second grade.

1948 ▩ The family moves to a house on Burns Avenue in
nearby Wyoming, another suburb of Cincinnati. Giovanni begins
kindergarten at Oak Avenue School, where her teacher is Mrs.
Elizabeth Hicks; her sister enters third grade there.

1949–52 ▩ Giovanni completes the first, second, and third
grades at Oak Avenue School, while her sister completes the
fourth, fifth, and sixth grades. In 1951 her mother accepts a
third-grade teaching position at St. Simon's School, an all-Black
Episcopal school in the nearby Black suburb of Lincoln Heights.

1952 ▓ Gus Giovanni makes a down payment on a home at 1167 Jackson Street in Lincoln Heights and moves his family there. Giovanni's parents had hoped to build a home in a new all-Black housing development called Hollydale. But after several years they realize that obtaining a loan is not going to be possible in the foreseeable future; racist lending practices simply cannot be circumvented. With the money he makes from selling his stock in this venture, her father is able to make the down payment on the Jackson Street house. During World War II, Lincoln Heights had been known as the Valley Homes, affordable housing for employees of General Electric, but with the economic boom following the war, white residents began moving to other suburbs. The U.S. government sold the homes to a corporation of Black citizens, and Lincoln Heights was born.

Giovanni enters fourth grade at St. Simon's School. Her sister enrolls in seventh grade at South Woodlawn School, where their father teaches.

1953–57 ▓ Giovanni continues her schooling at St. Simon's School, where she completes the fifth through eighth grades. Her seventh-grade teacher, Sister Althea Augustine, is an important influence on her and ultimately becomes a lifelong friend. Her sister enters Wyoming High School as one of the three Black students who desegregate the previously all-white school. In 1955, when Emmett Till is killed, Gary's teacher makes the comment "He got what he deserved." Gary and her friend Beverly Waugh walk out in protest. Eventually the school makes an official apology. Also during this period, Giovanni's father quits his teaching job to take a better-paying position as a probation officer in the Hamilton County Juvenile Detention Office. Through his contacts in that position, he is able to help Giovanni's mother obtain a position with the Hamilton County Welfare Department, which carries better wages than the one hundred dollars a month she has been earning at St. Simon's School.

1957–58 ▓ Giovanni enters the ninth grade at Lockland High School, an all-Black school. Her sister's negative experiences in desegregating Wyoming High School make her and her parents uninterested in having her try to attend one of the white high schools. Gary leaves home to attend Central State University. Meanwhile, the tensions between her parents are difficult for Giovanni to handle. So in 1958 she asks her grandmother Watson if she can come to Knoxville for the summer. Once there, she tells her grandparents her real plan: to stay with them and attend school in Knoxville.

1958–60 ▓ Giovanni enrolls in Austin High School, where her grandfather taught Latin for many years. Her grandmother, who is involved in numerous charitable and political endeavors, becomes an increasing influence on her, teaching her the importance of helping others and fighting injustice. When a demonstration is planned to protest segregated dining facilities at downtown Rich's department store, her grandmother cheerfully volunteers Nikki. In high school Giovanni has two influential teachers: her French teacher, Mrs. Emma Stokes, and her English teacher, Miss Alfredda Delaney. They persuade her to apply for early admission to college. Meanwhile, Gary has a son, Christopher, in April 1959. That summer Giovanni returns to Cincinnati to take care of Christopher, who is living with her parents.

1960–61 ▓ Giovanni goes to Nashville to enroll in Fisk University—her grandfather's alma mater—as an early entrant. Academics present no problem to her, but she is unprepared for the conservatism of this small Black college. Almost from the outset she runs into trouble with the dean of women, Ann Cheatam, whose ideas about the behavior and attitudes appropriate to a Fisk woman are diametrically opposed to Giovanni's ideas about the intellectual seriousness and political awareness appropriate to a college student. She goes back to

Knoxville to spend Thanksgiving with her grandparents—without obtaining permission from Dean Cheatam. To compound the problem, when she visits Dean Cheatam the Monday after Thanksgiving, she articulates her contempt for the rules. Not surprisingly, she is expelled on February 1. She goes back to Cincinnati, where she lives with her parents. Her grandmother, far from uttering any reproach, travels to Nashville to meet with Dean Cheatam and later writes a letter protesting her decision.

1961–63 ■ Giovanni lives with her parents in Cincinnati, takes care of her nephew, and works at Walgreens. She also takes courses at the University of Cincinnati and does volunteer work with children and parents among her mother's clients. Her parents move into a better house at 1168 Congress Avenue, just a few blocks from the house on Jackson. In March 1962, her grandfather Watson dies, and she drives her mother and nephew to Knoxville for the funeral.

1964–66 ■ Giovanni's grandmother Louvenia is obliged to move from her home at 400 Mulvaney Street, which is sacrificed to "urban renewal." Although her new house on Linden Avenue is nice, it lacks the accumulated memories of the old house, which Giovanni has come to regard as home. Giovanni travels to Fisk to explore the possibility of reenrolling. She discovers that Dean Cheatam is gone and that her replacement, Blanche McConnell Cowan ("Jackie") is completely different. Dean Cowan purges the file Dean Cheatam collected on Giovanni and encourages her to come back, which she does in the fall of 1964. Giovanni does well academically and becomes a leader on campus. She majors in history but takes writers' workshops with the writer in residence John Oliver Killens. In spring 1966, at the First Writers Conference at Fisk, she meets Dudley Randall, who will soon launch Broadside Press; Robert Hayden; Melvin Tolson; Margaret Walker; and LeRoi Jones, now Amiri Baraka. She edits a student literary journal (titled *Élan*) and reestablishes the campus chapter of SNCC (Student Nonviolent Coordinating Committee). She publishes an essay in *Negro Digest* on gender questions in the movement.

1967 ■ Having completed her undergraduate coursework in December, Giovanni moves back to Cincinnati and rents her own apartment. She receives her B.A. in history, with honors, on January 28. Her grandmother Louvenia Watson dies on March 8, just two days before she was to have come for a visit. Giovanni drives her mother, sister, and nephew to Knoxville for the funeral, marking the most significant loss of her life. She turns to writing as a refuge and produces most of the poems that will make up her first volume, *Black Feeling Black Talk*. She edits *Conversation*, a Cincinnati revolutionary art journal. She attends the Detroit Conference of Unity and Art, where she meets H. Rap Brown (1943–), now Jamil Abdullah Al-Amin, and other movement leaders. She organizes a Black Arts Festival, Cincinnati's first, for which she adapts and directs Virginia Hamilton's *Zeely* for the stage. Moves to Wilmington, Delaware and, with the help of a Ford Foundation fellowship, enrolls in the University of Pennsylvania's School of Social Work. Works at a People's Settlement House in Wilmington as a part of her graduate studies.

1968 ■ Giovanni borrows money to publish her first volume of poetry, *Black Feeling Black Talk*. She drops out of the University of Pennsylvania but continues working at the settlement house. Continues writing poems at a prodigious rate. Goes to Atlanta for the funeral of Martin Luther King, Jr., who was assassinated on April 4. Receives a grant from the National Endowment for the Arts. Moves to New York City, where she begins almost immediately to attract attention. Enrolls in an M.F.A. program at Columbia University's School of Fine Arts. At the end of the year, uses money from sales of *Black Feeling Black Talk* and a grant from the Harlem Arts Council to privately publish her second volume of poetry, *Black Judgement;* Broadside Press offers to distribute it.

1969   ■   Giovanni teaches at Queens College. She has a
Sunday afternoon book party (to promote *Black Judgement*) at the
old Birdland jazz club, which attracts hundreds of people and
makes the next day's metro section of *The New York Times*. Gains
increasing attention from the media and begins receiving
invitations to read and speak. In April *The New York Times*
features her in an article entitled "Renaissance in Black Poetry
Expresses Anger." The *Amsterdam News* names her one of the ten
"most admired Black women." Regularly publishes book reviews
in *Negro Digest*. Travels to Cincinnati for Labor Day weekend and
gives birth to Thomas Watson Giovanni, her only child. Returns
to New York and begins teaching at Livingston College of Rutgers
University; frequently makes the commute with the struggling
writer Toni Cade Bambara (1939–95).

1970   ■   Giovanni edits and privately publishes *Night Comes
Softly,* one of the earliest anthologies of poetry by Black women; it
includes poems by new and relatively unknown writers as well as
by established poets such as Margaret Walker and Mari Evans.
Establishes NikTom, Ltd. Meets Ellis Haizlip (1929–91) and
begins making regular appearances on his television program,
Soul!, an entertainment-variety-talk show that promoted Black art
and culture and allowed political expression. (During the history
of the show—1967–72—which aired on WNET, many important
artists and leaders, including Muhammad Ali, Jesse Jackson,
Harry Belafonte, Sidney Poitier, Gladys Knight, Miriam Makeba,
and Stevie Wonder, made appearances. Giovanni was for several
years a "regular.") Giovanni publishes *Black Feeling Black
Talk/Black Judgement* as one volume with William Morrow & Co.
Publishes *Re: Creation* with Broadside Press. Writes and
publishes the broadside "Poem of Angela Yvonne Davis." Has
become a recognized figure on the Black literary scene; in the
anthology *We Speak as Liberators,* published this year, she is
referred to as an "established name." *Ebony* magazine names her
Woman of the Year.

1971 ▨ Giovanni publishes autobiography, *Gemini*, and poems for children, *Spin A Soft Black Song*. *Black Feeling Black Talk/Black Judgement* comes out in paperback. Records *Truth Is On Its Way* with the New York Community Choir. Performs with the choir in a concert to introduce the album at Canaan Baptist Church in Harlem before a crowd of 1,500. Continues regular appearances on *Soul!*, including an appearance in January with Lena Horne. The Mugar Memorial Library of Boston University approaches her about housing her papers and she accepts; today the Mugar has all her papers and memorabilia. *Contact* magazine names her Best Poet in its annual awards. *Mademoiselle* magazine names her Woman of the Year. Travels to Africa. *Truth* sells more than 100,000 copies in its first six months. Giovanni travels to London to tape special segments of *Soul!* with James Baldwin; these air on December 15 and 22. Falls ill from exhaustion after returning to the United States.

1972 ▨ Giovanni publishes *My House*. Joins National Council of Negro Women. Receives an honorary doctorate from Wilberforce University, becoming the youngest person so honored by the nation's oldest Black college. *Truth Is On Its Way* receives NATRA's (National Association of Television and Radio Announcers) Award for Best Spoken Word Album. Receives widespread attention from print media, including publications such as *Jet, Newsweek, The Washington Post*, and *Ebony*. Appears frequently on *Soul!* and is a guest on *The Tonight Show*. Plays an active role in a new publication undertaken by her friend Ida Lewis, *Encore*, later renamed *Encore American & Worldwide News*, a Black newsmagazine. Until 1980 Giovanni acts as consultant, contributes a regular column, and helps finance the magazine. Puts on a free Father's Day concert with La Belle at Canaan Baptist Church in Harlem. Performs at Alice Tully Hall in Lincoln Center with the New York Community Choir and La Belle. Receives key to Lincoln Heights, Ohio. Reads at the Paul Laurence Dunbar Centennial in Dayton, Ohio, where she and

Paula Giddings, then an editor at Howard University Press, conceive the idea of a book composed of a conversation between Giovanni and Margaret Walker (1915–98). Travels to Walker's home in Jackson, Mississippi, in November to begin taping.

1973 ■ Giovanni publishes *Ego-Tripping and Other Poems for Young People* and *A Dialogue: James Baldwin and Nikki Giovanni*, an edited transcription of the videotaping she did with Baldwin for two episodes of *Soul!* Releases the album *Like A Ripple On A Pond*. The American Library Association names *My House* one of the best books of 1973. *Gemini* is nominated for a National Book Award. Meets Margaret Walker in Washington, D.C., to complete the tapings for their book. On May 14 receives a Woman of the Year Award from the *Ladies' Home Journal*; the ceremony at the Kennedy Center in Washington, airs nationwide, and Giovanni is criticized for accepting the award. Throws a thirtieth birthday party for herself on June 21 at New York's Philharmonic Hall; the recital includes an introduction by Reverend Ike and guest appearances by Wilson Pickett and Melba Moore. Is initiated as an honorary member into Delta Sigma Theta, Inc., at its convention in Atlanta in August. Takes her sister to Paris to celebrate Gary's graduation from Xavier University (Cincinnati). Receives Life Membership and Scroll from the National Council of Negro Women. Goes on an African lecture tour sponsored by USIA; brings her son and his nanny, Deborah Russell, a former student of hers at Rutgers. They visit Ghana, Swaziland, Lesotho, Botswana, Zambia, Tanzania, Kenya, and Nigeria.

1974–77 ■ Giovanni publishes *A Poetic Equation: Conversations Between Nikki Giovanni and Margaret Walker* (1974) and *The Women and the Men* (1975). Releases the albums *The Way I Feel* (1975), *Legacies* (1976), and *The Reason I Like Chocolate* (1976). Receives honorary doctorates from Ripon University; the University of Maryland, Princess Anne Campus; and Smith College. Continues to write essays for *Encore American & Worldwide News*. Lectures extensively at colleges and universities across the country. Travels to Rome for the United Nations' First World Food Conference (1974).

1978–82 ▪ Giovanni publishes *Cotton Candy On A Rainy Day* and releases album with the same title (1978). Publishes *Vacation Time* in 1979. In 1978 her father has a stroke and is subsequently diagnosed with cancer. Giovanni moves with her son back to her parents' home in Lincoln Heights. Primary responsibility for her parents and her son, including steep medical bills, increases her speaking schedule and she has less time to devote to writing. Named an honorary commissioner for the President's Commission on the International Year of the Child. Father dies on June 8, 1982, one day after her thirty-ninth birthday.

1983–87 ▪ Giovanni publishes *Those Who Ride the Night Winds* (1983). Continues a heavy schedule of speaking engagements. Named Woman of the Year by the Cincinnati YWCA (1983). Teaches as a visiting professor at Ohio State University (1984–85) and as professor of creative writing at Mount Saint Joseph's College (1985–87). Receives honorary doctorates from Mount Saint Joseph's College (1985) and Mount Saint Mary College (1987). Makes a European lecture tour for USIA, visiting France, Germany, Poland, and Italy (1985). Is named to the Ohio Women's Hall of Fame (1985) and named Outstanding Woman of Tennessee (1985). Receives *The Cincinnati Post*'s Post-Corbett Award and serves as Duncanson artist in residence at the Taft Museum in Cincinnati (1986). Is the subject of a PBS documentary, *Spirit to Spirit* (1987). Thomas graduates from high school and enlists in the Army. Accepts position as Commonwealth Visiting Professor of English at Virginia Tech, in Blacksburg, Virginia. Her mother moves to California to live with Gary. Serves on the Ohio Humanities Council. Judges the Robert F. Kennedy Book Awards.

1988 ▪ Giovanni publishes *Sacred Cows . . . and Other Edibles*. Receives honorary doctorate from Fisk University.

Cincinnati bi-centennial honoree. *Spirit to Spirit* receives the Silver Apple Award from the Oakland Museum Film Festival. Receives the Ohioana Library Award for *Sacred Cows*. McDonald's institutes the Nikki Giovanni Poetry Award. USIA selects *Spin a Soft Black Song* for inclusion in its Exhibition to the Soviet Union. *Vacation Time* receives the Children's Reading Roundtable of Chicago Award. National Festival of Black Storytelling initiates the Nikki Giovanni Award for Young African American Storytellers. Begins a writing group at Warm Hearth Village, a retirement home.

1989–91 ▪ Giovanni accepts a permanent position as tenured full professor of English at Virginia Tech and relocates to Blacksburg, Virginia. Edits an anthology by her Warm Hearth writers group, *Appalachian Elders: A Warm Hearth Sampler*. Receives honorary doctorate from Indiana University. Attends Utrecht International Poetry Festival as the featured poet. "Two Friends" is incorporated as a permanent tile wall exhibit by the Oxnard Public Library in California. Thomas enrolls in Morehouse College. Continues to lecture on campuses across the country during the spring. Serves on the advisory board of the Virginia Foundation for the Humanities and Public Policy (1990–96).

1992–94 ▪ Giovanni publishes the twentieth-anniversary edition of *Ego-Tripping and Other Poems for Young Readers* (1993), which includes new poems. Publishes *Racism 101* (essays) and *Knoxville, Tennessee* (illustrated children's book). Edits and publishes *Grand Mothers: A Multicultural Anthology of Poems, Reminiscences, and Short Stories About the Keepers of Our Traditions*. Receives honorary doctorates from Otterbein College (1992), Rockhurst College (1993), and Widener University (1993). Featured Poet at Portland (Oregon) Art Beat Festival. Receives Community Volunteer of the Year Award from Warm Hearth Village. Writes and presents a poem commemorating the tenth anniversary of the Mount Vernon Slave Memorial ("But

Since You Finally Asked"). Conducts interview with the astronaut Mae Jemison for *Essence* magazine. Is Martin Luther King, Jr., Visiting Professor at the University of Oregon (1992). Is Hill Visiting Professor at the University of Minnesota (1993). Continues to receive keys to the major cities in America; to date, these include Dallas, Miami, New York, New Orleans, Baltimore, Los Angeles, Mobile, and a dozen or so more. Receives the Tennessee Writer's Award from the *Nashville Banner*. Thomas graduates magna cum laude from Morehouse College (1994). Her mother and sister relocate to Virginia (1994).

1995 ▪ In mid-January Giovanni is diagnosed with lung cancer. Travels to Cincinnati for a second opinion and has surgery at Jewish Hospital. Receives honorary doctorates from Albright College and Cabrini College. Is a week-long writer in residence for the National Book Foundation's Family Literacy Program at the Family Academy in Harlem. In summer is visiting professor at Indiana University, Kokomo.

1996–97 ▪ Giovanni publishes *The Selected Poems of Nikki Giovanni, The Genie in the Jar* (illustrated children's book), *The Sun Is So Quiet* (illustrated children's book), *Shimmy Shimmy Shimmy Like My Sister Kate: Looking at the Harlem Renaissance Through Poems* (all 1996), and *Love Poems* (1997). Releases *Nikki in Philadelphia* (1997). Receives honorary doctorate from Allegheny College (1997). Reads for "A Celebration of Lorraine Hansberry," a benefit sponsored by the Schomburg Library. *Selected Poems of Nikki Giovanni* nominated for NAACP Image Award. Reads for Literacy Partners Benefit Reading at Lincoln Center. Receives the Langston Hughes Award. Is Artist in Residence for the Philadelphia Clef Club of Jazz and Performing Arts. Travels on book tour. Continues to do a spring lecture tour. Named Gloria D. Smith Professor of Black Studies at Virginia Tech (1997–99). Serves on the national advisory board of the National Underground Museum and Freedom Center (1997–).

1998–99 ■ Giovanni publishes *Blues: For All the Changes* (1999) and edits and publishes *Grand Fathers: Reminiscences, Poems, Recipes, and Photos of the Keepers of Our Tradition* (1999). Receives honorary doctorates from Delaware State University (1998), and Martin University and Wilmington University (1999). Named University Distinguished Professor at Virginia Tech, the highest honor the university confers (1999). Wins NAACP Image Award for *Love Poems* (1998). Attends Millennium Evening at the White House. Inducted into the National Literary Hall of Fame for Writers of African Descent. Receives Appalachian Medallion Award. Wins the 1998 Tennessee Governor's Award in the Arts.

2000–01 ■ Giovanni receives NAACP Image Award for *Blues: For All the Changes* (2000). Wins the 2000 Virginia Governor's Award for the Arts. Receives honorary doctorates from Manhattanville College, State University of West Georgia (2000), and Central State University (2001). Named to the Gihon Foundation's 2000 Council of Ideas. Serves as poetry judge for the National Book Awards (2000). Receives Certificate of Commendation from the U.S. Senate (2000). Serves on the board of trustees of Cabrini College (2001–03). Serves on the board of directors of Mill Mountain Theater (of Roanoke, Virginia) (2001–).

2002–03 ■ Giovanni publishes *Quilting the Black-Eyed Pea: Poems and Not Quite Poems* (2002). Caedmon records and releases *The Nikki Giovanni Poetry Collection* (2002). Receives honorary doctorates from Pace University (2002) and West Virginia University (2003). Featured in *Foundations of Courage . . . A Cry to Freedom!* on BET. Appears in A&E television's *Witness: James Baldwin*. Wins NAACP Image Award for *Quilting the Black-Eyed Pea* (2003). Judge for the Robert F. Kennedy Book Awards (2002). Serves on Multimedia Advisory Panel for the Virginia Museum of Fine Arts (2002–). Receives the first Rosa Parks Woman of Courage Award (2002). Inducted into Phi Beta Kappa, Delta of Tennessee Chapter, Fisk University (2003). Performs a tribute to Gwendolyn Brooks with Elizabeth Alexander, Ruby Dee, and Yusef Komunyakaa (2003). Contributes to a Smithsonian special exhibition, *In the Spirit of Martin: The Living Legacy of Dr. Martin Luther King, Jr.*

Black Feeling
Black Talk

1 9 6 8

Detroit Conference of Unity and Art ■

(For HRB)

We went there to confer
On the possibility of
Blackness
And the inevitability of
Revolution

We talked about
Black leaders
And Black Love

We talked about
Women
And Black men
No doubt many important
Resolutions
Were passed
As we climbed Malcolm's ladder

But the most
Valid of them
All was that
Rap chose me

On Hearing "The Girl with
the Flaxen Hair"

He has a girl who has flaxen hair
My woman has hair of gray
I have a woman who wakes up at dawn
His girl can sleep through the day

His girl has hands soothed with perfumes sweet
She has lips soft and pink
My woman's lips burn in midday sun
My woman's hands—black like ink

He can make music to please his girl
Night comes I'm tired and beat
He can make notes, make her heart beat fast
Night comes I want off my feet

Maybe if I don't pick cotton so fast
Maybe I'd sing pretty too
Sing to my woman with hair of gray
Croon softly, Baby it's you.

You Came, Too

I came to the crowd seeking friends
I came to the crowd seeking love
I came to the crowd for understanding

I found you

I came to the crowd to weep
I came to the crowd to laugh

You dried my tears
You shared my happiness

I went from the crowd seeking you
I went from the crowd seeking me
I went from the crowd forever

You came, too

Poem ■

(For TW)

For three hours (too short for me)
I sat in your home and enjoyed
Your own special brand of Southern
Hospitality

And we talked

I had come to learn more about you
To hear a human voice without the Top Ten in the background

You offered me cheese and Horowitz and
It was relaxing
You gave me a small coke
And some large talk about being Black
   And an individual

You had tried to fight the fight I'm fighting
And you understood my feelings while you
Picked my brains and kicked my soul

It was a pleasant evening
When He rises and Black is king
I won't forget you

Poem ■

(For BMC No. 1)

I stood still and was a mushroom on the forest green
With all the *moiles* conferring as to my edibility
It stormed and there was no leaf to cover me
I was water-logged (having absorbed all that I could)
I dreamed I was drowning
That no sun from Venice would dry my tears
But a silly green cricket with a pink umbrella said
Hello   Tell me about it
And we talked our way through the storm

Perhaps we could have found an inn
Or at least a rainbow somewhere over
But they always said
Only one   Only one more
And Christmas being so near
We over identified

Though I worship nothing (save myself)
You were my savior—so be it
And it was
Perhaps not never more or ever after
But after all—once you were mine

Our Detroit Conference

(For Don L. Lee)

We met in
The Digest
Though I had
Never Known You

Tall and Black
But mostly in
The Viet Cong
Image

You didn't smile

Until we had traded
Green stamps
for Brownie Points

Poem

(For Dudley Randall)

So I met this man
Who was a publisher
When he was young

Who is a poet now

Gentle and loving and
Very patient
With a Revolutionary
Black woman

Who drags him
to meetings

But never quite
Gets around to
saying

I love you

Poem ■

(For BMC No. 2)

There were fields where once we walked
Among the clover and crab grass and those
Funny little things that look like cotton candy

There were liquids expanding and contracting
In which we swam with amoebas and other Afro-Americans

The sun was no further than my hand from your hair

Those were barefoot boy with cheeks of tan days
And I was John Henry hammering to get in

I was the camel with a cold nose

Now, having the tent, I have no use for it
I have pushed you out

Go 'way
Can't you see I'm lonely

Personae Poem ▪

(For Sylvia Henderson)

I am always lonely
for things I've never had
and people I've never been

But I'm not really
sad
because you once said
Come
and I did
even though I don't like
you

Poem ■

(For PCH)

And this silly wire
(which some consider essential)
Connected us
And we came together

So I put my arms around you to keep you
From falling from a tree
(there is evidence that you have climbed
too far up and are not at all functional
with this atmosphere or terrain)
And if I had a spare
I'd lend you my oxygen tent

But you know how selfish people are
When they have something at stake

So we sit between a line of
Daggers
And if all goes well

They will write Someday
That you and I did it

And we never even thought for sure
(if thought was one of the processes we employed)
That it could be done

Poem ▪

(No Name No. 1)

And every now and then I think
About the river

Where once we sat
Upon the bank
Which
You robbed

And I let you

Wasn't it fun

Poem

(For BMC No. 3)

But I had called the office
And the voice across the line
Swore up and down (and maybe
all the way 'round)
That you wouldn't be in

Until 11:00 A.M.

So I took a chance
And dialed your phone

And was really quite content
After you said
Hello

But since I had previously
Been taught
By you especially
That you won't say
Hello
More than once

I picked a fight

Black Separatism ▪

It starts with a hand
Reaching out in the night
And pretended sleep

We may talk about our day
At the office
Then again
Baseball scores are just
As valid
As the comic page
At break fast

The only thing that really
Matters
Is that it comes

And we talk about the kids
Signing our letters

YOURS FOR FREEDOM

A Historical Footnote to Consider
Only When All Else Fails

(For Barbara Crosby)

While it is true
(though only in a factual sense)
That in the wake of a
Her-I-can comes a
Shower
Surely I am not
The gravitating force
that keeps this house
full of panthers

Why, LBJ has made it
quite clear to me
He doesn't give a
Good goddamn what I think
(else why would he continue to *masterbate* in public?)

Rhythm and Blues is not
The downfall of a great civilization
And I expect you to
Realize
That the Temptations
have no connection with
The CIA

We must move on to
the true issues of
Our time
like the mini-skirt
Rebellion
And perhaps take a
Closer look at
Flour Power

It is for Us
to lead our people
out of the
Wein-Bars
   into the streets
into the streets
(for safety reasons only)
Lord knows we don't
Want to lose the
support
of our Jewish friends

So let us work
for our day of Presence
When Stokely is in
The Black House
And all will be right with
Our World

Poem ▪

(No Name No. 2)

Bitter Black Bitterness
Black Bitter Bitterness
Bitterness Black Brothers
Bitter Black Get
Blacker Get Bitter
Get Black Bitterness
   NOW

The True Import of Present Dialogue, ▪ Black vs. Negro

(For Peppe, Who Will Ultimately Judge Our Efforts)

Nigger
Can you kill
Can you kill
Can a nigger kill a honkie
Can a nigger kill the Man
Can you kill nigger
Huh? nigger can you
kill
Do you know how to draw blood
Can you poison
Can you stab-a-Jew
Can you kill huh? nigger
Can you kill
Can you run a protestant down with your
'68 El Dorado
(that's all they're good for anyway)
Can you kill
Can you piss on a blond head
Can you cut it off
Can you kill
A nigger can die
We ain't got to prove we can die
We got to prove we can kill
They sent us to kill
Japan and Africa
We policed europe
Can you kill
Can you kill a white man
Can you kill the nigger
in you
Can you make your nigger mind
die

Can you kill your nigger mind
And free your black hands to
strangle
Can you kill
Can a nigger kill
Can you shoot straight and
Fire for good measure
Can you splatter their brains in the street
Can you kill them
Can you lure them to bed to kill them
We kill in Viet Nam
for them
We kill for UN & NATO & SEATO & US
And everywhere for all alphabet but
BLACK
Can we learn to kill WHITE for BLACK
Learn to kill niggers
Learn to be Black men

A Short Essay of Affirmation ▪
Explaining Why
(With Apologies to the Federal Bureau of Investigation)

Honkies always talking 'bout
Black Folks
Walking down the streets
Talking to themselves
(They say we're high—
or crazy)

But recent events have shown
We know who we're talking
to

That little microphone
In our teeth
Between our thighs
Or anyplace
That may have needed
Medical attention
Recently
My mail has been stopped
And every morning
When I awake
I speak to
Lessy-in-the-wall
Who bangs behind
My whole Rap

This is a crazy country

They use terms like
Psychosis and paranoid
With us

But we can't be Black
And not be crazy
How the hell would anyone feel
With a mechanical dick
in his ass
lightening the way
for   whitey

And we're supposed to jack off
behind it

Well I'm pissed
off

They ain't getting
Inside
My bang
or
My brain
I'm into my Black Thing
And it's filling all
My empty spots

Sorry 'bout that,
Miss Hoover

Poem ■
(No Name No. 3)

The Black Revolution is passing you bye
negroes
Anne Frank didn't put cheese and bread away for you
Because she knew it would be different this time
The naziboots don't march this year
Won't march next year
Won't come to pick you up in a
honka honka VW bus
So don't wait for that
negroes
They already got Malcolm
They already got LeRoi
They already strapped a harness on Rap
They already pulled Stokely's teeth
They already here if you can hear properly
negroes
Didn't you hear them when 40 thousand Indians died
from exposure to
honkies
Didn't you hear them when Viet children died from
exposure to napalm
Can't you hear them when Arab women die from exposure to
    isrealijews
You hear them while you die from exposure to wine
and poverty programs
If you hear properly
negroes
Tomorrow was too late to properly arm yourself
See can you do an improper job now
See can you do now something, anything, but move now
negro
If the Black Revolution passes you bye it's for damned
sure
the whi-te reaction to it won't

Wilmington Delaware

Wilmington is a funni Negro
He's a cute little gingerbread man who stuffs his pipe
with
Smog and gas fumes and maybe (if you promise
not to tale)
Just a little bit of . . . pot
Because he has to meet his maker each and everyday
LORD KNOWS HE'S A GOOD BOY
AND TRIES HARD
While most of us have to go to church only once a week

They tell me he's up for the coloredman-of-the-year
award
And he'll probably win
(If he'd just stop wetting on himself each and
everytime he
meets a Due-pontee)
LORD KNOWS HE TRIES

Why just the other day I heard him say NO
But he was only talking to the janitor and I believe
they
expect him to exercise some control over the
excretionary
facilities around here
(But it's a start)
My only real criticism is that he eats his daily
nourishment at the "Y"
And I was taught that's not proper to do in public

But he's sharp, my but that boy is sharp
Why it took the overlords two generations to recognize
that negroes had moved to the East side of town (which is
    similar to

but not the same as the wrong side of the tracks)
And here he is making plans for future whites who
haven't even
reclaimed the best land yet

"Don't say nothing Black or colored or look unhappy"
I heard him tell his chief joints
And every bone bopped in place but quick
(He can really order some colored people around—
a sight to behold)
And does a basically good militant shuffle
when dancing is in order

I'd really like to see him party more but he swears
Asphalt is bad for his eye-talian shoes
And we all appreciate eye-tal
don't we

I tried to talk to him once but he just told me
"Don't be emotional"
And all the while he was shaking and crying
and raining blows on
poor black me

So I guess I'm wrong again
Just maybe I don't know the coloure of my
truefriends
As Wilmington pointed out to me himself
But I'm still not going to anymore banquits

The last one they replaced jello with
jellied gas (a Due-pontee specialty; housewise)
And I couldn't figure out what they were trying
to tell me
Wilmington said they were giving me guest treat-meants

But somehow I don't feel welcome
So I'm going to pack my don-key (asswise) and split
before they start to do me favors too

Letter to a Bourgeois
Friend Whom Once
I Loved

(And Maybe Still
Do If Love Is Valid)

The whole point of writing you is pointless
and somewhere in the back of my mind I really do
accept that. But on the other hand the whole point
of points is pointless when it's boiled all the way down
to the least common denominator. But I was never one
to deal with fractions when there are so many wholes
that cannot be dissected—at least these poor hands
lack both skill and tool and perhaps this poor heart
lacks even the inclination to try because emotion is in
and of itself a wasteful thing because it lacks the power
to fulfill itself. And power is to be sought.
I see, after talking with you I did see, that Johnson
sent his storm troopers into Detroit and that's wrong
and the wrong is not what we have done but what
Johnson and all the johnsons before him have done
and it's wrong that we hate but it's even more wrong
to love when neither love nor hate have anything to do
with what must be done. And Rap does love and
maybe he won't tomorrow or the next day and if
he does maybe it won't be with me but if we must love
then I must love you and him and all other people.

Or I must not deal with love at all. And if we are not
to deal with love then we must not deal with emotion
because if not love then we deal with hate or fear
or anxiety or just anything but The Problem which is
what we must deal with if we are to get back to love
and hate and anxiety and all those foolish emotions.
Which is what we're talking about. And you are angry

with me maybe because you think I'll get hurt
(if indeed you care) or maybe because you think
you'll get hurt but not at all because I hate
because you know I don't hate and not because
I'm violent because you know I'm not violent
so perhaps you are not angry at all but just give
slightly a shade left of a good goddamn what the hell
happens to me and whether or not I want to share it
with you and the truth being that I should give
a bout face and act like an adult except that adulthood
has no room for me because adulthood implies another
adult to relate to and there are no adults
only children whose balloons are bursting spit
all over their faces and having never tasted spit
let alone eaten any shit or licked any ass
you think that liquid on your face is rain from Heaven
and maybe you hope if it rains hard enough
all the wrinkles will disappear and the fountain
of youth, having been presented to you by our friend
and neighbor, will be yours for-ever surrounded by
flashing lights on the outside instead of the terrible
hammer inside which beats the sweat or fans the cold
and sometimes buckles your knees. So we move to
needs which must be met and I confess with a smile
on my lips that my needs are far more important to me
than your needs are to me and even though your needs
mean something to me they are only important
insofar as your needs have a need to meet mine.

And your needs lack significance to me when your
need is to get away from me and my needs.
Which is why I'm currently going through a thing
which is the only accurate description of my emotional
goulash, as if you've never been lonely and basically
afraid but recognizing that fear is an invalid emotion
and so is loneliness but being afraid and lonely

nonetheless. I called you but you have a job.
Which is no longer inclusive of me or maybe I just
developed a bad case of paranoia which in the next
thousand years may be understood by all the people
everywhere who can understand how it feels to be
lonely and afraid when there is no place for emotion.
And that has to upset your world which I fully intend
to do even if I don't like doing it because likes or
dislikes have nothing to do with what has to be done
—even to you with whom I'd dearly like to do nothing
at all. My, but you hurt.

I'm Not Lonely ▪

i'm not lonely
sleeping all alone

you think i'm scared
but i'm a big girl
i don't cry
or anything

i have a great big bed
to roll around
in and lots of space
and i don't dream
bad dreams
like i used
to have that you
were leaving me
anymore

now that you're gone
i don't dream
and no matter
what you think
i'm not lonely
sleeping
all alone

Love Poem ▪

(For Real)

it's so hard to love
people
who will die soon

the sixties have been one
long funeral day
the flag flew at half-mast
so frequently
seeing it up
i wondered what was wrong

it will go back
to half
on inauguration day
(though during the johnson love
in the pole
was cut
the mourning wasn't
official)

the Jews are seeking
sympathy
cause there isn't one Jew
(and few circumcised women)
in the cabinet
old mother no dick plans
to keep it
bare
it's impossible to love
a Jew

united quakers and crackers
for death, inc.

are back in the driver's seat
it hertz
and i pledge allegiance
to the removal of all
pain

it's masochistic
(derived from colored
meaning sick to kiss massa)
to love honkies

riderless horses
backward boots
the eternal flame of the flammable
Black Man
who does not plan to screw
honkies to death

it's so easy to love
Black Men
they must not die anymore

and we must not die
with america
their day of mourning
is our first international
holiday

it's a question of power
which we must wield
if it is not
to be wielded
against
us

For
an Intellectual
Audience

i'm a happy *moile*
the opposite of which
is an unhappy
womblie

and the only way you'll ever
understand
this poem
is if you sit
on your ear
three times a day
facing south
justa whistling
dixie
while nikki picks
her nose

if you miss nose
picking time
then you must collect
three and one half milograms
of toe jam
and give it to barbara's cat

and if you can't find
barbara's cat

then how you gonna call
yourself
a black man?

Black Power ▪

*(For All the Beautiful
Black Panthers East)*

But the whole thing is a miracle—See?

We were just standing there
talking—not touching or smoking
Pot
When this cop told
Tyrone
Move along buddy—take your whores
outa here

And this tremendous growl
From out of nowhere
Pounced on him

Nobody to this very day
Can explain
How it happened

And none of the zoos or circuses
Within fifty miles
Had reported
A panther
Missing

Seduction ▪

one day
you gonna walk in this house
and i'm gonna have on a long African
gown
you'll sit down and say "The Black . . ."
and i'm gonna take one arm out
then you—not noticing me at all—will say "What about
this brother . . ."
and i'm going to be slipping it over my head
and you'll rap on about "The revolution . . ."
while i rest your hand against my stomach
you'll go on—as you always do—saying
"I just can't dig . . ."
while i'm moving your hand up and down
and i'll be taking your dashiki off
then you'll say "What we really need . . ."
and i'll be licking your arm
and "The way I see it we ought to . . ."
and unbuckling your pants
"And what about the situation . . ."
and taking your shorts off
then you'll notice
your state of undress
and knowing you you'll just say
"Nikki,
isn't this counterrevolutionary . . . ?"

Word Poem ■

(Perhaps Worth Considering)

as things be / come
let's destroy
then we can destroy
what we be / come
let's build
what we become
when we dream

Black

Judgement

1 9 6 8

The Dance Committee ■

(Concerning Jean-Léon Destiné)

I am the token negro
I sit in the colored section with Fanon in hand
(to demonstrate my militancy)
and a very dry martini
(ingredients: yellow grass and a green faggot
over lightly)
while circumcised flies buzz brassy smells over my head

The women (obviously my superiors)
White sharp lines
and light-blue mascara
reaching all the way down beyond the red neck
crossing the middle age spread
form a double V (at home and the office)
spinning spidery daydreams of cloth
once covering and once removed
dripping babies

I asked why
the group wouldn't be in the Black community
(it was Black French—which I should point out
has nothing to do with sex)
And was told quite soundlee
that just because they're colored don't
mean they're not artists too
THEY'RE ARTISTS TOO AND COLOR
AIN'T GOT NOTHING TO DO WITH IT
AND WHY OH WHY WON'T YOU PEOPLE
LET US FORGET YOU'RE COLORED TOO

Token Negroes
I do believe, at least I was told,

and it is very important
for future exchanges
And again I must point out sex is not the issue
that we should simply fuck
tokenism

Of Liberation ▪

Dykes of the world are united
Faggots got their thing together
(Everyone is organized)
Black people these are facts
Where's your power

Honkies rule the world
Where's your power Black people
(There are those who say it's found in the root of all evil)
You are money
You seek property
Own yourself
3/5 of a man
100% whore
Chattel property
All of us
The most vital commodity in america
Is Black people
Ask any circumcised honkie

There are relevant points to be considered, Black People
Honkies tell niggers don't burn
"violence begets you nothing my fellow americans"
But they insist on straightened hair
They insist on bleaching creams
It is only natural that we would escalate

It has been pointed out:
"If we can't out fight them, we can't out vote them"
These are relevant points to consider
If 10% honkies can run south africa
        then
10% Black people (which has nothing to do with negroes)
can run america

These are facts
Deal with them

It has been pointed out:
"The last bastion of white supremacy
is in the Black man's mind"
(Note—this is not a criticism of brothers)

Everything comes in steps
Negative step one: get the white out of your hair
Negative step two: get the white out of your mind
Negative step three: get the white out of your parties
Negative step four: get the white out of your meetings

BLACK STEP ONE:
Get the feeling out (this may be painful—endure)
BLACK STEP TWO:
Outline and implement the program
All honkies and some negroes will have to die
This is unfortunate but necessary

Black law must be implemented
The Black Liberation Front must take responsibility
For Black people
If the choice is between the able and the faithful
The faithful must be chosen
Blackness is its own qualifier
Blackness is its own standard
There are no able negroes
White degrees do not qualify negroes to run
The Black Revolution

The Black Liberation Front must set the standards
These are international rules

Acquaint yourself with the Chinese, The Vietnamese,

The Cubans
And other Black Revolutions
We have tried far too long to ally with whites
Remember the rule of thumb:
WILD ANIMALS CAN BE TRAINED
BUT NEVER TAMED
The honkie is this category
Like any beast he can be trained with varying degrees
of excellence to
1) eat from a table
2) wash his hands
3) drive an automobile or bicycle
4) run a machine
5) And in some rare cases has been known to speak
This is training, Black people,
And while it is amusing
It is still a circus we are watching
Barnum and Bailey are the minds
behind president Johnson

You would not trust your life to a wolf or a tiger
no matter how many tricks they can learn
You would not turn your back on a cobra
Even if it can dance
Do not trust a honkie
They are all of the same family
The Black Liberation Front has free jobs to offer
for those concerned about the unemployed
The sisters need to make flags
(there are no nations without a flag)
The Red Black and Green must wave from all our
buildings as we build our nation
Even the winos have a part—they empty the bottles
    which the children can collect
Teen-age girls can fill with flammable liquid
and stuff with a rag

Professor Neal says a tampax will do just fine
Ammunition for gun and mind must be smuggled in
Support your local bookstore
Dashikis hide a multitude of Revolution
Support your local dress shop

As all reports have indicated our young men are primary
On the job training is necessary
Support your local rebellion—
send a young man into the streets

Our churches must bless these efforts in the name
of our Black God
Far too long we have been like Jesus
Crucified
It is time for The Resurrection of Blackness
"A little child shall lead them" for the Bible tells me so
And we shall follow our children into battle

Our choice a decade ago was war or dishonor
(another word for integration)
We chose dishonor
We got war

Mistakes are a fact of life
It is the response to error that counts
Erase our errors with the Black Flame
Purify our neighborhoods with the Black Flame
We are the artists of this decade
Draw a new picture with the Black Flame
Live a new life within the Black Flame

Our choice now is war or death
Our option is survival
Listen to your own Black hearts

Poem for Black Boys ▪
(With Special Love to James)

Where are your heroes, my little Black ones
You are the Indian you so disdainfully shoot
Not the big bad sheriff on his faggoty white horse

You should play run-away-slave
or Mau Mau
These are more in line with your history

Ask your mothers for a Rap Brown gun
Santa just may comply if you wish hard enough
Ask for CULLURD instead of Monopoly
DO NOT SIT IN DO NOT FOLLOW KING
GO DIRECTLY TO STREETS
This is a game you can win

As you sit there with your all understanding eyes
You know the truth of what I'm saying
Play Back-to-Black
Grow a natural and practice vandalism

These are useful games (some say a skill is even learned)
There is a new game I must tell you of
It's called Catch The Leader Lying
(and knowing your sense of the absurd
you will enjoy this)

Also a company called Revolution has just issued
a special kit for little boys
called Burn Baby
I'm told it has full instructions on how to siphon gas
and fill a bottle

Then our old friend Hide and Seek becomes valid
Because we have much to seek and ourselves to hide
from a lecherous dog

And this poem I give is worth much more
than any nickel bag
or ten cent toy
And you will understand all too soon
That you, my children of battle, are your heroes
You must invent your own games and teach us old ones
how to play

Concerning
One Responsible Negro
with Too Much Power

scared?
are responsible negroes running
scared?

i understand i'm to be sued
and you say you can't fight fifteen hundred national
guards men
so you'll beat the shit
out of poor Black me
(no doubt because i've castrated you)

dynamite came to your attention
and responsible negroes tell the cops

your tongue must be removed
since you have no brain
to keep it in check

aren't you turned around
teaching tolerance
how can i tolerate
genocide
my cup is full
and you already know
we have no ability
to delay gratification

i only want to reclaim myself
i even want you
to reclaim yourself
but more and more i'm being convinced
that your death

responsible negro
is the first step
toward my reclamation

it's very sad
i'd normally stop and cry
but evening is coming
and i've got to negotiate
for my people's freedom

Reflections on April 4, 1968 ■

What can I, a poor Black woman, do to destroy america? This is a question, with appropriate variations, being asked in every Black heart. There is one answer—I can kill. There is one compromise—I can protect those who kill. There is one cop-out—I can encourage others to kill. There are no other ways.

The assassination of Martin Luther King is an act of war. President johnson, your friendly uncandidate, has declared war on Black people. He is not making any distinction between us and negroes. The question—does it have rhythm? The answer—yes. The response—kill it. They have been known to shoot at the wind and violate the earth's gravity for these very reasons.

Obviously the first step toward peace is the removal of at least two fingers, and most probably three, from both hands of all white people. Fingers that are not controlled must be removed. This is the first step toward a true and lasting peace. We would also suggest blinding or the removal of at least two eyes from one of the heads of all albino freaks.

And some honkie asked about the reaction? What do you people want? Isn't it enough that you killed him? You want to tell me how to mourn? You want to determine and qualify how I, a lover, should respond to the death of my beloved? May he rest in peace. May his blood choke the life from ten hundred million whites. May the warriors in the streets go ever forth into the stores for guns and tv's, for whatever makes them happy (for only a happy people make successful Revolution) and this day begin the Black Revolution.

How can one hundred and fifty policemen allow a man to be shot? Police were seen coming from the direction of the shots. And there was no conspiracy? Just as there was no violent reaction to his death. And no city official regretted his death but only that it occurred in Memphis. We heard similar statements from Dallas—this country has too many large Southern cities.

Do not be fooled, Black people. Johnson's footprints are the footprints of death. He came in on a death, he is presiding over a death, and his own death should take him out. Let us pray for the whole state of Christ's church.

Zeus has wrestled the Black Madonna and he is down for the count. Intonations to nadinolia gods and a slain honkie will not overcome. Let america's baptism be fire this time. Any comic book can tell you if you fill a room with combustible materials then close it up tight it will catch fire. This is a thirsty fire they have created. It will not be squelched until it destroys them. Such is the nature of revolution.

America has called itself the promised land—and themselves God's chosen people. This is where we come in, Black people. God's chosen people have always had to suffer—to endure—to overcome. We have suffered and america has been rewarded. This is a foul equation. We must now seek our reward. God will not love us unless we share with others our suffering. Precious Lord—Take Our Hands—Lead Us On.

The Funeral of Martin Luther King, Jr.

His headstone said
FREE AT LAST, FREE AT LAST
But death is a slave's freedom
We seek the freedom of free men
And the construction of a world
Where Martin Luther King could have lived
and preached non-violence.

A Litany for Peppe ▪

They had a rebellion in Washington this year
because white people killed Martin Luther King
Even the cherry blossoms wouldn't appear

Black Power and a sweet Black Peace

Just about 200 white people died
because they conspired to kill Martin Luther King

And peace and power to you my child

Blessed be machine guns in Black hands
All power to grenades that destroy our oppressor
Peace Peace, Black Peace at all costs

We're having our spring sale
200 honkies for one non-violent

Even Wilmington Delaware
(a funni negro at best)
Responded appropriately

And to you my Black boy
A Revolution
My gift of love
Blessed is he who kills
For he shall control this earth.

Nikki-Rosa ▪

childhood remembrances are always a drag
if you're Black
you always remember things like living in Woodlawn
with no inside toilet
and if you become famous or something
they never talk about how happy you were to have
your mother
all to yourself and
how good the water felt when you got your bath
from one of those
big tubs that folk in chicago barbecue in
and somehow when you talk about home
it never gets across how much you
understood their feelings
as the whole family attended meetings about Hollydale
and even though you remember
your biographers never understand
your father's pain as he sells his stock
and another dream goes
And though you're poor it isn't poverty that
concerns you
and though they fought a lot
it isn't your father's drinking that makes any difference
but only that everybody is together and you
and your sister have happy birthdays and very good
Christmases
and I really hope no white person ever has cause
to write about me
because they never understand
Black love is Black wealth and they'll
probably talk about my hard childhood
and never understand that
all the while I was quite happy

The Great Pax Whitie ∎

In the beginning was the word
And the word was
Death
And the word was nigger
And the word was death to all niggers
And the word was death to all life
And the word was death to all
   peace be still

The genesis was life
The genesis was death
In the genesis of death
Was the genesis of war
   be still peace be still

In the name of peace
They waged the wars
   ain't they got no shame

In the name of peace
Lot's wife is now a product of the Morton company
   nah, they ain't got no shame

Noah packing his wife and kiddies up for a holiday
row row row your boat
But why'd you leave the unicorns, noah
Huh? why'd you leave them
While our Black Madonna stood there
Eighteen feet high holding Him in her arms
Listening to the rumblings of peace
   be still be still

CAN I GET A WITNESS? WITNESS? WITNESS?
He wanted to know
And peter only asked who is that dude?

Who is that Black dude?
Looks like a troublemaker to me
And the foundations of the mighty mighty
Ro Man Cat holic church were laid

hallelujah jesus
nah, they ain't got no shame

Cause they killed the Carthaginians
in the great appian way
And they killed the Moors
"to civilize a nation"
And they just killed the earth
And blew out the sun
In the name of a god
Whose genesis was white
And war wooed god
And america was born
Where war became peace
And genocide patriotism
And honor is a happy slave
cause all god's chillun need rhythm
And glory hallelujah why can't peace
  be still

The great emancipator was a bigot
  ain't they got no shame
And making the world safe for democracy
Were twenty million slaves
  nah, they ain't got no shame

And they barbecued six million
To raise the price of beef
And crossed the 38th parallel
To control the price of rice
  ain't we never gonna see the light

And champagne was shipped out of the East
While kosher pork was introduced
To Africa
    Only the torch can show the way

In the beginning was the deed
And the deed was death

And the honkies are getting confused
    peace be still

So the great white prince
Was shot like a nigger in texas
And our Black shining prince was murdered
like that thug in his cathedral
While our nigger in memphis
was shot like their prince in dallas
And my lord
ain't we never gonna see the light
The rumblings of this peace must be stilled
    be stilled be still

ahh Black people
ain't we got no pride?

Intellectualism ▪

sometimes i feel like i just get in
everybody's way
when i was a little girl
i used to go read
or make fudge
when i got bigger i
read
or picked my nose
that's what they called
intelligence
or when i got older
intellectualism
but it was only
that i was in the way

Universality ▪

You see boy
is universal
It can be a
man
a woman
a child
or anything—
but normally it's
a
nigger
I was told

Knoxville, Tennessee

I always like summer
best
you can eat fresh corn
from daddy's garden
and okra
and greens
and cabbage
and lots of
barbecue
and buttermilk
and homemade ice-cream
at the church picnic
and listen to
gospel music
outside
at the church
homecoming
and go to the mountains with
your grandmother
and go barefooted
and be warm
all the time
not only when you go to bed
and sleep

it's so important to record
i sit here trying to record
trying to find a new profound
way to say
johnson is the vilest
germiest beast
the world has ever
known
in the alleged civilized
times
trying to record
how i feel about a
family
being wiped out
trying to explain
that they have nothing
against bobby
he's a white
millionaire
several hundred times over
so it must be me
they are killing
trying to record
the feeling of shame
that we Black people
haven't yet
committed a
major assassination
which very desperately
must be
done
trying to record the
ignorance of the
voices

that say
i'm glad a negro
didn't do it
a negro needs to kill
something
trying to record
that this country must be
destroyed
if we are to live
must be destroyed if we are to live
must be destroyed if we are to live

Adulthood ▪

(For Claudia)

i usta wonder who i'd be
when i was a little girl in indianapolis
sitting on doctors' porches with post-dawn pre-debs
(wondering would my aunt drag me to church sunday)
i was meaningless
and i wondered if life
would give me a chance to mean

i found a new life in the withdrawal from all things
not like my image

when i was a teen-ager i usta sit
on front steps conversing
the gym teacher's son with embryonic eyes
about the essential essence of the universe
(and other bullshit stuff)
recognizing the basic powerlessness of me

but then i went to college where i learned
that just because everything i was was unreal
i could be real and not just real through withdrawal
into emotional crosshairs or colored bourgeois
intellectual pretensions
but from involvement with things approaching reality
i could possibly have a life

so catatonic emotions and time wasting sex games
were replaced with functioning commitments to logic
and
necessity and the gray area was slowly darkened into
a Black thing

for a while progress was being made along with a certain
degree
of happiness cause i wrote a book and found a love
and organized a theatre and even gave some lectures on
Black history
and began to believe all good people could get
together and win without bloodshed
then
hammarskjöld was killed
and lumumba was killed
and diem was killed
and kennedy was killed
and malcolm was killed
and evers was killed
and schwerner, chaney and goodman were killed
and liuzzo was killed
and stokely fled the country
and le roi was arrested
and rap was arrested
and pollard, thompson and cooper were killed
and king was killed
and kennedy was killed
and i sometimes wonder why i didn't become a
debutante
sitting on porches, going to church all the time,
wondering
is my eye make-up on straight
or a withdrawn discoursing on the stars and moon
instead of a for real Black person who must now feel
and inflict
pain

From a Logical ■
Point of View

I mean it's only natural that if
water seeks its own level
The honkie would not bother with
Viet Nam
It's unworthy of him
Cause they are not ready
for the revolutionary
advanced technology
that america is trying
to put on them
and nothing is worse
than a
dream deferred

It's just those simple
agrarian people
trying to invoke
simple land
reform
and maybe bring
a new level
of consciousness
to their people

And here america is
trying
to teach them
how to
read and
write
and be
capitalists

when it's fairly obvious
to the naked
untrained
eye
that they aren't
ready
for meaningful
change
and the revolution
is only
in the honkies'
mind

I mean
if it was me
I wouldn't
try to enlighten
those
slant-eyed
bastards
who only want
to sing and
dance
and be happy
all the time
I would have had enough fooling
around with niggers

I mean really
if I had at my
disposal
a means to get
out of this world
I'd go
and let those un
grateful

coloreds
try to get
along
without
me

Dreams ■

in my younger years
before i learned
black people aren't
suppose to dream
i wanted to be
a raelet
and say "dr o wn d in my youn tears"
or "tal kin bout tal kin bout"
or marjorie hendricks and grind
all up against the mic
and scream
"baaaaaby nightandday
baaaaaby nightandday"
then as i grew and matured
i became more sensible
and decided i would
settle down
and just become
a sweet inspiration

Revolutionary Music ■

you've just got to dig sly
and the family stone
damn the words
you gonna be dancing to the music
james brown can go to
viet nam
or sing about whatever he
has to
since he already told
the honkie
"although you happy you better try
to get along
money won't change you
but time is taking you on"
not to mention
doing a whole
song they can't even snap
their fingers to
"good god! ugh!"
talking bout
"i got the feeling baby i got the feeling"
and "hey everybody let me tell you the news"
martha and the vandellas dancing in the streets
while shorty long is functioning at that junction
yeah we hip to that
aretha said they better
think
but she already said
"ain't no way to love you"
(and you know she wasn't talking to us)
and dig the o'jays asking "must i always be a stand in
for love"
i mean they say "i'm a fool for being myself"

While the might mighty impressions have told the
world
for once and for all
"We're a Winner"
even our names—le roi has said—are together
impressions
temptations
supremes
delfonics
miracles
intruders (i mean intruders?)
not beatles and animals and white bad things like
young rascals and shit
we be digging all
our revolutionary music consciously or un
cause sam cooke said "a change is gonna come"

Beautiful Black Men ■

(With compliments and apologies
to all not mentioned by name)

i wanta say just gotta say something
bout those beautiful beautiful beautiful outasight
black men
with they afros
walking down the street
is the same ol danger
but a brand new pleasure

sitting on stoops, in bars, going to offices
running numbers, watching for their whores
preaching in churches, driving their hogs
walking their dogs, winking at me
in their fire red, lime green, burnt orange
royal blue tight tight pants that hug
what i like to hug

jerry butler, wilson pickett, the impressions
temptations, mighty mighty sly
don't have to do anything but walk
on stage
and i scream and stamp and shout
see new breed men in breed alls
dashiki suits with shirts that match
the lining that complements the ties
that smile at the sandals
where dirty toes peek at me
and i scream and stamp and shout
for more beautiful beautiful beautiful
black men with outasight afros

Woman Poem ■

you see, my whole life
is tied up
to unhappiness
it's father cooking breakfast
and me getting fat as a hog
or having no food
at all and father proving
his incompetence
again
i wish i knew how it would feel
to be free

it's having a job
they won't let you work
or no work at all
castrating me
(yes it happens to women too)

it's a sex object if you're pretty
and no love
or love and no sex if you're fat
get back fat black woman be a mother
grandmother strong thing but not woman
gameswoman romantic woman love needer
man seeker dick eater sweat getter
fuck needing love seeking woman

it's a hole in your shoe
and buying lil' sis a dress
and her saying you shouldn't
when you know
all too well—that you shouldn't

but smiles are only something we give
to properly dressed social workers
not each other
only smiles of i know
your game sister
which isn't really
a smile

joy is finding a pregnant roach
and squashing it
not finding someone to hold
let go get off get back don't turn
me on you black dog
how dare you care
about me
you ain't got no good sense
cause i ain't shit you must be lower
than that to care

it's a filthy house
with yesterday's watermelon
and monday's tears
cause true ladies don't
know how to clean

it's intellectual devastation
of everybody
to avoid emotional commitment
"yeah honey i would've married
him but he didn't have no degree"

it's knock-kneed mini-skirted
wig wearing died blond mamma's scar
born dead my scorn your whore
rough heeled broken nailed powdered
face me

whose whole life is tied
up to unhappiness
cause it's the only
for real thing
i
know

Ugly Honkies, or
The Election Game
and How to Win It

ever notice how it's only the ugly
honkies
who hate
like Hitler was an ugly dude
same with lyndon
ike nixon hhh wallace maddox
and all the governors of mississippi
and you don't ever see a good-looking
cop
perhaps this only relates to the physical
nature of the beast
at best interesting for a beast
and never beautiful
by that black standard

if dracula came to town now
he'd look like daley
booing senator ribicoff
no pretty man himself
but at least out of the beast
category
yet all had to describe julian bond
as the handsome black legislator
which is, of course, redundant

life put muskie and huskie humphrey
on the cover
and we were struck by a thought:
"if we must be screwed—they could at least be pretty"
but the uglies kill
all the pretties
like john and bobby

and evers and king
and if caroline don't look
out she'll be next

arthur miller spoke of the white things
jumping wildly on their feet
banging their paws together
hating the young
only this time they were hating
their young
a salute to the chicago kids
now you and the world knows
we weren't lying
a cracked skull in time
may save mine
(though i doubt it)
and hhh says we ought to quit pretending
what daley did was wrong
We aren't pretending
We didn't give a damn
you guys ought to get yourselves
together
eating your kids is a sexual
perversion

the politics of '68 remind us grievously
of the politics of '64
the deal to put the bird
and his faggoty flock in the white nest
(which began in dallas)
is being replayed and repaid
(the downpayment being made in los angeles)
with tricky dicky to win this time
(the final payment chicago)
cause there's only two parties in this country
anti-nigger and pro-nigger

most of the pro-niggers are now dead
this second reconstruction is being aborted
as was the first
the pro-niggers council voting
the anti-niggers have guns
if we vote this season we ought to seek to make it
effective
the barrel of a gun is the best
voting machine
your best protest vote
is a dead honkie
much more effective than a yes
for gregory or cleaver

this negative bullshit
they run on us
is to tie us up in identification
"you don't want nixon-agnew do you?"
"well vote for humphrey-muskie"
but all you honkies are alien
to me
and i reject the choice
it's the same game they run
about nigeria
"whose side are you on?"
the black side, fool
how many times must i show that?
taking sides is identifying
and that is commitment
be committed to us
and don't deal with them
as long as we choose one evil over another
(on some bullshit theory that it's lesser)
we'll have bullshit evil to deal with
let's build a for real black thing
called revolution

known to revolutionists as
love

the obvious need is a new liberal white party
to organize liberal and radical honkies
this will lessen but not remove the clear and present
danger
to us
we need to continue our fight to control
all of america
honkies are just not fit to rule
these are sorry but true facts—not one honkie is fit to
rule
the worst junkie or black businessman is more humane
than the best honkie
no black person would have allowed
his troops to be so slaughtered
and before you scream "king king"
his promise was your picture in the paper
and your head in bandages
mccarthy (the administration's official dissident
candidate)
was not so honest
there are those who say he began with lyndon's blessings
and the promise of good speaking engagements
and since we have witnessed the assassination of one who
didn't need the money
or have the blessing
we are inclined to agree

and daley talked of teddy not making up his mind
he said no
that's pretty definite

only it's sad that once again
we have a chance we aren't fully

utilizing
the honkies are at war to decide what to do
about us
and here we are
trying to get
into what every sensible person should be running
from
when we integrated the schools
they began moving away from public education
when we integrated the churches
they started the god is dead bit
now we're integrating politics
and they're moving to a police state
we ought to beat them to the punch
and pull off our coup
and take over, with arms and everything necessary,
our communities

post-election note:

those of us breathing easy now that wallace
wasn't elected
check again
that's gas you're smelling
survival is still the name of the game
black people still our only allies
life or death still our only option
let's me and you do that thing
please?

Cultural Awareness ▪

as we all probably realize
on some level
people are basically selfish
and perhaps in some cases
a little more than thoughtless
mostly i would suppose
because of the nature of life
under this and most other
systems

but someone came by
and brought to my attention
how ridiculously mean
i was being

most people
he assured me
have followed the teachings
of the honorable maulana elijah el shabbaz
and do not have anything at all
to do with pork

and here he found
when visiting me
that i didn't have
zig-zag papers
for a kosher
substitute

For Saundra ▪

i wanted to write
a poem
that rhymes
but revolution doesn't lend
itself to be-bopping

then my neighbor
who thinks i hate
asked—do you ever write
tree poems—i like trees
so i thought
i'll write a beautiful green tree poem
peeked from my window
to check the image
noticed the school yard was covered
with asphalt
no green—no trees grow
in manhattan

then, well, i thought the sky
i'll do a big blue sky poem
but all the clouds have winged
low since no-Dick was elected

so i thought again
and it occurred to me
maybe i shouldn't write
at all
but clean my gun
and check my kerosene supply

perhaps these are not poetic
times
at all

Balances ▪

in life
one is always
balancing

like we juggle our mothers
against our fathers

or one teacher
against another
(only to balance our grade average)

3 grains salt
to one ounce truth

our sweet black essence
or the funky honkies down the street

and lately i've begun wondering
if you're trying to tell me something

we used to talk all night
and do things alone together

and i've begun
(as a reaction to a feeling)
to balance
the pleasure of loneliness
against the pain
of loving you

For a Poet I Know ■

if you sang songs i could make a request
does the same hold true of poems

i'd like a poem about me
i'm black and exist and for real
i'd like a poem about your uncle
who got out of his bed to let us screw
yeah and maybe a poem
about how i tried
to talk to you one night
and you suggested i read my own poems
what were you really thinking

i'd like to hear a poem about your wig
everybody's got a wig
aretha's is on her head
james brown's is humphrey
mine is columbia
yours is the college you teach at
or the people who sent you there

i want a poem telling how tired you are
of fucking women
and relating to your hospital
experiences
or maybe a poem about who you'd like
to lay beside and dream with
and a real long poem on what you dream about

i really need a rare book poem
and what they mean to you
and a new book poem about what you read
and a joe goncalves poem about a hardworking brother
and a carolyn rodgers poem about a beautiful sister

and a father poem for hoyt fuller
and a jet poem because we've never been in it
and a scared poem about me taking your clothes off
then offering an excuse
and a man poem about how you reached your Blackness
or perhaps an alcoholic poem about your mother
and a climbing poem about how you reached the heights
and a you poem mostly
cause your other poems
don't tell me who you are
and i
having felt and tasted you know
what you should know and relate to
that you should write and are capable of writing
a tall lean explosive poem
not just a quiet half white hating poem
about a black poem
called a black poet
that i know and would like to love
again

For Teresa ▪

and when i was all alone
facing my adolescence
looking forward
to cleaning house
and reading books
and maybe learning bridge
so that i could fit
into acceptable society
acceptably
you came along
and loved me
for being black and bitchy
hateful and scared
and you came along
and cared that i got
all the things necessary
to adulthood
and even made sure
i wouldn't hate
my mother
or father
and you even understood
that i should love
peppe
but not too much
and give to gary
but not all of me
and keep on moving
'til i found me
and now you're sick
and have been hurt
for some time
and i've felt guilty
and impotent

for not being able
to give yourself
to you
as you gave
yourself
to me

My Poem ▪

i am 25 years old
black female poet
wrote a poem asking
nigger can you kill
if they kill me
it won't stop
the revolution

i have been robbed
it looked like they knew
that i was to be hit
they took my tv
my two rings
my piece of african print
and my two guns
if they take my life
it won't stop
the revolution

my phone is tapped
my mail is opened
they've caused me to turn
on all my old friends
and all my new lovers
if i hate all black
people
and all negroes
it won't stop
the revolution

i'm afraid to tell
my roommate where i'm going
and scared to tell
people if i'm coming

if i sit here
for the rest
of my life
it won't stop
the revolution

if i never write
another poem
or short story
if i flunk out
of grad school
if my car is reclaimed
and my record player
won't play
and if i never see
a peaceful day
or do a meaningful
black thing
it won't stop
the revolution

the revolution
is in the streets
and if i stay on
the 5th floor
it will go on
if i never do
anything
it will go on

Black Judgements ▪

(Of bullshit niggerish ways)

You
with your bullshit niggerish ways
want to destroy me

You want to preach
responsible revolution
along with progressive
procreation

Your desires will not be honored
this season

Shivering under the armour
of your
white protector
fear not
for thou art evil
The audacity of wanting
to be near the life
of what you seek to kill

Can you love
can you hate
is your game any damn good

Black Judgements are upon you
Black Judgements are upon you

Re: Creation

1970

For Tommy ▪

to tommy who:
eats chocolate cookies and lamb chops
climbs stairs and cries when i change
   his diaper
lets me hold him only on his schedule
defined my nature
and gave me a new name (mommy)
which supersedes all others
controls my life
and makes me glad
that he does

Two Poems: ■

From Barbados

the mother palm had plaited her daughter's
hair for us
to sit under
while her bad little boy
cloud wet
in public grape trees
stretched the moon
across the sand shadows

each nation sharing its natural
gift
to enhance a cultural
exchange

my use of english
has not always been
spoken
as you now know
and your english
cast in the middle of salt and sand
isn't just the "little" the guide
book tells us of

there is something more Bajan
to your language
and more african to my response

in muted conversation
we met
and i take with me
your english
gift

For Harold Logan ▪

*(Murdered by "persons unknown" cause he
wanted to own a Black club on Broadway)*

he was just a little
gangster with a high
voice
and a poetic mind that recognized
genius and let it grow

but someone pruned
his life

he didn't lie or steal
could give you measure
for emotion he paid
for what he wanted and had

but someone stole
his life

the sanitation committee had a big meeting
concerning broadway
said the lights weren't bright like
they used to be

a cleaning man came
and removed his life
said Broadway was getting
too dusty

No Reservations

(for Art Jones)

there are no reservations
for the revolution

no polite little clerk
to send notice
to your room
saying you are WANTED
on the battlefield

there are no banners
to wave you forward
no blaring trumpets
not even a blues note
moaning wailing lone blue note
to the yoruba drums saying
strike now   shoot
strike now   fire
strike now   run

there will be no grand
parade
and a lot thrown round
your neck
people won't look up and say
"why he used to live next to me
isn't it nice
it's his turn now"

there will be no recruitment
station
where you can give
the most convenient hours
"monday wednesday i play ball

friday night i play cards
any other time i'm free"
. there will be no reserve
of energy
no slacking off till next time
"let's see—i can come back
next week
better not wear myself out
this time"

there will be reservations
only
if we fail

Alone ■

i can be
alone by myself
i was
lonely alone
now i'm lonely
with you
something is wrong
there are flies
everywhere
i go

For Two Jameses ■
(Ballantine and Snow)
In iron cells

we all start
as a speck
nobody notices us
but some may hope
we're there
some count days and wait

we grow
in a cell that spreads
like a summer cold
to other people
they notice and laugh
some are happy
some wish to stop
our movement

we kick and move
are stubborn and demanding
completely inside
the system

they put us in a cell
to make us behave
never realizing it's from cells
we have escaped
and we will be born
from their iron cells
new people with a new cry

For Gwendolyn Brooks ▪

brooks start with cloud condensation
allah crying
for his lost children

brooks babble
from mountain tops to settle
in collecting the earth's essence

pure spring fountain
of love knowledge
for those who find
and dare drink
of it

Autumn Poems ▪

the heat
you left with me
last night
still smolders
the wind catches
your scent
and refreshes
my senses

i am a leaf
falling from your tree
upon which i was
impaled

Rain ▪

rain is
god's sperm falling
in the receptive
woman how else
to spend
a rainy day
other than with you
seeking sun and stars
and heavenly bodies
how else to spend
a rainy day
other than with you

Poem for Lloyd ▪

it's a drag
sitting around waiting
for death
gotta do something before
i die

it's so lonely dying
all alone
gotta do something
before i die
gotta gotta get a gun
walking talking thinking gun
before i die

they're so lonely
funeral dirges
hip black angry funeral
dirges
gotta gotta get a gun
it's so lonely
when you die
gotta gotta get a gun to kill
death

Housecleaning

i always liked house cleaning
even as a child
i dug straightening
the cabinets
putting new paper on
the shelves
washing the refrigerator
inside out
and unfortunately this habit has
carried over and i find
i must remove you
from my life

Poem for Aretha ▪

cause nobody deals with Aretha—a mother with four
   children—having to hit the road
they always say "after she comes
home" but nobody ever says what it's like
to get on a plane for a three week tour
the elation of the first couple of audiences the good
feeling of exchange the running on the high
you get from singing good
and loud and long telling the world
what's on your mind

then comes the eighth show on the sixth day the beginning
to smell like the plane or bus the if-you-forget-your-tooth-
   brush
in-one-spot-you-can't-brush-until-the-second-show the
   strangers
pulling at you cause they love you but you having no love
to give back
and singing the same songs night after night day after day
and if you read the gossip columns the rumors that your
   husband
is only after your fame
the wondering if your children will be glad to see you and
   maybe
the not caring if they are the scheming to get out
of just one show and go just one place where some doe-doe-
   dupaduke
won't say "just sing one song, please"

nobody mentions how it feels to become a freak
because you have talent and how
no one gives a damn how you feel
but only cares that aretha franklin is here like maybe that'll
stop:

chickens from frying
eggs from being laid
crackers from hating

and if you say you're lonely or scared or tired how they always
    just say "oh come off it" or "did you see
how they loved you did you see huh did you?"
which most likely has nothing to do with you anyway
and i'm not saying aretha shouldn't have talent and i'm
    certainly
not saying she should quit
singing but as much as i love her i'd vote "yes" to her
doing four concerts a year and staying home or doing what-
    ever
she wants and making records cause it's a shame
the way we are killing her
we eat up artists like there's going to be a famine at the end
of those three minutes when there are in fact an abundance
of talents just waiting let's put some
of the giants away for a while and deal with them like they
    have
a life to lead

Aretha doesn't have to relive billie holiday's life doesn't have
to relive dinah washington's death but who will
stop the pattern

she's more important than her music—if they must be
separated—
and they should be separated when she has to pass out
before
anyone recognizes she needs
a rest and i say i need
aretha's music
she is undoubtedly the one person who put everyone on

notice
she revived johnny ace and remembered lil green aretha sings
   "i say a little prayer" and dionne doesn't
want to hear it anymore
aretha sings "money won't change you"
but james can't sing "respect" the advent
of Aretha pulled ray charles from marlboro country
and back into
the blues made nancy wilson
try one more time forced
dionne to make a choice (she opted for the movies)
and diana ross had to get an afro wig pushed every
Black singer into Blackness and negro entertainers
into negroness you couldn't jive
when she said "you make me/feel" the blazers
had to reply "gotta let a man be/a man"
aretha said "when my soul was in the lost and found/you came
   along to claim it" and joplin said "maybe"
there has been no musician whom her very presence hasn't
affected when humphrey wanted her to campaign she said
"woeman's only hueman"
and he pressured james brown
they removed otis cause the combination was too strong
the impressions had to say "lord have mercy/we're moving
on up"
the Black songs started coming from the singers on stage and
   the dancers
in the streets
aretha was the riot was the leader if she had said "come
let's do it" it would have been done
temptations say why don't we think about it
                think about it
                think about it

Revolutionary Dreams ▪

i used to dream militant
dreams of taking
over america to show
these white folks how it should be
done
i used to dream radical dreams
of blowing everyone away with my perceptive powers
of correct analysis
i even used to think i'd be the one
to stop the riot and negotiate the peace
then i awoke and dug
that if i dreamed natural
dreams of being a natural
woman doing what a woman
does when she's natural
i would have a revolution

Walking Down Park ▪

walking down park
amsterdam
or columbus do you ever stop
to think what it looked like
before it was an avenue
did you ever stop to think
what you walked
before you rode
subways to the stock
exchange (we can't be on
the stock exchange
we are the stock
exchanged)

did you ever maybe wonder
what grass was like before
they rolled it
into a ball and called
it central park
where syphilitic dogs
and their two-legged tubercular
masters fertilize
the corners and side-walks
ever want to know what would happen
if your life could be fertilized
by a love thought
from a loved one
who loves you

ever look south
on a clear day and not see
time's squares but see
tall Birch trees with sycamores
touching hands

and see gazelles running playfully
after the lions
ever hear the antelope bark
from the third floor apartment

ever, did you ever, sit down
and wonder about what freedom's freedom
would bring
it's so easy to be free
you start by loving yourself
then those who look like you
all else will come
naturally

ever wonder why
so much asphalt was laid
in so little space
probably so we would forget
the Iroquois, Algonquin
and Mohicans who could caress
the earth

ever think what Harlem would be
like if our herbs and roots and elephant ears
grew sending
a cacophony of sound to us
the parrot parroting black is beautiful black is beautiful
owls sending out whooooo's making love . . .
and me and you just sitting in the sun trying
to find a way to get a banana tree from one of the monkeys
koala bears in the trees laughing at our listlessness

ever think it's possible
for us to be
happy

Kidnap Poem

ever been kidnapped
by a poet
if i were a poet
i'd kidnap you
put you in my phrases and meter
you to jones beach
or maybe coney island
or maybe just to my house
lyric you in lilacs
dash you in the rain
blend into the beach
to complement my see
play the lyre for you
ode you with my love song
anything to win you
wrap you in the red Black green
show you off to mama
yeah if i were a poet i'd kid
nap you

The Genie in the Jar ▪

(for Nina Simone)

take a note and spin it around spin it around don't
prick your finger
take a note and spin it around
on the Black loom on the Black loom
careful baby
don't prick your finger

take the air and weave the sky
around the Black loom around the Black loom
make the sky sing a Black song sing a blue song
sing my song make the sky sing a Black song
from the Black loom from the Black loom
careful baby
don't prick your finger

take the genie and put her in a jar
put her in a jar
wrap the sky around her
take the genie and put her in a jar
wrap the sky around her
listen to her sing
sing a Black song our Black song
from the Black loom
singing to me
from the Black loom
careful baby
don't prick your finger

All I Gotta Do ■

all i gotta do
is sit and wait
sit and wait
and it's gonna find
me
all i gotta do
is sit and wait
if i can learn
how

what i need to do
is sit and wait
cause i'm a woman
sit and wait
what i gotta do
is sit and wait
cause i'm a woman
it'll find me

you get yours
and i'll get mine
if i learn
to sit and wait
you got yours
i want mine
and i'm gonna get it
cause i gotta get it
cause i need to get it
if i learn how

thought about calling
for it on the phone
asked for a delivery
but they didn't have it

thought about going
to the store to get it
walked to the corner
but they didn't have it

called your name
in my sleep
sitting and waiting
thought you would awake me
called your name
lying in my bed
but you didn't have it
offered to go get it
but you didn't have it
so i'm sitting

all i know
is sitting and waiting
waiting and sitting
cause i'm a woman
all i know
is sitting and waiting
cause i gotta wait
wait for it to find
me

The Game
Of Game

when all the cards are in
when all the chips are counted
the smiles smiled
the pictures taken
i wonder
if they'll say
you played a fair
game
of game?

Master Charge: Blues ■

it's wednesday night baby
and i'm all alone
wednesday night baby
and i'm all alone
sitting with myself
waiting for the telephone

wanted you baby
but you said you had to go
wanted you yeah
but you said you had to go
called your best friend
but he can't come 'cross no more

did you ever go to bed
at the end of a busy day
look over and see the smooth
where your hump usta lay
feminine odor and no reason why
i said feminine odor and no reason why
asked the lord to help me
he shook his head "not i"

but i'm a modern woman baby
ain't gonna let this get me down
i'm a modern woman
ain't gonna let this get me down
gonna take my master charge
and get everything in town

The Lion
In Daniel's Den

(for Paul Robeson, Sr.)

on the road to damascus
to slay the christians
saul saw the light
and was blinded by that light
and looked into the Darkness
and embraced that Darkness
and saul arose from the great white way
saying "I Am Paul
who would slay you
but I saw the Darkness
and I am that Darkness"
then he raised his voice
singing red black and green songs
saying "I am the lion
in daniel's den
I am the lion thrown to slaughter"

do not fear the lion
for he is us
and we are all
in daniel's den

For A Lady of Pleasure ▪
Now Retired

some small island birthed
her and a big (probably) white ship took her
from mother to come
to america's recreation

she lives in the top of my building
i only know her through her eyes
she is old now not only from years
but from aging

one gets the impression she was most
beautiful and like good wine
or a semiprecious jewel touted out
for the pleasure of those
who could afford
her recreation

her head is always high
though the set of her mouth shows
it's not easy
she asks nothing
seems to have something
to give but no one to give it
to if ever she gave it
to anyone

age requires happy memories like louvenia smiled
when she died and though her doctor had told her not
to there was pork cooking
on the stove
there are so many new mistakes
for a lady of pleasure
that can be made it shouldn't be

necessary to repeat the old
ones

and it was cold
on the elevator that morning
when i spoke to her and foolishly asked
    how are you
she smiled and tilted her head
    at least, i said, the sun is
    shining
and her eyes smiled   yes
and i was glad to be
there to say through spirits
    there is a new creation
to her

2nd Rapp

they ain't gonna never get
rap
he's a note turned himself
into a million songs listen
to aretha call
his name

he's a light
turned himself into our homes
look how well we see
since he came

he's a spirit turned
pisces to aries
alpha to omega

he's a man
turned himself into Black
women
and we turn little hims
loose on the world

A Robin's Poem ▪

if you plant grain
you get fields of flour
if you plant seeds
you get grass
or babies
i planted once
and a robin red breast flew
in my window
but a tom cat wouldn't let it
stay

Alabama Poem

if trees could talk
  wonder what they'd say
met an old man
  on the road late after noon
  hat pulled over to shade
  his eyes
  jacket slumped over his
  shoulders
  told me "girl! my hands seen
  more than all
  them books they got
  at Tuskegee"
  smiled at me
  half waved his hand
  walked on down the dusty road
met an old woman
  with a corncob pipe
  sitting and rocking
  on a spring evening
  "sista" she called to me
  "let me tell you—my feet
  seen more than yo eyes
  ever gonna read"
  smiled at her and kept
  on moving
  gave it a thought and went
  back to the porch
  "i say gal" she called down
  "you a student at the institute?
  better come here and study
  these feet
  i'm gonna cut a bunion off
  soons i gets up"

i looked at her
  she laughed at me
if trees would talk
  wonder what they'd tell me

Poem For ■
Unwed Mothers

(to be sung to
"The Old F.U. Spirit")

it was good for the virgin mary
it was good enough for mary
it was good for the virgin mary
it's good enough for me

Chorus

12 Gates: ▪
To The City

the white man is
nocturnal that's why
he wants to get to the moon
it's his rising sign

he's a vampire see
how he strikes between
dusk and dawn preying
on us day light
comes he has to be back
in his casket or office as
they call them now but
dracula would be quite comfortable

if the cracker were natural then the by
products from his body would grow
natural plants like when we are
buried flowers grow see
the stones that spring up among
their dead

nothing violates nature all
the time and even white
people came south for warmth
when the ice age hit
europe
christians should note that
it was ice water and now
fire cause the cracker is playing
with atomic matches

allah told us all
we need to know when he called

mankind hueman beings just because
they dropped the "e" the concept remains
colored cause we recognize
if we add "s" to hisstory why we ain't
a part of it or put "n" back in
democracy and you'll understand
the present system war
is raw any way you look
at it even with a spanish touch
and god is a dog

when the romans started counting
they started with one and went to x
an unknown mathematically speaking
so we know they couldn't deal
with twelve zodiac signs

aquarius died when
they buried atlantis this
is the age of pisces
check it out

Ego Tripping

(there may be a reason why)

I was born in the congo
I walked to the fertile crescent and built
    the sphinx
I designed a pyramid so tough that a star
    that only glows every one hundred years falls
    into the center giving divine perfect light
I am bad

I sat on the throne
    drinking nectar with allah
I got hot and sent an ice age to europe
    to cool my thirst
My oldest daughter is nefertiti
    the tears from my birth pains
    created the nile
I am a beautiful woman

I gazed on the forest and burned
    out the sahara desert
    with a packet of goat's meat
    and a change of clothes
I crossed it in two hours
I am a gazelle so swift
    so swift you can't catch me

For a birthday present when he was three
I gave my son hannibal an elephant
    He gave me rome for mother's day
My strength flows ever on

My son noah built new/ark and
I stood proudly at the helm
    as we sailed on a soft summer day

I turned myself into myself and was
    jesus
    men intone my loving name
    All praises All praises
I am the one who would save

I sowed diamonds in my back yard
My bowels deliver uranium
    the filings from my fingernails are
    semi-precious jewels
    On a trip north
I caught a cold and blew
My nose giving oil to the arab world
I am so hip even my errors are correct
I sailed west to reach east and had to round off
    the earth as I went
    The hair from my head thinned and gold was laid
    across three continents

I am so perfect so divine so ethereal so surreal
I cannot be comprehended
    except by my permission

I mean . . . I . . . can fly
    like a bird in the sky . . .

A Poem/Because It Came ■ As A Surprise To Me

homosexuality
(an invention of saul
as played to perfection by the pope)
is two people
of similar sex
DOING IT
that's all

Oppression ▪

i wish i could have been oppressed
by straightened hair
then i wouldn't have had no problems
till after emancipation when mme. walker
captured our kinks

i think it would have been hip to be oppressed
by greek letter organizations from APA to GDI
then the very earliest i would have had problems
was with the founding of howard university

or really i could dig oppression by the pig
greasy though he is he always fed me
or yeah let me bring it on down oppression
by diana ross leaving the supremes would be choice
then i wouldn't have had no problems at all till the mafia
took over motown
and my number one choice i swear would be neo-colonialism
by bell bottom pants cause we all recognize how they have
kept us in bondage for the last four hundred years

i mean i could really dig being oppressed by Black men
cause that would mean at least someone i love
is in power

what i'm gonna say one more time is i'm
oppressed by crackers
and that's what i've gotta deal
with

Toy Poem ▪

if they put you in a jack-in-the-box poet
would you pop up poeming a positive poem on
positive Blackness
would you poet a loving rawls poem and a real
st. jacques poem before they put them in a box

could you poet beyond the greek symbol into
the need for fraternity

if they put you in a wind up toy would you spin out liberated
woman
would you spin out a feminist or feminine
women have a different reality from men
would you spin into the arms of a Black man
or the clutch of white women

could you spin into an orphan home and liberate
a Black baby

if they took our insides out would we be still
Black people or would we become play toys
for master players
there's a reason we lose a lot it's not our game
and we don't know how to score

listen here
i wanna take you higher

Some Uses ■
For Them Not Stated

the white man sent me
the EVERYTHING card
so i called the jew
to buy my house
he said: is you colored
i says: yeah! i wanna
charge my house
he said: you give me a charge
and we'll work it out
burned EVERYTHING up

the mailman brought me
the bankamericard to guarantee
my checks
checked myself and sent it
back

then on a weak day they sent
the UNICard and i really needed
something
so i worked my juju
and turned it
into a man

Poem For Flora ■

when she was little
and colored and ugly with short
straightened hair
and a very pretty smile
she went to sunday school to hear
'bout nebuchadnezzar the king
of the jews

and she would listen

shadrach, meshach and abednego in the fire

and she would learn

how god was neither north
nor south east or west
with no color but all
she remembered was that
Sheba was Black and comely

and she would think

i want to be
like that

Sometimes ■

sometimes
when i wake up
in the morning
and see all the faces
i just can't
breathe

Poem For My Nephew

(Brother C. B. Soul)

i wish i were
a shadow
oh wow! when they put
the light on
me i'd grow
longer and taller and
BLACKER

Yeah . . . But . . . ▪

i don't want you to think
that i don't know the pain
when you say sister diana don't sing
like she used to
cause i heard dionne making way for just like me
and i remembered the expectation
and the little surprises her albums
used to bring
the little love notes that told someone
what i felt and the ultimate surprise
when she didn't sing for me and my love
no more and the pain was deep
cause the pleasure had been so complete
and i can dig when you say sing
like you used to but maybe we can
remember
we don't poet like that
no more either

Poem For A Lady ∎
Whose Voice I Like

so he said: you ain't got no talent
  if you didn't have a face
  you wouldn't be nobody

and she said: god created heaven and earth
  and all that's Black within them

so he said: you ain't really no hot shit
  they tell me plenty sisters
  take care better business than you

and she said: on the third day he made chitterlings
  and all good things to eat
  and said: "that's good"

so he said: if the white folks hadn't been under
  yo skirt and been giving you the big play
  you'd a had to come on uptown like everybody else

and she replied: then he took a big Black greasy rib
  from adam and said we will call this woeman and her
  name will be sapphire and she will divide into four parts
  that simone may sing a song

and he said: you pretty full of yourself ain't chu

so she replied: show me someone not full of herself
  and i'll show you a hungry person

How Do You Write A Poem?

how do you write a poem
about someone so close
to you that when you say ahhhhh
they say chuuuu
what can they ask you to put
on paper that isn't already written
on your face
and does the paper make it
any more real
that without them
life would be not
impossible but certainly
more difficult
and why would someone need
a poem to say when i come
home if you're not there
i search the air
for your scent
would i search any less
if i told the world
i don't care at all
and love is so complete
that touch or not we blend
to each other the things
that matter aren't all about
baaaanging (i can be baaaanged all
day long) but finding a spot
where i can be free
of all the physical
and emotional bullshit
and simply sit with a cup
of coffee and say to you
"i'm tired" don't you know

those are my love words
and say to you "how was your
day" doesn't that show
i care or say to you "we lost
a friend" and not want to share
that loss with strangers
don't you already know
what i feel and if
you don't maybe
i should check my feelings

And Sometimes ■
I Sit

and sometimes i sit
down at my typewriter
and i think
not of someone
cause there isn't anyone
to think
about and i wonder
is it worth it

I Want To Sing

i want to sing
a piercing note
lazily throwing my legs
across the moon
my voice carrying all the way
over to your pillow
      i want you

i need i swear to loll
about the sun
and have it smelt me
the ionisphere carrying
my ashes all
the way over
to your pillow
      i want you

Ever Want ■
To Crawl

ever want to crawl
in someone's arms
white out the world
in someone's arms
and feel the world
of someone's arms
it's so hot in hell
if i don't sweat
i'll melt

My House

1972

Legacies ∎

her grandmother called her from the playground
    "yes, ma'am"
    "i want chu to learn how to make rolls" said the old
woman proudly
but the little girl didn't want
to learn how because she knew
even if she couldn't say it that
that would mean when the old one died she would be less
dependent on her spirit so
she said
    "i don't want to know how to make no rolls"
with her lips poked out
and the old woman wiped her hands on
her apron saying "lord
    these children"
and neither of them ever
said what they meant
and i guess nobody ever does

Mothers ▪

the last time i was home
to see my mother we kissed
exchanged pleasantries
and unpleasantries pulled a warm
comforting silence around
us and read separate books

i remember the first time
i consciously saw her
we were living in a three room
apartment on burns avenue

mommy always sat in the dark
i don't know how i knew that but she did

that night i stumbled into the kitchen
maybe because i've always been
a night person or perhaps because i had wet
the bed
she was sitting on a chair
the room was bathed in moonlight diffused through
those thousands of panes landlords who rented
to people with children were prone to put in windows
she may have been smoking but maybe not
her hair was three-quarters her height
which made me a strong believer in the samson myth
and very black

i'm sure i just hung there by the door
i remember thinking: what a beautiful lady

she was very deliberately waiting
perhaps for my father to come home
from his night job or maybe for a dream

that had promised to come by
"come here" she said "i'll teach you
a poem: *i see the moon*
   the moon sees me
   god bless the moon
   and god bless me"
i taught it to my son
who recited it for her
just to say we must learn
to bear the pleasures
as we have borne the pains

A Poem for Carol ▪

(*May She Always Wear Red Ribbons*)

when i was very little
though it's still true today
there were no sidewalks in lincoln heights
and the home we had on jackson street
was right next to a bus stop and a sewer
which didn't really ever become offensive
but one day from the sewer a little kitten
with one eye gone
came crawling out
though she never really came into our yard but just
sort of hung by to watch the folk
my sister who was always softhearted but able
to act effectively started taking milk
out to her while our father would only say
don't bring *him* home and everyday
after school i would rush home to see if she was still
there and if gary had fed her but i could never
bring myself to go near her
she was so loving
and so hurt and so singularly beautiful and i knew
i had nothing to give that would
replace her one gone eye

and if i had named her which i didn't i'm sure
i would have called her carol

A Fishy Poem ▪

i have nine guppies
there were ten but the mother died shortly
after the birth
the father runs up and down the aquarium
looking

at first i thought i wasn't feeding
them enough
so i increased and increased
until the aquarium was very very dirty
then i realized he was just a guppie
whose father was a goldfish
and he was only following
his nature

Winter Poem ■

once a snowflake fell
on my brow and i loved
it so much and i kissed
it and it was happy and called its cousins
and brothers and a web
of snow engulfed me then
i reached to love them all
and i squeezed them and they became
a spring rain and i stood perfectly
still and was a flower

Conversation ■

"yeah" she said "my man's gone too
been dead longer than you is old"
"what do you do" i asked
"sit here on the porch and talk to the old folk
i rock and talk and go to church most times"
"but aren't you lonely sometimes" i asked
"now you gotta answer yo own question"
"i guess the children help a lot   you got grandchildren
haven't you"
"oh the children they come and go always in a hurry
got something to do ain't no time for old folks
like me"
she squinted at the sun packing her jaw
with *bruton* snuff
"the old days done gone . . . and i say good-bye
peoples be going to the moon and all . . . ain't that
wonderful . . . to the moon"
and i said "i see stars all the time aretha franklin
and sly were at madison square garden recently"
"what you doing here" she asked
"i'm a poet" i said
"that ain't no reason to be uppity"
and the sun beat down on my head while
a dragonfly admonished my flippancy
but a blue and yellow butterfly sat on my knee
i looked her square in the eye
"i ain't gonna tell you" she said and turned her head
"ain't gonna tell me what" i asked
"what you asking me you gotta live to be seventy-nine
fore you could understand anyhow"
"now you being uppity" i said
"yeah but i earned it" she replied and shifting her wad
she clapped her hands and smiled
"you been here before"

and i said "yes ma'am but would you tell me just one thing
what did i learn"
and she spat out her juice
"honey if you don't know how can i"
i wanted to argue but the sun was too hot and the sky
too lazy and god heaved a sigh that swept under my blouse
and i felt me feeling a feeling
she crossed her legs at the ankle
and straightened her back
"tell you this" she said
"keep yo dress up and yo pants down and you'll be all right"
and i said impatiently "old lady you got it all wrong"
"honey, ain't never been wrong yet
you better get back to the city cause you one of them
technical niggers and you'll have problems here"

Rituals ■

i always wanted to be a bridesmaid
honest to god
i could just see me floating
down that holy aisle leading
some dear friend to heaven
in pink and purple organza with lots and lots
of crinoline pushing the violets out from my dress
hem
or maybe in a more sophisticated endeavor
one of those lovely sky blue slinky numbers
fitting tight around my abounding twenty-eights
holding a single red rose white gloves open in the back
always forever made of nylon and my feet nestled gently
in *chandlers* number 699 which was also the price plus
one dollar to match it pretty near the dress color

wedding rituals have always intrigued me
and i'd swear to friends i wouldn't say goddamn not even
once no matter what neither would i give a power
sign but would even comb my hair severely
back and put that blue shit under my eyes
i swear i wanted to be in a wedding

Poem for Stacia ▪

i see wonder
in little things
like thorn figurines rowing
across my table
or stacia caring
by imposing which being
such a little thing wasn't
a big imposition
and i saw a rainbow
after a very cloudy day
but i looked down to swat
a mosquito and lost
it in the midst

The World Is Not
a Pleasant Place to Be

the world is not a pleasant place
to be without
someone to hold and be held by

a river would stop
its flow if only
a stream were there
to receive it

an ocean would never laugh
if clouds weren't there
to kiss her tears

the world is not
a pleasant place to be without
someone

The Only Song I'm Singing ▪

they tell me that i'm beautiful i know
i'm Black and proud
the people ask for autographs
i sometimes draw a crowd
i've written lots of poetry and other
kinds of books
i've heard that white men crumble
from one of my mean looks
i study hard and know my facts
in fact the truth is true
the only song i'm singing now is my song
of you

    and i'm asking you baby please
    please somehow show me what i need
    to know so i can love you right
    now

i've had great opportunities to move
the world around
whenever they need love and truth they call
me to their town
the president he called me up and asked
me to come down
but if you think you want me home i think
i'll stick around

    and i'm asking you baby please baby baby show me
    right now most of the things i need to know
    so i can love you somehow

The Butterfly ▪

those things
which you so laughingly call
hands are in fact two
brown butterflies fluttering
across the pleasure
they give
my body

I Remember

i remember learning you jump
in your sleep and smile
when you wake up

at first you cuddle
then one arm across my stomach
then one leg touching my leg then
you turn your back

but you smile when you wake up

i was surprised to know you don't care
if your amp burns all night and that you could
play *ohmeohmy* over and over again just
because you remembered

i discovered you don't like hair
in your bathroom sink and never step
your wet feet onto a clean rug

you will answer your phone
but you don't talk too long and you do
rub my toes and make faces
while you talk
and your voice told her anyway
that i was there

you can get up at three and make sandwiches
and orange juice and tell jokes
you sometimes make incoherent sentences
you snore
and you smile when you wake up

i know you cry when you're hurt
and curse when you're angry
and try when you don't feel
like it and smile at me
when you wake up

these things i learned through
a simple single touch
when fleshes clashed

A Certain Peace ▪

it was very pleasant
not having you around
this afternoon

not that i don't love you
and want you and need you
and love loving and wanting and needing you

but there was a certain peace
when you walked out the door
and i knew you would do something
you wanted to do
and i could run
a tub full of water
and not worry about answering the phone
for your call
and soak in bubbles
and not worry whether you would want something
special for dinner
and rub lotion all over me
for as long as i wanted
and not worry if you had a good idea
or wanted to use the bathroom
and there was a certain excitement
when after midnight you came home
and we had coffee
and i had a day of mine
that made me as happy
as yours did you

When I Nap ▪

when i nap
usually after 1:30
because the sun comes
in my room then
hitting the northeast
corner

i lay at the foot
of my bed and smell
the sweat of your feet
in my covers
while i dream

Mixed Media ■

on my bedroom wall hang a poster
two pen and inks one oil one framed photograph
something with a lot of color that i don't
quite know its substance
and you
cause i got tired of bathing and oiling
and waiting for you to be too tired or
too drunk and when i realized it was your smile
that turned me on i engraved it
just above the shelf where the ash tray sits
i cut your eyes and ears and nose away
leaving your lips to open me
to a very energetic
sober brother

Just a New York Poem ▪

i wanted to take
your hand and run with you
together toward
ourselves down the street to your street
i wanted to laugh aloud
and skip the notes past
the marquee advertising "women
in love" past the record
shop with "The Spirit
In The Dark" past the smoke shop
past the park and no
parking today signs
past the people watching me in
my blue velvet and i don't remember
what you wore but only that i didn't want
anything to be wearing you
i wanted to give
myself to the cyclone that is
your arms
and let you in the eye of my hurricane and know
the calm before

and some fall evening
after the cocktails
and the very expensive and very bad
steak served with day-old baked potatoes
after the second cup of coffee taken
while listening to the rejected
violin player
maybe some fall evening
when the taxis have passed you by
and that light sort of rain
that occasionally falls
in new york begins

you'll take a thought
and laugh aloud
the notes carrying all the way over
to me and we'll run again
together
toward each other
yes?

[Untitled] ▪

there is a hunger
    often associated with pain
    that you feel
    when you look at someone
    you used to love and enjoyed
    loving and want
    to love again
    though you know you can't
that gnaws at you
    as steadily as a mosquito
    some michigan summer
    churning his wings
    through your window screen
because the real world
    made up of baby

clothes	*to be washed*
food	*to be cooked*
lullabies	*to be sung*
smiles	*to be glowed*
hair	*to be plaited*
ribbons	*to be bowed*
coffee	*to be drunk*
books	*to be read*
tears	*to be cried*
loneliness	*to be borne*

says you are a strong woman
    and anyway he never thought you'd really miss him

The Wonder Woman ▪

(A New Dream—for Stevie Wonder)

dreams have a way
of tossing and turning themselves
around and the times
make requirements that we dream
real dreams for example
i wanted to be
a sweet inspiration in my dreams
of my people but the times
require that i give
myself willingly and become
a wonder woman

Categories ▪

sometimes you hear a question like "what is
your responsibility as an unwed mother"
and some other times you stand sweating profusely before
going on stage and somebody says "but you are used
   to it"
or maybe you look into a face you've never seen
or never noticed and you know
the ugly awful loneliness of being
locked into a mind and body that belong
to a *name* or *non-name*—not that it matters
cause *you* feel and *it* felt but you have
a planetrainbussubway—it doesn't matter—something
to catch to take your arms away from someone
you might have thought about
putting them around if you didn't
have all that shit to take you safely away

and sometimes on rainy nights you see
an old white woman who maybe you'd really care about
except that you're a young Black woman
whose job it is to kill maim or seriously
make her question
the validity of her existence
and you look at her kind of funny colored eyes
and you think
if she weren't such an aggressive bitch she would see
that if you weren't such a Black one
there would be a relationship but anyway—it doesn't matter
much—except you started out to kill her and now find
you just don't give a damn cause it's all somewhat
   of a bore
so you speak of your mother or sister or very good friend
and really you speak of your feelings which are too
   personal

for anyone else
to take a chance on feeling
and you eat that godawful food and you get somehow
through it and if this seems
like somewhat of a tentative poem it's probably
because i just realized that
i'm bored with categories

Straight Talk ▪

i'm giving up
on language
my next book will be blank
pages of various textures and hues
i have touched in
certain spots and patterns
and depending upon the mood the reader can come
with me or take me somewhere else

    i smell blood a'cookin

"but why" i asked when she said "i'm afraid
to see men cry"
"because i depend" she replied "on their strength"
"but are they any less strong for crying
nylon stockings wear better if they're washed first"

    mommy said it's only pot
    luck but you can have some

science teaches us matter
is neither created nor destroyed
and as illogical as it is there is nothing
worthwhile but people
and lord knows how irrational we are

    i'll just have a scrambled egg
    if it's all right

the question turns on a spelling problem
i mean i hate
to squash a roach and thought about giving up
meat between the shadow
and the act falls the essence   encore!

the preceding paragraph was brought to you by the letter E
in the name of huemanity

an acorn to an ant
is the same as a white man to a Black JOB
enjoyed waiting on
the lord tell me
why can't i

and i'm glad i'm smart cause i know
smart isn't enough and i'm glad
i'm young cause "youth and truth are making love" i'm glad
i'm Black not only
because it's beautiful but because it's me
and i can be dumb and old and petty and ugly
and jealous but i still need love

    your lunch today was brought to you
    by the polytech branch of your local
    spear o agnew association
    HEY! this is straight talk!

have a good day

Scrapbooks ■

it's funny that smells and sounds return
so all alone uncalled unneeded
on a sweaty night as i sit armed
with coffee and cigarettes waiting

sometimes it seems
my life is a scrapbook

i usta get 1.50 per week
for various duties unperformed
while i read *green dolphin street*
and *the sun is my undoing*
never understanding my exclusion
but knowing quite clearly the hero
is always misunderstood
though always right in the end

roy gave me a yellow carnation
that year for the junior prom

the red rose was from michael
who was the prettiest boy i'd ever known
he took me to the *jack* and *jill* dance
and left me sitting in the corner until
the slow drags came on then he danced
real tight and sweated out my bangs
i had a white leather monstrosity that passed
for taste in my adolescence pressed with dances
undanced though the songs were melodious

and somehow three or four books were filled
with proms and parties and programs that
my grandmother made me go to
for "culture" so that i could be
a lady

my favorite is the fisk book with clippings
of the *forum* and notes from the dean of women
saying "you are on social probation" and "you are
suspended from fisk"
and letters from my mother saying "behave yourself"
and letters from my grandmother reminding me
"your grandfather graduated fisk in 1905" and not
to try to run the school
but mostly notes from alvin asking when
was i coming over
again
i purchased a blue canvas notebook for the refrain

it's really something when you sit
watching dawn peep over apartment buildings
that seemed so ominous during the night and see
pages of smiling pictures   groups of girls throwing
pillows   couples staring nervously ahead as if they
think the kodak will eat them   someone with a ponytail
and a miles davis record   a lady with an afro pointing
joyously to a diploma   a girl in a brown tan and red
bathing suit holding a baby that looks like you
and now there is a black leather book filled
efficiently by a clipping service
and a pile of unanswered letters that remind
you to love those who love you
and i sit at dawn
all my defenses gone sometimes
listening to *something cool* sometimes
hearing *tears on my pillow*
and know there must be other books
filled with failures and family and friends
that perhaps one day i can unfold
for my grandchildren

When I Die ■

when i die i hope no one who ever hurt me cries
and if they cry i hope their eyes fall out
and a million maggots that had made up their brains
crawl from the empty holes and devour the flesh
that covered the evil that passed itself off as a person
that i probably tried
to love

when i die i hope every worker in the national security
   council
the interpol the fbicia foundation for the development
   of black women gets
an extra bonus and maybe takes one day off
and maybe even asks why they didn't work as hard for us
   as they did
them
but it always seems to be that way

please don't let them read "nikki-roasa" maybe just let
some black woman who called herself my friend go around
   and collect
each and every book and let some black man who said it was
negative of me to want him to be a man collect every picture
and poster and let them burn—throw acid on them—shit
   on them as
they did me while i tried
to live

and as soon as i die i hope everyone who loved me learns
   the meaning
of my death which is a simple lesson
don't do what you do very well very well and enjoy it
   it scares white folk
and makes black ones truly mad

but i do hope someone tells my son
his mother liked little old ladies with
their blue dresses and hats and gloves that sitting
    by the window
to watch the dawn come up is valid that smiling at an
    old man
and petting a dog don't detract from manhood
do
somebody please
tell him i knew all along that what would be
is what will be but i wanted to be a new person
and my rebirth was stifled not by the master
but the slave

and if ever i touched a life i hope that life knows
that i know that touching was and still is and will always
    be the true
revolution

[Untitled]

(For Margaret Danner)

one ounce of truth benefits
like ripples on a pond
one ounce of truth benefits like a ripple
on a pond
one ounce of truth
benefits like ripples on
a pond
as things change remember my smile

the old man said my time is getting near
the old man said my time
is getting near
he looked at his dusty cracked boots to say
sister my time is getting near
and when i'm gone remember i smiled
when i'm gone remember
i smiled
i'm glad my time is getting there

the baby cried wanting some milk
the baby cried needing some milk
the baby he cried for wanting
his mother kissed him gently
when i came they sang a song
when i was born they sang a song
when i was saved they sang a song
remember i smiled when i'm gone
remember i smiled when i'm gone
sing a good song when i'm gone
we ain't got long to stay

My Tower ▪

(For Barb and Anthony)

i have built my tower on the wings of a spider
spinning slippery daydreams of paperdoll fantasies
i built my tower on the beak of a dove
pecking peace to a needing woman

i have built my dreams on the love of a man
holding a nation in his palm asking me the time of day

i built my castle by the shore thinking
i was an oyster clammed shut forever
when this tiny grain i hardly noticed
crept inside and i spit around
and spit around and spun a universe inside
with a black pearl of immeasurable worth
that only i could spin around

i have borne a nation on my heart
and my strength shall not be my undoing
cause this castle didn't crumble
and losing my pearl made me gain
and the dove flew with the olive branch by harriet's route
to my breast and nestled close and said "you are mine"
and i was full and complete while emptying my wombs
and the sea ebbed ohhhhhhhh
what a pretty little baby

Poem ▪

(For Nina)

we are all imprisoned *in the castle of our skins*
and some of us have said so be it
if i am in jail my castle shall become
my rendezvous
my courtyard will bloom with hyacinths and jack-in-the-
    pulpits
my moat will not restrict me but will be filled
with dolphins sitting on lily pads and sea horses ridden by
    starfish
goldfish will make love
to Black mollies and color my world Black Gold
the vines entwining my windows will grow butterflies
and yellow jackets will buzz me to sleep
the dwarfs imprisoned will not become my clowns
for me to scorn but my dolls for me to praise and fuss
with and give tea parties to
my gnomes will spin cloth of spider web silkness
my wounded chocolate soldiers will sit in evening coolness
or stand gloriously at attention during that midnight sun
for i would have no need of day patrol
if i am imprisoned in my skin let it be a dark world
with a deep bass walking a witch doctor to me for spiritual
consultation
let my world be defined by my skin and the skin of my people
for we   spirit to spirit   will embrace
this world

on the bite of a kola nut
i was so high the clouds blanketing
   africa
in the mid morning flight were pushed
away in an angry flicker
of the sun's tongue

a young lioness sat smoking a pipe
while her cubs waved up at the plane
look ida i called a lion waving
but she said there are no lions
in this part of africa
it's my dream dammit i mumbled

but my grandmother stood up
from her rocker just then
and said you call it
like you see it
john brown and i are with you
and i sat back for my morning
coffee

we landed in accra and the people
clapped and i almost cried wake up
we're home
and something in me said shout
and something else said quietly
your mother may be glad to see you
but she may also remember why
you went away

Africa II ■

africa is a young man bathing
in the back of a prison fortress

the guide said "are you afro-american
cape coast castle holds a lot for your people"

and the 18th century clock keeps perfect
time for the time it has

i watched his black skin turn foaming
white and wanted to see this magnificent
man stand naked and clean before me
but they called me to the dungeons where above
the christian church an african stood listening
for sounds of revolt

the lock the guide stated indicated a major once ran
the fort and the british he said had recently demanded
the lock's return
and i wanted the lock maybe for a door
stop to unstop the 18th century clock

"and there is one African buried
here   we are proud of him" he said
and i screamed NO there are thousands
but my voice was lost in the room
of the women with the secret passageway
leading to the governor's quarters

so roberta flack recorded a song
and les mccann cried but
a young african man on the rock
outside the prison where my people were
born bathed in the sunlight

and africa is a baby to be
tossed about and disciplined and loved
and neglected and bitten on its bottom
as i wanted to
sink my teeth into his thigh
and tell him he would never be
clean until he can
possess me

They Clapped ▪

they clapped when we landed
thinking africa was just an extension
of the black world
they smiled as we taxied home to be met
black to black face not understanding africans lack
color prejudice
they rushed to declare
cigarettes, money, allegiance to the mother land
not knowing despite having read fanon and davenport
hearing all of j.h. clarke's lectures, supporting
nkrumah in ghana and nigeria in the war that there was once
a tribe called afro-americans that populated the whole
of africa
they stopped running when they learned the packages
on the women's heads were heavy and that babies didn't
cry and disease is uncomfortable and that villages are fun
only because you knew the feel of good leather on good
pavement
they cried when they saw mercedes benz were as common
in lagos as volkswagens are in berlin
they shook their heads when they understood there was no
difference between the french and the english and the
    americans
and the afro-americans or the tribe next door or the country
across the border
they were exasperated when they heard sly and the family
    stone
in francophone africa and they finally smiled when little
    boys
who spoke no western tongue said "james brown" with
    reverence
they brought out their cameras and bought out africa's
    drums
when they finally realized they are strangers all over

and love is only and always about the lover not the beloved
they marveled at the beauty of the people and the richness
of the land knowing they could never possess either

they clapped when they took off
for home despite the dead
dream they saw a free future

Poem ▪

(For Anna Hedgeman and Alfreda Duster)

thinning hair
estee laudered
deliberate sentences
chubby hands
glasses resting atop ample softness
dresses too long
beaded down
elbow length gloves   funny hats
ready smiles
    diamond rings
hopeful questions
needing to be needed
my ladies over fifty
who birthed and nursed
my Blackness

in an age of napalmed children
with words like *the enemy is whatever moves*
as an excuse for killing vietnamese infants

at a time when one president one nobel prize winner
one president's brother four to six white students
dozens of Black students and various hippies
would be corralled maimed and killed

in a day where the c.i.a. could hire Black hands to pull
the trigger on malcolm

during a decade that saw eight nurses in chicago
sixteen people at the university of texas along with
the boston strangler do a fantastic death
dance matched only by the murders of john coltrane
sonny liston jimi hendrixs and janis joplin

in a technological structure where featherstone
and che would be old-fashioned bombed

at a moment when agnew could define hard and soft
drugs on the basis of his daughter's involvement
with them

in a nation where eugene robinson could testify
against his own panther recruits and eldridge cleaver
could expel a martyr from that martyr's creation
where the president who at least knows
the law would say manson who at least tried
is guilty

it is only natural that joe frazier
would emerge

Nothing Makes Sense ■

a bright sun flower yellow tiger
was at my bedroom door teeth bared ready to pounce
when the child cried "the bear is gonna get me!"
and i completely understood cause i had to really
wake up fast to keep that tiger back

nothing is real especially
tones i heard
a rumbling and thought
the world was coming
to an end

and saw my body blown to bits and crushed under
the rubbish that had been the 100th street apartment
complex my guppies struggled for one last breath
and my turtle   head hidden in his shell   never
to fuss again at me for not cleaning him

the blinding light started in the 96th street subway
and quickly swept up to my house melting my flesh
into the cactus plant at my bedside and as my hand blended
into a thorn i wondered what it would be like to never
hold anyone again

what never was cannot be
though it engulfed me and i cried
"what always is   is not the answer!"

they came from all over the world in planes
in boats and dirigibles
on kites and pollen seeds riding bikes
and horses bare back on electric roller skates
and lionel trains all carrying an instrument to play
or blow and bleat and the sound called all the carnivores

from all over the world the aardwolf and the puma playing
the talking drum even the snow leopard with a long thin
hollowed ice flute came from his himalayan retreat
and all the snakes over ten feet long slithered through
the heavy traffic to my house to play a mass
and through the altos and basses and your condescending
attitude aretha started a low moan

the outline of a face on a picture isn't really
a face or an image of a face but the idea of an image
of a dream that once was dreamed by some artist
who never knew how much more real is a dream than reality

so julian bond was elected president and rap brown chief
justice of the supreme court and nixon sold himself
on 42nd street for a package of winstons
(with the down home taste) and our man on the moon said
    alleluia
and we all raised our right fist in the power sign
and the earth was thrown off course and crashed into the sun
but since we never recognize the sun
we went right on to work in our factories
and offices and laundry mats and record shops
the next morning and only the children
and a few poets knew
that a change had come

I Laughed When I Wrote It ▪

(Don't You Think It's Funny?)

the f.b.i. came by my house three weeks ago
one white agent one black (or i guess negro would be
more appropriate) with two three-button suits on (one to a
    man)
thin ties—cuffs in the bottoms—belts at their waists
they said in unison:
    ms. giovanni you are getting to be quite important
    people listen to what you have to say
i said nothing
    we would like to have you give a different message
i said: gee are all you guys really shorter than hoover
they said:
    it would be a patriotic gesture if you'd quit saying
    you love rap brown and if you'd maybe give us some
    leads
    on what some of your friends are doing
i said: fuck you
a week later the c.i.a. came by two unisexes one blond afro
one darker one three bulges on each showing lovely bell-
    bottoms and boots
they said in rounds:
    sister why not loosen up and turn on
    fuck the system up from the inside
    we can turn you on to some groovy
    trips and you don't have to worry
    about money or nothing   take the commune
    way and a few drugs it'll be good for you
    and the little one
after i finished a long loud stinky fart i said serenely
definitely though with love
    fuck you
yesterday a representative from interpol stopped me in the
    park

tall, neat afro, striped hip huggers bulging only in the right
place
    i really dig you, he said, i want to do something for you
    and you alone
i asked what he would like to do   for me
    need a trip around the world a car bigger apartment
    are you lonely i mean we need to get you comfortable
    cause a lot of people listen to you and you
    need to be comfortable to put forth a positive image
and digging the scene i said listen i would sell
out but i need to make it worth my while you understand
    you just name it and i'll give it to you, he assured me
well, i pondered, i want aretha franklin and her piano
    reduced to fit next to my electric
typewriter on my desk and i'll do anything you want
he lowered his long black eyelashes and smiled a whimsical
    smile
    fuck you, nikki, he said

On Seeing Black Journal ▪ and Watching Nine Negro Leaders "Give Aid and Comfort to the Enemy" to Quote Richard Nixon

it wouldn't have been
so bad if there had
been a white rock group singing
"steal away" from the side lines
(at least that would have made it
honest)

it is not too late/is too/is not/yah yah/so yo mama/is not
"Sir would you keep your remarks
succinct" said straight face
to people who were used to talking hours and never
sucking cint

"come with me—i mean come to me—that is i got rhythm
    —i mean
i can orchestrate and harmonize and ooo wee can i do a
    militant
shuffle"

"well i'm from small plains oklahoma and i want
to know about the sewer problem
just how should black people approach them"
"would whoever answers please
just be brief   we have important calls
from all over the country!"
"i want the integrationists to go on
record   just where do you stand
on sewers?!!!??!*?
    chorus

oh jesus was a lovely cat
he taught us how to pray
and every night we get on our knees
and this is what we say:
    oh i hate the white man
    i love the white man
    and it's just a natural fact
    that one way or other if you stick around
    he'll get on your back
and what about naomi?
for the answers to these and other important questions
like: do we have any Black leaders
stay tuned to (music please————)

the sets were turned off
the white men stood up   scratched themselves
and said well we're good for another
four hundred years or so

the Black youngsters turned off
their sets got down
on their knees and prayed
    oh Lord please
    don't take the honkie
    away

And Another Thing ▪

i'm leaving at five
she said why
are niggers always
late

a circle he replied is
a sunbeam that saw
itself and fell
in love

niggers would be
late for their own
damned funerals

it's the early bird
he whispered in her
ear that catches the worm
but no one ever said why
the worm gets up

how we gonna get this
country moving when we can't
get together
on such simple shit

sometimes he said brushing
her afro back with his rough hands
you scrub clothes to remove
a spot and sometimes you soak
them first

you not even listening to me

you're not listening to me

they looked at each other
for a moment

and another thing
she began

We ▪

we stood there waiting
    on the corners
    in the bars
    on the stoops
    in the pews
    by the cadillacs
    for buses
    wanting for love
    watching to see if hope would come by
we stood there hearing
    the sound of police sirens
    and fire engines
    the explosions
    and babies crying
    the gas escaping
    and the roaches breeding
    the garbage cans falling
    and the stairways creaking
we listened
    to the books opening
    and hearts shutting
    the hands rubbing
    the bodies sweating
we were seeing the revolution screeeeeeeeeeeching
    to a halt
    trying to find a clever way
    to be empty

My House ▪

i only want to
be there to kiss you
as you want to be kissed
when you need to be kissed
where i want to kiss you
cause it's my house
and i plan to live in it

i really need to hug you
when i want to hug you
as you like to hug me
does this sound like a silly poem

i mean it's my house
and i want to fry pork chops
and bake sweet potatoes
and call them yams
cause i run the kitchen
and i can stand the heat

i spent all winter in
carpet stores gathering
patches so i could make
a quilt
does this really sound
like a silly poem
i mean i want to keep you
warm

and my windows might be dirty
but it's my house
and if i can't see out sometimes
they can't see in   either

english isn't a good language
to express emotion through
mostly i imagine because people
try to speak english instead
of trying to speak through it
i don't know maybe it is
a silly poem

i'm saying it's my house
and i'll make fudge and call
it love and touch my lips
to the chocolate warmth
and smile at old men and call
that revolution cause what's real
is really real
and i still like men in tight
pants cause everybody has some
thing to give and more ,
important needs something to take

and this is my house and you make me
happy
so this is your poem

The Women and
the Men

1975

The Women Gather

(for Joe Strickland)

the women gather
because it is not unusual
to seek comfort in our hours of stress
    a man must be buried

it is not unusual
that the old bury the young
    though it is an abomination

it is not strange
that the unwise and the ungentle
carry the banner of humaneness
    though it is a castration of the spirit

it no longer shatters the intellect
that those who make war
call themselves diplomats

we are no longer surprised
that the unfaithful pray loudest
every sunday in every church
and sometimes in rooms facing east
    though it is a sin and a shame

    so how do we judge a man

most of us love from our need to love not
because we find someone deserving

most of us forgive because we have trespassed not
because we are magnanimous

most of us comfort because we need comforting
our ancient rituals demand that we give
what we hope to receive

and how do we judge a man

we learn to greet when meeting
to cry when parting
and to soften our words at times of stress

the women gather
with cloth and ointment
their busy hands bowing to laws that decree
willows shall stand swaying but unbroken
against even the determined wind of death

we judge a man by his dreams
not alone his deeds
we judge a man by his intent
not alone his shortcomings
we judge a man because it is not unusual
to know him through those who love him

the women gather strangers
to each other because
they have loved a man

it is not unusual to sift
through ashes
and find an unburnt picture

Once a Lady Told Me ▪

like my mother and her grandmother before
i paddle around the house
in soft-soled shoes
chasing ghosts from corners
with incense
they are such a disturbance my ghosts
they break my bric-a-brac and make
me forget to turn my heating stove

the children say you must come to live
with us   all my life i told them i've lived
with you   now i shall live with myself

the grandchildren say it's disgraceful
you in this dark house with the curtains
pulled   snuff dripping from your chin
would they be happier if i smoked   cigarettes

i was very exquisite once   very small and well courted
some would say a beauty when my hair was plaited
and i was bustled up

my children wanted my life
and now they want my death

but i shall pad around my house
in my purple soft-soled shoes
i'm very happy now
it's not so very neat, you know, but it's my
life

Each Sunday ▪

if she wore her dresses
the same length as mine
people would gossip viciously
about her morals

if i slept   head barely touching
the string of freshwater fake pearls
mouth slightly open   eyebrows knitted
almost into a frown
people would accuse me of running around
too much

suddenly her eyes springing away
from her sleep intensely
scope the pulpit and fall
on me

i wonder did she dream
while baking cold-water cornbread
of being a great reporter churning
all the facts together and creating
the truth
did she think   while patching the torn pants
and mending the socks of her men   of standing
arms outstretched before a great world
body offering her solution for peace
what did she feel wringing the neck
of Sunday's chicken breaking the beans
of her stifled life

she sits each sunday black
dress falling below her knees which have drifted
apart defining a void

in the temple of her life in the church of her god
strong and staunch and hopeful
that we never change
places

The December of My Springs ■

in the december of my springs
i long for the days
i shall somehow have
free from children and dinners
and people i have grown stale with

this time i think i'll face love
with my heart instead of my glands
rather than hands clutching to satiate
my fingers will stroke to satisfy
i think it might be good
to decide rather than to need

that pitter-patter rhythm of rain
sliding on city streets is as satisfying
to me as this quiet has become
and like the raindrop i accede to my nature

perhaps there will be no
difference between the foolishness of age
and the foolishness of youth
some say we are responsible
for those we love
others know we are responsible
for those who love us

so i sit waiting
for a fresh thought
to stir the atmosphere

i'm glad i'm not iron
else i would be burned
by now

Communication

[...]ic is the most universal language
[...]ink of me as one whole note

[...]nce has the most perfect language
[...]e me as MC²

[...]mathematics can speak to the infinite
[...]ne me as 1 to the first power

[...]i mean is   one day
[...]onna grab your love
[...]ou'll be
[...]fied

The Life I Led

i know my upper arms will grow
flabby it's true
of all the women in my family

i know that the purple veins
like dead fish in the Seine
will dot my legs one day
and my hands will wither while
my hair turns grayish white   i know that
one day my teeth will move when
my lips smile
and a flutter of hair will appear
below my nose   i hope
my skin doesn't change to those blotchy
colors

i want my menses to be undifficult
i'd very much prefer staying firm and slim
to grow old like a vintage wine fermenting
in old wooden vats with style
i'd like to be exquisite   i think

i will look forward to grandchildren
and my flowers   all my knickknacks in their places
and that quiet of the bombs not falling in cambodia
settling over my sagging breasts

i hope my shoulder finds a head that needs nestling
and my feet find a footstool after a good soaking
with epsom salts

i hope i die
warmed
by the life that i tried
to live

Mother's Habits

i have all
my mother's habits
i awake in the middle of night
to smoke a cigarette
i have a terrible fear of flying
and i don't like being alone
in the dark
sleep is a sport we all
participate in
it's the scourge of youth
and a necessity of old age
though it only hastens the day
when dissolution is inevitable
i grow tired
like my mother doing without
even one small word
that says i care
and like my mother i shall fade
into my dreams
no longer caring
either

i've noticed i'm happier
when i make love
with you
and have enough left
over to smile at my doorman

i've realized i'm fulfilled
like a big fat cow
who has just picked
for a carnation contentment
when you kiss your special place
right behind my knee

i'm as glad as mortar
on a brick that knows
another brick is coming
when you walk through
my door

most time when you're around
i feel like a note
roberta flack is going to sing

in my mind you're a clock
and i'm the second hand sweeping
around you sixty times an hour
twenty-four hours a day
three hundred sixty-five days a year
and an extra day
in leap year
cause that's the way
that's the way
that's the way i feel
about you

if mu
just t

if sci
pict

sinc
ima

wha
i'm
and
sati

Luxury

i suppose living
in a materialistic society
luxury
to some would be having
more than what you need

living in an electronic age seeing
the whole world by pushing a button
the *nth* degree might perhaps be
adequately represented by having
someone there to push
the buttons for you

i have thought if only
i could become rich and famous i would
live luxuriously in new york knowing
famous people eating
in expensive restaurants calling
long distance anytime i want

but you held me
one evening and now i know
the ultimate luxury
of your love

Poem ◾

like a will-o'-the-wisp in the night
on a honeysuckle breeze
a moment sticks
us together

like a dolphin being
tickled on her stomach
my sea of love flip-flops all
over my face

like the wind blowing
across a field of wheat
your smile whispers to my inner ear

with the relief of recognition
i bend to your eyes
casually
raping me

Hampton, Virginia

the birds flew south
earlier this year
and flowers wilted under the glare
of frost
nature puts her house in order

the weather reports say this
will be the coldest winter
already the perch have burrowed
deep into the lakes
and the snails are six instead
of three feet under

i quilted myself
one blanket and purchased five
pounds of colored popcorn
in corners i placed dried
flowers and in my bathroom a jar
of lavender smells
my landlord stripped my windows
and i cut all my old sox for feet pads

they say you should fight the cold with the cold
but since i never do anything right
i called you

Poetry Is a Trestle ▪

poetry is a trestle
spanning the distance between
what i feel
and what i say

like a locomotive
i rush full speed ahead
trusting your strength
to carry me over

sometimes we share a poem
because people are near
and they would notice me
noticing you
so i write X and you write O
and we both win

sometimes we share a poem
because i'm washing the dishes
and you're looking at your news

or sometimes we make a poem
because it's Sunday and you want
ice cream while i want cookies

but always we share a poem
because belief predates action
and i believe
the most beautiful poem
ever heard is your heart
racing

The Laws of Motion

(for Harlem Magic)

The laws of science teach us a pound of gold weighs as
much as a pound of flour though if dropped from any
undetermined height in their natural state one would
reach bottom and one would fly away

Laws of motion tell us an inert object is more difficult to
propel than an object heading in the wrong direction is to
turn around. Motion being energy—inertia—apathy.
Apathy equals hostility. Hostility—violence. Violence
being energy is its own virtue. Laws of motion teach us

Black people are no less confused because of our
Blackness than we are diffused because of our
powerlessness. Man we are told is the only animal who
smiles with his lips. The eyes however are the mirror of
the soul

The problem with love is not what we feel but what we
wish we felt when we began to feel we should feel
something. Just as publicity is not production: seduction
is not seductive

If I could make a wish I'd wish for all the knowledge of all
the world. Black may be beautiful Professor Micheau
says but knowledge is power. Any desirable object is
bought and sold—any neglected object declines in value.
It is against man's nature to be in either category

If white defines Black and good defines evil then men
define women or women scientifically speaking describe
men. If sweet is the opposite of sour and heat the
absence of cold then love is the contradiction of pain and
beauty is in the eye of the beheld

Sometimes I want to touch you and be touched in return. But you think I'm grabbing and I think you're shirking and Mama always said to look out for men like you

So I go to the streets with my lips painted red and my eyes carefully shielded to seduce the world my reluctant lover

And you go to your men slapping fives feeling good posing as a man because you know as long as you sit very very still the laws of motion will be in effect

The Life I Led ▪

i know my upper arms will grow
flabby it's true
of all the women in my family

i know that the purple veins
like dead fish in the Seine
will dot my legs one day
and my hands will wither while
my hair turns grayish white   i know that
one day my teeth will move when
my lips smile
and a flutter of hair will appear
below my nose   i hope
my skin doesn't change to those blotchy
colors

i want my menses to be undifficult
i'd very much prefer staying firm and slim
to grow old like a vintage wine fermenting
in old wooden vats with style
i'd like to be exquisite   i think

i will look forward to grandchildren
and my flowers   all my knickknacks in their places
and that quiet of the bombs not falling in cambodia
settling over my sagging breasts

i hope my shoulder finds a head that needs nestling
and my feet find a footstool after a good soaking
with epsom salts

i hope i die
warmed
by the life that i tried
to live

Mother's Habits

i have all
my mother's habits
i awake in the middle of night
to smoke a cigarette
i have a terrible fear of flying
and i don't like being alone
in the dark
sleep is a sport we all
participate in
it's the scourge of youth
and a necessity of old age
though it only hastens the day
when dissolution is inevitable
i grow tired
like my mother doing without
even one small word
that says i care
and like my mother i shall fade
into my dreams
no longer caring
either

The Way I Feel ∎

i've noticed i'm happier
when i make love
with you
and have enough left
over to smile at my doorman

i've realized i'm fulfilled
like a big fat cow
who has just picked
for a carnation contentment
when you kiss your special place
right behind my knee

i'm as glad as mortar
on a brick that knows
another brick is coming
when you walk through
my door

most time when you're around
i feel like a note
roberta flack is going to sing

in my mind you're a clock
and i'm the second hand sweeping
around you sixty times an hour
twenty-four hours a day
three hundred sixty-five days a year
and an extra day
in leap year
cause that's the way
that's the way
that's the way i feel
about you

Communication ■

if music is the most universal language
just think of me as one whole note

if science has the most perfect language
picture me as MC^2

since mathematics can speak to the infinite
imagine me as 1 to the first power

what i mean is   one day
i'm gonna grab your love
and you'll be
satisfied

Luxury

i suppose living
in a materialistic society
luxury
to some would be having
more than what you need

living in an electronic age seeing
the whole world by pushing a button
the *nth* degree might perhaps be
adequately represented by having
someone there to push
the buttons for you

i have thought if only
i could become rich and famous i would
live luxuriously in new york knowing
famous people eating
in expensive restaurants calling
long distance anytime i want

but you held me
one evening and now i know
the ultimate luxury
of your love

Poem ■

like a will-o'-the-wisp in the night
on a honeysuckle breeze
a moment sticks
us together

like a dolphin being
tickled on her stomach
my sea of love flip-flops all
over my face

like the wind blowing
across a field of wheat
your smile whispers to my inner ear

with the relief of recognition
i bend to your eyes
casually
raping me

Hampton, Virginia ▪

the birds flew south
earlier this year
and flowers wilted under the glare
of frost
nature puts her house in order

the weather reports say this
will be the coldest winter
already the perch have burrowed
deep into the lakes
and the snails are six instead
of three feet under

i quilted myself
one blanket and purchased five
pounds of colored popcorn
in corners i placed dried
flowers and in my bathroom a jar
of lavender smells
my landlord stripped my windows
and i cut all my old sox for feet pads

they say you should fight the cold with the cold
but since i never do anything right
i called you

Poetry Is a Trestle ▪

poetry is a trestle
spanning the distance between
what i feel
and what i say

like a locomotive
i rush full speed ahead
trusting your strength
to carry me over

sometimes we share a poem
because people are near
and they would notice me
noticing you
so i write X and you write O
and we both win

sometimes we share a poem
because i'm washing the dishes
and you're looking at your news

or sometimes we make a poem
because it's Sunday and you want
ice cream while i want cookies

but always we share a poem
because belief predates action
and i believe
the most beautiful poem
ever heard is your heart
racing

Something to Be Said for Silence ■

there is something
to be said for silence
    it's almost as sexual as moving
    your bowels

i wanted to be in love
when winter came
like a groundhog i would burrow
under the patchwork pieces
of your love
but the threads are slender
and they are being stretched

i guess it's all right
to want to feel
though it's better to really feel
and sometimes i wonder
did i ever love anyone

i like my house my job i gave up
my car
but i bought a new coat
and somewhere something is missing
    i do all the right things
maybe i'm just tired
maybe i'm just tired of being tired
i feel sometimes so inert
and laws of motion being what they are
i feel we won't feel again

it's all right with me
if you want to love
it's all right with me if you don't

my silence is at least
as sexy as your love
and twice as easy
to take

Africa

i am a teller of tales
a dreamer of dreams
   shall i spin a poem around you
human beings grope to strangers
to share a smile
complain to lovers of their woes
and never touch
those who need to be touched
   may i move on
the african isn't independent
he's emancipated
and like the freedman he explores
his freedom rather than exploits
his nation
worrying more about the condition
of the women than his position in the world
   i am a dreamer of dreams
in my fantasy i see a person
not proud for pride is a collection of lions
or a magazine in washington d.c.
but a person who can be wrong and go on
or a person who can be praised and still work
but a person who can let a friend share a joy as easily
as a friend shares a sorrow
it's odd that all welcome a tale of disappointment
though few a note of satisfaction
have none of us been happy
i am a teller of tales
i see kings and noblemen
slaves and serfs all selling
and being sold for what end
to die for freedom or live for joy
   i am a teller of tales
we must believe in each other's dreams

i'm told and i dream
of me accepting you and you accepting yourself
will that stroke the tension
between blacks and africans
i dream of truth lubricating our words
will that ease three hundred years
and i dream of black men and women walking
together side by side into a new world
described by love and bounded by difference
for nothing is the same except oppression and shame
    may i spin a poem around you
come let's step into my web
and dream of freedom together

Swaziland

i am old and need
to remember
you are young and need
to learn
if i forget the words
will you remember the music

i hear a drum speaking of a stream
the path is crossing the stream
the stream is crossing the path
which came first the drums ask
the music is with the river

if we meet does it matter
that i took the step toward you

the words ask are you fertile
the music says let's dance

i am old and need to remember
you are young and want to learn
let's dance together
let's dance
together
let's
dance
together

A Very Simple Wish ▪

i want to write an image
like a log-cabin quilt pattern
and stretch it across all the lonely
people who just don't fit in
   we might make a world
   if i do that

i want to boil a stew
with all the leftover folk
whose bodies are full
of empty lives
   we might feed a world
   if i do that

twice in our lives
we need direction
when we are young and innocent
when we are old and cynical
but since the old refused
to discipline us
we now refuse
to discipline them
which is a contemptuous way
for us to respond
to each other

i'm always surprised
that it's easier to stick
a gun in someone's face
or a knife in someone's back
than to touch skin to skin
anyone whom we like

i should imagine if nature holds true
one day we will lose our hands
since we do no work nor make
any love
if nature is true
we shall all lose our eyes
since we cannot even now distinguish
the good from the evil

i should imagine we shall lose our souls
since we have so blatantly put them up
for sale and glutted the marketplace
thereby depressing the price

i wonder why we don't love
not some people way on
the other side of the world with strange
customs and habits
not some folk from whom we were sold
hundreds of years ago
but people who look like us
who think like us
who want to love us   why
don't we love them

i want to make a quilt
of all the patches and find
one long strong pole
to lift it up

i've a mind to build
a new world

want to play

Night

in africa night walks
into day as quickly
as a moth is extinguished
by its desire for flame

the clouds in the caribbean carry
night like a young man
with a proud erection dripping
black dots across the blue sky
the wind a mistress of the sun howls
her displeasure at the involuntary
fertilization

but nights are white
in new york
the shrouds of displeasure
mask our fear of facing
ourselves between the lonely
sheets

Poetry ■

poetry is motion graceful
as a fawn
gentle as a teardrop
strong like the eye
finding peace in a crowded room

we poets tend to think
our words are golden
though emotion speaks too
loudly to be defined
by silence

sometimes after midnight or just before
the dawn
we sit typewriter in hand
pulling loneliness around us
forgetting our lovers or children
who are sleeping
ignoring the weary wariness
of our own logic
to compose a poem
   no one understands it
it never says "love me" for poets are
beyond love
it never says "accept me" for poems seek not
acceptance but controversy
it only says "i am" and therefore
i concede that you are too

a poem is pure energy
horizontally contained
between the mind
of the poet and the ear of the reader
if it does not sing discard the ear

for poetry is song
if it does not delight discard
the heart for poetry is joy
if it does not inform then close
off the brain for it is dead
if it cannot heed the insistent message
that life is precious

which is all we poets
wrapped in our loneliness
are trying to say

Always There Are the Children ■

and always   there are the children

there will be children in the heat of day
there will be children in the cold of winter

children   like a quilted blanket
are welcomed in our old age

children   like a block of ice to a desert sheik
are a sign of status in our youth

we feed the children with our culture
that they might understand our travail

we nourish the children on our gods
that they may understand respect

we urge the children on the tracks
that our race will not fall short

but children are not ours
nor we theirs   they are future   we are past

how do we welcome the future
not with the colonialism of the past
   for that is our problem
not with the racism of the past
   for that is their problem
not with the fears of our own status
   for history is lived not dictated

we welcome the young of all groups
as our own with the solid nourishment
of food and warmth

we prepare the way with the solid
nourishment of self-actualization

we implore all the young to prepare for the young
because always there will be children

Cotton Candy on a

Rainy Day

1978

Cotton Candy on a Rainy Day

Don't look now
I'm fading away
Into the gray of my mornings
Or the blues of every night

Is it that my nails
    keep breaking
Or maybe the corn
    on my second little piggy
Things keep popping out
    on my face
        or
    of my life

It seems no matter how
I try I become more difficult
    to hold
I am not an easy woman
    to want

They have asked
    the psychiatrists   psychologists   politicians and
    social workers
What this decade will be
    known for
There is no doubt   it is
    loneliness

If loneliness were a grape
    the wine would be vintage
If it were a wood
    the furniture would be mahogany
But since it is life   it is

Cotton Candy
on a rainy day
The sweet soft essence
of possibility
Never quite maturing

I have prided myself
On being in that great tradition
albeit circus
That the show must go on
Though in my community the vernacular is
One Monkey Don't Stop the Show

We all line up
at some midway point
To thread our way through
the boredom and futility
Looking for the blue ribbon and gold medal

Mostly these are seen as food labels

We are consumed by people who sing
the same old song   STAY:

as sweet as you are

in my corner

Or perhaps   *just a little bit longer*
But whatever you do   *don't change baby baby don't*
change
Something needs to change
Everything   some say   will change
I need a change
of pace   face   attitude and life
Though I long for my loneliness
I know I need something
Or someone
Or . . . . . .

I strangle my words as easily as I do my tears
I stifle my screams as frequently as I flash my smile
  it means nothing
I am cotton candy on a rainy day
    the unrealized dream of an idea unborn

I share with the painters the desire
To put a three-dimensional picture
On a one-dimensional surface

Introspection ■

she didn't like to think in abstracts
sadness happiness taking giving   all abstracts
she much preferred waxing the furniture
cleaning the shelves putting the plates away
something concrete to put her hands on
a job well done in a specific time span

her eyes were two bright shiny six guns
already cocked
prepared to go off at a moment's indiscretion
had she been a vietnam soldier or a mercenary
for Ian Smith   all the children and dogs and goodly
portions of grand old trees would have been demolished

she had lived both long and completely enough
not to be chained to truth
she was not pretty
she had no objections to the lies
lies were better than the silence that abounded
nice comfortable lies like   I need you
or   Gosh you look pretty this morning
the lies that make the lie of life real
or lies that make real life livable

she lived on the edge of an emotional abyss
or perhaps she lived in the well of a void
there were always things she wanted
like arms to hold her
eyes that understood
a friend to relax with
someone to touch
always   someone to touch

her life was a puzzle broken
into a hundred thousand little pieces
she didn't mind being emotionally disheveled
she was forever fascinated by putting the pieces
together   though most times
the center was empty

she never slept well
there wasn't a time
actually
when sleep refreshed her
perhaps it could have
but there were always dreams
or nightmares
and mostly her own acknowledgment
that she was meant to be tired

she lived
because she didn't know any better
she stayed alive
among the tired and lonely
not waiting   always wanting
needing a good night's rest

Forced Retirement ▪

all problems being
as personal as they are
have to be largely
of our own making

i know i'm unhappy
most of the time
nothing an overdose
of sex won't cure of course
but since i'm responsible
i barely have an average
intake

on the other hand
i'm acutely aware
there are those suffering
from the opposite affliction

some people die of obesity
while others starve to death
some commit suicide
because they are bored
others because of pressure
the new norm is as elusive
as the old

granting problems coming
from within
are no less painful
than those out of our hands
i never really do worry
about atomic destruction
of the universe

though i can be quite vexed
that Namath and Ali don't retire
my father has to
and though he's never made a million
or even hundreds of thousands
he too enjoys his work
and is good at it
but more   goes
even when he doesn't
feel like it

people fear boredom
not because they are   bored
rather more from fear
of boring
though minds are either sharp
or dull
and bodies available
or not
and there's something else
that's never wrong
though never quite right
either

i've always thought the beautiful
are as pitiful
as the ugly
but the average is no guarantee
of happiness

i've always wandered a bit
not knowing if this is a function
of creeping menopause
or incipient loneliness
i no longer correct my habits

nothing makes sense
if we are just a collection of genes
on a freudian altar to the species
i don't like those theories
telling me why i feel as i do
behaviorisms never made sense
outside feeling

i could say i am black female
and bright
in a white male mediocre world
but that hardly explains why
i sit on the beaches of st croix
feeling so abandoned

The New Yorkers ■

In front of the bank building
after six o'clock the gathering
of the bag people begins

In cold weather they huddle
around newspapers
when it is freezing they get
cardboard boxes

Someone said they are all rich eccentrics
Someone is   of course   crazy

The man and his buddy moved
to the truck port
in the adjoining building
most early evenings he visits
his neighbors awaiting
the return of his friend
from points unknown to me
they seem to be a spontaneous
combustion these night people
they evaporate during the light of day
only to emerge at evening glow
as if they had never been away

I am told there are people
who live underground
in the layer between the subways
and the pipes that run them
they have harnessed the steam
to heat their corner
and cook their food
though there is no electricity
making them effectively   moles

The twentieth century has seen
    two big wars and two small ones
    the automobile and the SST
    telephones and satellites in the sky
    man on the moon and spacecraft on Jupiter
How odd to also see the people
of New York City living
in the doorways of public buildings
as if this is an emerging nation
though of course it is

Look at the old woman
who sits on 57th Street and 8th Avenue
selling pencils
I don't know where she spends the night
she sits summer and winter
snow or rain humming
some white religious song
she must weigh over 250 pounds
the flesh on her legs has stretched
like a petite pair of stockings
onto a medium frame
beyond its ability to fit
there are tears and holes
of various purples in her legs
things and stuff ooze from them
drying and running again
there is never   though   a smell
she does not ask you to buy
a pencil nor will her eyes
condemn your health
it's easy really to walk by her
unlike the man in front
of Tiffany's she holds her pencils
near her knee

you take or not
depending upon your writing needs

He on the other hand is blind and walking
his german shepherd dog
his sign says THERE
BUT FOR THE GRACE OF GOD
GOES YOU and there is a long
explanation of his condition
It's rather easy for the Tiffany shopper
to see his condition
   he is Black

Uptown on 125th Street is an old blind Black woman
she is out only in good
   weather and clothes
her house is probably spotless
as southern ladies are wont to keep house
and her wig is always on straight
   You got something for me, she called
   What do you want, I asked
   What's yo name? I know yo family
   No, you don't, I said laughing   You don't know
      anything about me
   You that Eyetalian poet ain't you? I know yo voice. I seen
      you on television
I peered closely into her eyes
   You didn't see me or you'd know I'm black
   Let me feel yo hair   if you Black   Hold down yo head
I did and she did
   Got something for me, she laughed
   You felt my hair   that's good luck
   Good luck is money, chile   she said
   Good luck is money

Crutches ▪

it's not the crutches we decry
it's the need to move forward
though we haven't the strength

women aren't allowed to need
so they develop rituals
since we all know working hands idle
the devil
women aren't supposed to be strong
so they develop social smiles
and secret drinking problems
and female lovers whom they never touch
except in dreams

men are supposed to be strong
so they have heart attacks
and develop other women
who don't know their weaknesses
and hide their fears
behind male lovers
whom they religiously touch
each saturday morning on the basketball court
it's considered a sign of health doncha know
that they take such good care
of their bodies

i'm trying to say something about the human condition
maybe i should try again

if you broke an arm or leg
a crutch would be a sign of courage
people would sign your cast
and you could bravely explain
no it doesn't hurt—it just itches

but if you develop an itch
there are no salves to cover the area
in need of attention
and for whatever guilt may mean
we would feel guilty for trying
to assuage the discomfort
and even worse for needing the aid

i really want to say something about all of us
am i shouting   i want you to hear me

emotional falls always are
the worst
and there are no crutches
to swing back on

Boxes ▪

i am in a box
on a tight string
subject to pop
without notice

everybody says how strong
i am

only black women
and white men
are truly free
they say

it's not difficult to see
how stupid they are

i would not reject
my strength
though its source
is not choice
but responsibility

i would not reject my light
though my wrinkles are also illuminated

something within demands
action
or words
if action is not possible

i am tired
of being boxed
muhammad ali must surely be pleased
that leon spinks relieved him

most of the time
i can't breathe
i smoke too much
to cover my fears
sometimes i pick
my nose to avoid
the breath i need

i do also do the same
injustice to my poems

i write because
i have to

i have considered
my reluctance
to be a fear of death
there are all sorts of reasons
i don't want to die
   responsibility to family
   obligations to friends
   dreams of future greatness
i close my eyes and chant
on airplanes to calm
my fleeting heart
since we are riding on air
my will is as necessary
as the pilot's abilities
to keep us afloat

i have felt that way
about other endeavors

however do we justify
our lives
the president of the united states
says Faith not deeds will determine
our salvation
that's probably why larry flynt
a stand-in for carter
is without his insides now
i have faith   of course
in the deeds i do
and see done
one really can't hate
the act but love
the actor
only jewish theater and american politics

would even contemplate
such a contradiction
however will we survive
the seventies

i seize on little things
you can tell a lot about people
by the way they comb their hair
or the way they don't look
you in the eye

am i discussing nixon
again

he went to humphrey's funeral
and opened his house
(2.50 per head)
for the public to see
can't decide if anita bryant
should marry carter or nixon
they both are so bad
they deserve her

there must be something fun
worth sharing

there is a split
between the jewish and black community
the former didn't mind
until the latter put a name to it

i live in a city
that has turned into a garbage can
there is no disagreement
about that
there is some question

concerning the dog dung in the streets
as opposed to the dog dung in the administration

ahhhh   but you will say
how awful of the poet
such insinuations she does make
nobody is perfect
i do   after all   have
this   well   reluctance

A Poem Off Center ■

how do poets write
so many poems
my poems get decimated
in the dishes the laundry
my sister is having another crisis
the bed has to be made
there is a blizzard on the way go to the grocery store
did you go to the cleaners
then a fuse blows
a fuse always has to blow
the women soon find themselves
talking either to babies or about them
no matter how careful we are
we end up giving tips
on the latest new improved cleaner
and the lotion that will take the smell away

if you write a political poem
you're anti-semitic
if you write a domestic poem
you're foolish
if you write a happy poem
you're unserious
if you write a love poem
you're maudlin
of course the only real poem
to write
is the go to hell writing establishment poem
but the readers never know who
you're talking about which brings us back
to point one

i feel   i think   sorry for the women
they have no place to go

it's the same old story blacks
hear all the time
if it's serious a white man
would do it
when it's serious
he will
everything from writing a poem
to sweeping the streets
to cooking the food
as long as his family doesn't eat it

it's a little off center
this life we're leading
maybe i shouldn't feel sorry
for myself
but the more i understand women
the more i do

The Winter Storm ■

somewhere there was a piano playing
but not in the bar
where she was sitting

somewhere across the candlelights
like a ship threading its way
through the morning fog
two people were surely moving
toward completion

she knew she had feelings
that were unfulfilled

there must certainly be a revolution
somewhere
but she couldn't see it
the idea of fulfillment baffled her

most assuredly she remembered

the sheets were clean
and he was tender
it was an accident
that rush of red wine starting with her toes
that came over her ending with a sigh
she had always hated people
who had to talk and instruct
or give indiscreet encouragement
she had laughed and laughed
what a marvelous thing you have discovered
she told him

she looked to see if anyone was happy
in the bar in which she was sitting

how many aeons had it been
how many men
enough to make her secure
in her desirability
too many to allow herself to say
she loved them all
remembering the names was the hardest
though she always retained the ability
to rate them
what indeed made sex
so fascinating to everyone
at best it's a tooth in a pain
that rubbing the gums will ease
at worst it's a desire denied
like the eyes closing
to the evening's sunset

she looked and crossed her support-hosed legs
in the bar with the music just out of reach

one always remembers passion
whether fantasy or fact
that rush of pure glandular energy
what really did she feel

she straightened her gray flannel panel skirt
pulling her gray silk blouse tight against her breasts
rubbing her left arm with the square gold band
against the chill that settled on the right
she looked around at the lonely faces
in the bar without the music

what made people interested
in other people
in whom they have no interest
but yes she recalled

as the drink was served
there is an energy crisis that's why
i'm having this drink
amid a raging storm outside
there is one inside too
and spring will not lessen
its ferocity

unconsciously as black women
are wont to do
she hummed a tune and patted her foot
to the gospel beat
the tips of the black pumps were a grayish white
the ice and salt having taken
their measure

she examined her nails
noting the cuticles needed trimming
a dim reflection from the mirror on the wall
showed her the face and form of a coward
life   she justified   is not heroic
but survival

tonight through the storm
she would sit in a bar
with only the music in her head

in the morning   for sure   she would go
home

Age

we tend to fear old age
as some sort of disorder   that can be cured
with the proper brand of aspirin
or perhaps a bit of Ben Gay for the shoulders
it does   of course   pay to advertise

one hates the idea of the first gray hair
a shortness of breath
devastating blows to the ego
indications we are doing
what comes naturally

it's almost laughable
that we detest aging
when we first become aware
we want it
little girls of four or five push
with eyes shining brightly at gram or mommy
the lie that they are seven or eight
little girls at ten worry
that a friend has gotten her monthly
and she has not
little girls of twelve
can be socially crushed
by lack of nobs on their chests

little boys of fourteen want
to think they want
a woman
the little penis that simply won't erect
is shattering to their idea of manhood
if perhaps they get a little peach fuzz
on their faces they may survive

adolescence proving there may indeed be life
after high school
the children begin to play   older
without knowing the price is   weariness

age teaches us that our virtues
are neither virtuous nor our vices
foul
age doesn't matter   really
what frightens is mortality
it dawns upon us that we can die
at some point it occurs we surely shall

it is not death we fear
but the loss of youth
not the youth of our teens
where most of the thinking took place
somewhere between the navel and the knee
but the youth of our thirties where career
decisions were going well
and we were respected for our abilities
or the youth of our forties
where our decisions proved if not right
then not wrong either
and the house   after all   is half paid

it may simply be that work
is so indelibly tied
to age that the loss
of work brings the depression
of impending death
there are so many   too many
who have never worked
and therefore for whom death
is a constant companion

as lack of marriage
lowers divorce rates
lack of life
prevents death
the unwillingness to try
is worse than any failure

in youth our ignorance gives us courage
with age our courage gives us hope
with hope we learn that man is more
than the sum of what he does
we also are what we wish we did
and age teaches us
that even that doesn't matter

Because

i wrote a poem
for you because
you are
my little boy

i wrote a poem
for you because
you are
my darling daughter

and in this poem
i sang a song
that says
as time goes on
i am you
and you are me
and that's how life
goes on

Their Fathers ▪

i will be bitter
when i grow old
i have seen the weakness
of our race
though i   as with many others
am reluctant
to give it name

each day i face
the world through fantasies
of past glories
who i deceive i am not
at all sure
   not myself
   not the whites above
   surely even the children
know the sterility
of their fathers

there are both reasons
and excuses
none are lacking in
understanding the causes
a cold front meeting
a warm mass of air
causes rain also
but that reason offers
less comfort
than a simple raincoat

mankind alone
among the mammals
communicates with his species
justification for his behavior

none among us lack compassion
or understanding or even sympathy
emotion is not a response
to inaction
and undoubtedly there are those
who are so unfeeling
they cannot represent mental
or emotional health
we have seen the Germans
and the Israeli reaction
and the Palestinian response
in our own time
we know the truth
of the Africans and Indians
we know we have only begun
the horror that is waiting
south of our borders
and south of our latitude
blood perhaps should not
all ways be the answer
but perhaps it always is

my people have suffered
so much for so long
we are pitiful
in our misery

we boost our spirits
by changing our minds
rather than our condition
blacks are still rather cheap
to purchase
    unemployment insurance
    a grant for a program programmed to fail
    enough seed money to insure bankruptcy
my people like magnificent race

horses have blinders
there is always talk
of the mighty past
but no plans
for a decent future
if no man is an island
black americans stand to prove
a people can be a peninsula
we are extended   phallic like   in an ocean
of whiteness
though that is not our problem
our extension like arms on
the body or legs on
a trunk is essential to balance
one neither walks nor stands without
extensions
one is not black without white
nor male without female
what is true of the mass is no less
true of the individual

someone said the only emotion
black men show
is rage or anger
which is only partly true
the only rage and anger
they show are to those
who would want to love them
and bear their children
and with them walk into the future
why do we
who have offered expectation
have to absorb pain

i will grow bitter
in old age

because life is not a problem
but a process
and there are no formulas
to our situation
the dinosaurs became extinct
ripened fruit falls from the bough
and i grow tired of hoping

it's only natural
that bitterness rests within
my spirit
the air is polluted
streams are poisoned
and i have seen the hollow look
of hatred in the dull
worn faces
of their fathers

Life Cycles ■

she realized
she wasn't one
of life's winners
when   she wasn't sure
life to her was some dark
dirty secret that
like some unwanted child
too late for an abortion
was to be borne
alone

she had so many private habits
she would masturbate sometimes
she always picked her nose when upset
she liked to sit with silence
in the dark
sadness is not an unusual state
for the black woman
or writers

she took to sneaking drinks
a habit which displeased her
both for its effects
and taste
yet eventually sleep
would wrestle her in triumph
onto the bed

she was nervous
when he was there
and anxious
when he wasn't
life   to her
was a crude cruel joke

played on the livers
she boxed her life
like a special private seed
planting it in her emotional garden
to see what weeds
would rise
to strangle
her

Adulthood II ■

There is always something
of the child
in us that wants
a strong hand to hold
through the hungry season
of growing up

when she was a child
summer lasted forever
and christmas seemed never
to come
now her bills from easter
usually are paid
by the 4th of july
in time to buy the ribs
and corn and extra bag of potatoes
for salad

the pit is cleaned
and labor day is near
time to tarpaulin
the above ground pool

thanksgiving turkey
is no sooner soup
than the children's shoes
wear thin saying
christmas is near   again
bringing the february letters asking
"did you forget
us last month"

her life looks occasionally
as if it's owed to some

machine
and the only winning point
she musters is to tear
mutilate and twist
the cards demanding information
payment
and a review of her credit worthiness

she sits sometimes
in her cubicled desk
and recalls her mother
did the same things
what we have been given
we are now expected to return
and she smiles

Habits

i haven't written a poem in so long
i may have forgotten how
unless writing a poem
is like riding a bike
or swimming upstream
or loving you
it may be a habit that once acquired
is never lost

but you say i'm foolish
of course you love me
but being loved of course
is not the same as being loved because
or being loved despite
or being loved

if you love me why
do i feel so lonely
and why do i always wake up alone
and why am i practicing
not having you to love
i never loved you that way

if being loved by you is accepting always
    getting the worst
    taking the least
    hearing the excuse
and never being called when you say you will
then it's a habit
like smoking cigarettes
or brushing my teeth when i awake
something i do without
thinking
but something without
which i could just as well do

most habits occur
because of laziness
we overdrink
because our friends do
we overeat
because our parents think
we need more flesh
on the bones
and perhaps my worst habit
is overloving
and like most who live
to excess
i will be broken
in two
by my unwillingness
to control my feelings

but i sit writing
a poem
about my habits
which while it's not
a great poem
is mine
and some habits
like smiling at children
or giving a seat to an old person
should stay
if for no other reason
than their civilizing
influence

which is the ultimate
habit
i need
to acquire

Fascinations ■

finding myself still fascinated
by the falls and rapids
i nonetheless prefer the streams
contained within the bountiful brown shoreline
i prefer the inland waters
to the salty seas
knowing that journeys end
as they begin
the sailor and his sail
the lover and her beloved
the light of day and night's darkness

i walk the new york streets
the heat rising in waves
to singe my knees
my head is always down
for i no longer look for you
usually i am cold no matter
what the temperature
i hunch my hands in the pockets of my pants
hoping you will be home
when i get there

i know i'm on dangerous ground
i misread your smile all year
assured that you and therefore everything
was all right
i wade from the quiet
of your presence into the turbulence
of your emotions
i have now understood a calm day
does not preclude a stormy evening
con edison after all went out
why shouldn't you

and though it took longer than anyone thought
the lights did come back on
why shouldn't yours
electricity is a product of the sea
as much as the air
coming from turbulence
as much as generators

if you were a pure bolt
of fire cutting the skies
i'd touch you risking my life
not because i'm brave or strong
but because i'm fascinated
by what the outcome will be

Gus ∎
(for my father)

He always had pretty legs
Even now   though he has gotten fat
His legs have kept their shape

He swam
Some men get those legs from tennis
But he swam
In a sink-or-swim mud hole somewhere
In Alabama

When he was a young man
More than half a century ago
Talent was described by how well
A thing was done   not by whom
That is   considering
That Black men weren't considered
One achieved on merit

The fact that he is short
Was an idea late reaching his consciousness
He hustled the ball on the high school court
Well enough to win a college scholarship
Luckily for me
Since that's where he met my mother

I have often tried to think lately
When I first met him
I don't remember
He was a stranger
As Black or perhaps responsible fathers
Are wont to be

He worked three jobs   a feat
Without precedence though not unknown
In the hills of West Virginia or the Red Clay of Georgia
What happens to a dream
When it must tunnel under
Langston says it might explode
It might also just die
Shriveling to the here and now
Confusing the dreamer til he no longer knows
Whether he is awake or asleep

Before we ourselves:
    Meet the man
    Lie to the bill collectors
    Don't know where the mortgage payment is coming from
It's difficult to understand
A weakness

Before our mettle is tested
We easily consider ourselves strong
Before we see our children want
Not elaborate things
But a christmas bike or easter shoes
It's easy to say
what should have been done

Before we see our own possibility shrink
Back into the unclonable cell
From which dreams spring
It's easy to condemn

If the first sign of spring is the swallows
Then the first sign of maturity is the pride
We gulp when we realize
There are few choices in life
That are clear

Seldom is good pitted against evil
Or even better against best
Mostly it's bad versus worse
And while some may intone
   life is not fair
"Choice" by definition implies
Equally attractive alternatives
Or mutually exclusive experiences

Boxers protect themselves from blows
   with heavily greased shoulders
Football players wear helmets
Joggers have specially made shoes
   to absorb the shocks
The problem with the Life game
For unprotected players
Is not what you don't have
But what you can't give
Though ultimately there is the understanding
That even nothing is something
As long as you are there
To give the nothing   personally

Black men grow inverse
To the common experience

He grew younger as his children left home
He has both time and money to buy
The toys he never had
Lawn mowers   saws   garden equipment   CB's
   Steroes
Whatever is new and exciting
He smiles more often too
And his legs are still
quite exceptional
For a Grandfather

Choices ▪

if i can't do
what i want to do
then my job is to not
do what i don't want
to do

it's not the same thing
but it's the best i can
do

if i can't have
what i want   then
my job is to want
what i've got
and be satisfied
that at least there
is something more
to want

since i can't go
where i need
to go   then i must   go
where the signs point
though always understanding
parallel movement
isn't lateral

when i can't express
what i really feel
i practice feeling
what i can express
and none of it is equal

i know
but that's why mankind
alone among the mammals
learns to cry

Photography ▪

the eye we are told
is a camera
but the film is the heart
not the brain
and our hands joining
those that reach
develop the product

it's easy sitting in the sun
to forget that cold exists
let alone envelops
the lives of people
it's easy sitting in the sun
to forget the ice and ravages
of winter yet
there are those who would have
no other season
it's always easy when thinking
we have the best to assume
others covet it
yet surf or sea each has
its lovers and its meaning
for love

watching the red sun bleed
into the ocean
one thinks of the beauty that fire brings
if the eye is a camera and the film is the heart
then the photo assistant is god

The Beep Beep Poem ▪

I should write a poem
but there's almost nothing
that hasn't been said
and said and said
beautifully, ugly, blandly
excitingly
   stay in school
   make love not war
   death to all tyrants
   where have all the flowers gone
and don't they understand at kent state
the troopers will shoot . . . again

i could write a poem
because i love walking
in the rain
and the solace of my naked
body in a tub of warm water
cleanliness may not be next
to godliness but it sure feels
good

i wrote a poem
for my father but it was so constant
i burned it up
he hates change
and i'm baffled by sameness

i composed a ditty
about encore american and worldwide news
but the editorial board
said no one would understand it
as if people have to be tricked
into sensitivity
though of course they do

i love to drive my car
hours on end
along back country roads
i love to stop for cider and apples and acorn squash
three for a dollar
i love my CB when the truckers talk
and the hum of the diesel in my ear
i love the aloneness of the road
when I ascend descending curves
the power within my toe delights me
and i fling my spirit down the highway
i love the way i feel
when i pass the moon and i holler to the stars
i'm coming through

Beep Beep

A Poem for Ed and Archie ▪

I dreamed of you last night
standing near the Drugstore on the St.-Germain-des-Prés
You popped out of the pastry shop
wiping some exotic créme from your lips
showing off your new cigarette holder
"Got one yet?"
and your smile lit up the city of lights
Southern men cannot be generalized about
I know you all as liars and lynchers
I have accepted the myth that though you may wear a suit
beneath it the blood runs hot
and your hair   so similar to those whom Darwin said were
   all our ancestors   mats against your heaving chest
It's unpatriotic not to smoke tobacco
we both agreed   at least in North Carolina
and poor Ed   who will some day be a great man
just sat there confused

without laughter what is the purpose
my ancestors once worked for yours
involuntarily
and I laugh because it is only what happened
not nearly the truth

I've seen Paris and you've seen me
and last night in my dream
we both smiled

Woman ■

she wanted to be a blade
of grass amid the fields
but he wouldn't agree
to be the dandelion

she wanted to be a robin singing
through the leaves
but he refused to be
her tree

she spun herself into a web
and   looking for a place to rest
turned to him
but he stood straight
declining to be her corner

she tried to be a book
but he wouldn't read

she turned herself into a bulb
but he wouldn't let her grow

she decided to become
a woman
and though he still refused
to be a man
she decided it was all
right

Space

a flying saucer landed
in my living room
i too am an astronaut
having applied for my own space
i welcomed the visitor
i need something intelligent
to talk to   not for long
but maybe just through dinner

not being afraid
of what i don't know
i unanxiously awaited the emergence

should i call him a space man
or might not it be a woman
probably not
her menses on jupiter
no less than earth
causes excuses for exclusion

should i shake hands
and offer a glass of white wine
i always wanted to know space
people but how do we proceed

i think i should tell you
she reported as she stepped from her craft
you possibly are not seeing me
depending upon the solar year
you may only be seeing my aura

don't worry i assured her
happy it was a woman

depending upon my aura
you are most likely only seeing
my solar years

we sat down
to talk

Poem

(for EMA)

though i do wonder
why you intrigue me
i recognize that an exceptional moth
is always drawn
to an exceptional flame

you're not at all what you appear
to be
though not so very different

I've not learned
the acceptable way of saying
you fascinate me
I've not even learned
how to say i like you
without frightening people
away

sometimes I see things
that aren't really there
like warmth and kindness
when people are mean
but sometimes i see things
like fear and want to soothe it
or fatigue and want to share it
or love and want to receive it

is that weird
you think everyone is weird
though you're not really hypocritical
you just practice not being
what you want to be
and fail to understand

how others would dare
to be otherwise
that's weird to me
flames don't flicker
forever
and moths are born to be burned

it's an unusual way
to start a friendship
but nothing lasts forever

The Rose Bush ▦

(for Gordon)

i know i haven't grown but
i don't fit beneath the rose
bush by my grandmother's porch

i couldn't have grown so much though
i don't see why the back of the couch
doesn't hide me from my sister

the lightning that would flash
on summer days brought shouts
of you children be still   the lightning's
gonna get you

we laughed my cousins and sister and i
at the foolish old people
and their backward superstitions
though lightning struck me
in new york city
and i ran
to or from what   i'm not sure
but i was hit
and now i don't fit
beneath the rose bushes
anymore
anyway   they're gone

Patience ▪

there are sounds
which shatter
the staleness of lives
transporting the shadows
into the dreams

raindrops falling
on leaves shatter
the dust of the city
as soap washed off
bodies shatters
the complacent dirt

she waited for him
to take away that quiet

she waited for his call
with the patience of a slave
woman quilting or a jewish mother
simmering chicken broth

there would be no other
sound than his voice
to shatter the quiet
of her heart

she waited for him
to come

Make Up ∎

we make up our faces
for lots of reasons
to go to the movies
or some junior prom
to see ice hockey
or watch the Dodgers come home again
defeated

going to the grocery store
only requires lipstick
while a bridge game
can mean a quick trip
to the hairdresser for a touch up

i clean my make up
before going to bed
alone
and if my mood is foul
i spray the sheets
with Ultra Ban

most faces are made up
before the public is faced
whether male female or child
it's always so appropriate
don'tcha know
to put a little mascara
around the eyes

we make up fantasies
to face life
we need to believe
we are good on the job
or at least in the bed

we make up lies
to impress people
who are making up lies
to impress us
and if either took all
the make up off
life would not be
worth living

we make up excuses
to say i'm sorry *that*
forgive me *because*
and after all didn't i tell you
why

and i make up with you
because you aren't strong
enough to reach out
to say
come home   i need you

Frogs burrow the mud
snails bury themselves
and I air my quilts
preparing for the cold

Dogs grow more hair
mothers make oatmeal
and little boys and girls
take Father John's Medicine

Bears store fat
chipmunks gather nuts
and I collect books
For the coming winter

You Are There ▪

i shall save my poems
for the winter of my dreams
i look forward to huddling
in my rocker with my life
i wonder what i'll contemplate
lovers—certainly those
i can remember
and knowing my life
you'll be there

you'll be there in the cold
like a Siamese on my knee
proud purring when you let me stroke you

you'll be there in the rain
like an umbrella over my head
sheltering me from the damp mist

you'll be there in the dark
like a lighthouse in the fog
seeing me through troubled waters

you'll be there in the sun
like coconut oil on my back
to keep me from burning

i shall save a special poem
for you to say
you always made me smile
and even though i cried sometimes
you said i will not let you
down

my rocker and i on winter's porch
will never be sad if you're gone
the winter's cold has been stored
against
you will always be
there

A Statement on Conservation

Scarcity in oil and gas
Can bring about a cold spell
No one cares if you conserve
As long as you can pay well

Cash is not the only tool
To purchase what we need
Dollar bills and jingling change
Are very cheap indeed

Buying power in our world
Speaks to white illusion
Understanding what I need
I've come to this conclusion

Love is in short supply
Like leaves on a winter vine
Whether it's right or whether it's wrong
I'll pay the price for mine

Spring is late and summer soon
Will come in with its heat wave
We will all need energy
Unless we have a cool cave

I don't mind the cold or heat
And I've got a reason
Love when it's spread all around
Can tackle any season

Turning ▪
(I need a better title)

she often wondered why people spoke
of gaining years as turning
when she celebrated her thirtieth birthday she knew
she had turned though
she hadn't gained

the rain turned on her windowsill
and it didn't gain
and he like her face gaining
wrinkles
turned indifferent

she became happier without
the big apartment
the stereo components
and the ten pounds she shed
while adjusting to the loss
of his love

her fault lay
in her honesty
it was always his sexiness
that held her not
his arms
it was his lovemaking not
his love she missed

she compacted her
life into one
tiny room with kitchen   bed and roaches
in the four corners which contained nothing
that couldn't be stolen

or left in case
she had to run
for her sanity

so she turned thirty-one
with all
the introspections that nothing
not even them was meant
not to turn
and from that understanding
she gained
knowledge

A Response ▪

(to the rock group Foreigner)

you say i'm as cold
as ice
but ice is good
for a burn
if you were a woman
you would have known that
and rubbed me
the right way
to let me cool
your passion

A Poem of Friendship

We are not lovers
because of the love
we make
but the love
we have

We are not friends
because of the laughs
we spend
but the tears
we save

I don't want to be near you
for the thoughts we share
but the words we never have
to speak

I will never miss you
because of what we do
but what we are
together

Being and Nothingness

(to quote a philosopher)

i haven't done anything
meaningful in so long
it's almost meaningful
to do nothing

i suppose i could fall in love
or at least in line
since i'm so discontented
but that takes effort
and i don't want to exert anything
neither my energy nor my emotions

i've always prided myself
on being a child of the sixties
and we are all finished
so that makes being
nothing

The Moon Shines Down ■

the moon shines down
on new york city
while i smile over
at you

the moon is still
against the night
and i am still
against you

surely you must sometimes wonder
won't i ever go home
surely you must sometimes say
poet please leave me alone

but my bad rhyme
and love of night
retain me here with you
and though it's so sad to admit
without you what would i do

of course you are no panacea
for my lack of friends
but if i were a hallmark card
here's where we'd begin

    the moon shines down
    on new york city
    while i smile over
    at you

That Day

if you've got the key
then i've got the door
let's do what we did
when we did it before

if you've got the time
i've got the way
let's do what we did
when we did it all day

you get the glass
i've got the wine
we'll do what we did
when we did it overtime

if you've got the dough
then i've got the heat
we can use my oven
til it's warm and sweet

i know i'm bold
coming on like this
but the good things in life
are too good to be missed

now time is money
and money is sweet
if you're busy baby
we can do it on our feet

we can do it on the floor
we can do it on the stair
we can do it on the couch
we can do it in the air

we can do it in the grass
and in case we get an itch
i can scratch it with my left hand
cause i'm really quite a witch

if we do it once a month
we can do it in time
if we do it once a week
we can do it in rhyme
if we do it every day
we can do it everyway
we can do it like we did it
when we did it
that day

Those Who Ride the

Night Winds

1983

Charting the Night Winds ▪

The first poem . . . ever written . . . was probably carved . . . on a cold damp cave . . . by a physically unendowed cave man . . . who wanted to make a good impression . . . on a physically endowed . . . cave woman . . . But maybe not . . . Maybe it was she . . . trying to gain the notice . . . of a hunk . . . who was in demand . . . Or perhaps . . . it was simply someone . . . who admired the motion . . . of a sabertooth tiger . . . and wanting to capture the beauty . . . picked up a sharpened rock . . . to draw . . . We know so very little . . . about the origin of the written word . . . let alone the language . . . that all conjecture deserves some consideration . . .

The fears . . . of the human race . . . are legion . . . Perhaps our size . . . strength . . . and speed . . . coupled with our ability . . . to see our weakness . . . have made us an anxious species . . . There are smaller mammals . . . There are more vulnerable life-forms . . . Yet we alone can give vent to our understanding . . . of the tenuousness of Life . . .

Nature is a patient teacher . . . She slowly changes . . . winter to summer . . . by proper use . . . of spring and fall . . . That's kind . . . of nature . . . Humans fear . . . sudden change . . . Hurricanes . . . Volcanoes . . . Earthquakes . . . Tornadoes . . . all are generally perceived . . . as aberrant . . . Blizzards . . . in winter . . . Electrical storms . . . in summer . . . are a part of the season . . . But change . . . both gradual . . . and violent . . . is a necessary ingredient . . . with Life . . .

Art . . . and by necessity . . . artists . . . are on the cutting edge . . . of change . . . The very fact . . . that something has been done . . . over and over again . . . is one reason . . . to change . . . Everything . . . must change . . . If only through perception . . . Honor thy Father and Mother . . . does not change . . . though the understanding of long life has . . . Do unto others as you would have them do unto you . . . has not changed . . . though the application must move from the individual to the nation . . . What goes up must come down . . . will not change . . . though our rock stars and superathletes seem impervious . . . to the lessons of Telstar . . . There is . . . in reality . . . very little that is new . . . under the yellow sun . . . We have only rearranged the matter . . . and reconceptualized the thought . . . Greed . . . is a terrible thing . . . Envy . . . is not an acceptable emotion . . . Jealousy . . . is dangerous to your emotional life . . . and the physical and mental well-being . . . of your loved one . . . Though people say . . . they cannot change . . . change we do . . . in our abilities . . . desires . . . understanding . . . The need to force . . . humans to change . . . may be one reason we all grow . . . older . . . though there is no corresponding gene . . . to make us grow . . . wiser . . .

In the written arts . . . language has opened . . . becoming more accessible . . . more responsive . . . to what people really think . . . and say . . . We are now free . . . to use any profane word . . . or express any profound thought . . . we may wish . . . Sexuality . . . once a great taboo in language . . . and act . . . is fully explored . . . through fiction . . . and nonfiction . . . through poetry . . . and plays . . . Different and same gender . . . different and same age . . . different and same race . . . religion . . . or creed . . . all take their places . . . on the bookshelves . . . Ideas that once allowed the State to poison Socrates . . . Ideas that once allowed the Church to force Copernicus to recant . . . Ideas that once encouraged McCarthy to destroy the lives of men and women . . . are now as acceptable as a stop-and-go light . . . or at least as well understood . . . as fluoride . . . While there is surely much . . . to be done . . . some change has rent . . . its ways . . . I changed . . . I chart the night winds . . . glide with me . . . I am the walrus . . . the time has come . . . to speak of many things . . .

Lorraine Hansberry: ▪
An Emotional View

It's intriguing to me that "bookmaker" is a gambling . . . an under-
world . . . term somehow associated with that which is both ille-
gal . . . and dirty . . . Bookmakers . . . and those who play with
them . . . are dreamers . . . are betting on a break . . . a lucky
streak . . . that something will come . . . their way—something
good . . . something clean . . . something wonderful . . . We who
make books . . . we who write our dreams . . . confess our
fears . . . and witness our times are not so far . . . from the under-
world . . . are not so far . . . from illegality . . . are not so far from
the root . . . the dirt . . . the heart of the matter.

Writers . . . I think . . . live on that fine line between insanity and
genius . . . Either scaling the mountains . . . or skirting the
valleys . . . Riding that lonely train of truth . . . with just enough of
the player in us . . . to continue to hope . . . for the species . . .
Writers are . . . perhaps . . . congenital hypocrites . . . I don't think
preachers . . . priests . . . rabbis . . . and ayatollahs are hypocriti-
cal . . . because they have tubular vision . . . are indeed . . .
myopic . . . They know the answer . . . before you ask the ques-
tion . . . But the writer . . . the painter . . . the sculptor . . . the
creator . . . those who work . . . with both the mind . . . and the
heart of mankind . . . have no reason . . . to be hopeful . . . We
have . . . in fact . . . no right to write the happy ending . . . or the
love poem . . . no reason . . . to sculpt David . . . or paint . . . like
Charles White . . . We who have seen . . . all sides of the coin . . .
the front . . . the back . . . and the ribbed edge . . . know what the
ending . . . will surely be . . . Yet we speak . . . to and of . . .
courage . . . love . . . hope . . . something better . . . in mankind . . .
When we are perfectly honest . . . with ourselves . . . we cannot jus-
tify . . . our faith . . . Yet faith we do have . . . and continue to share.

Bookmaking is shooting craps . . . with the white boys . . . down-
town on the stock exchange . . . is betting a dime you can win . . .

a hundred . . . Making books is shooting craps . . . with God . . . is wandering into a casino where you don't even know the language . . . let alone the rules of the game . . . And that's proper . . . that's as it should be . . . If you wanted to be safe . . . you would have walked into the Post Office . . . or taken a graduate degree in Educational Administration . . . If you want to share . . . a vision . . . or tell the truth . . . you pick up . . . your pen . . . And take your chances . . . This is not . . . after all . . . tennis . . . where sets can be measured by points . . . or football . . . where games run on time . . . or baseball . . . where innings structure the play . . . It is life . . . open-ended . . . And once the play has begun . . . the book made . . . time . . . is the only judge.

Time . . . to the Black American . . . has always been . . . a burden . . . from 1619 to now . . . we have played out our drama . . . before a reluctant time . . . We were either too late . . . or too early . . . No people on Earth . . . in all her history . . . has ever produced so many people . . . so generally considered . . . "ahead of their time." . . . From the revolts in Africa . . . to our kidnapping . . . to the martyrs of freedom today . . . our people have been burdened . . . by someone else's sense . . . of the appropriate . . . There are . . . of course . . . all the jokes . . . about C. P. time . . . and there are the reminders . . . by the keepers of our souls . . . that God "is never late . . . but He always comes . . . on time." . . . To be Black . . . in America . . . is to not at all understand . . . time . . . Little Linda Brown was told . . . her school would be desegregated . . . "with all deliberate speed" . . . and twenty-five years later . . . this is still . . . untrue . . . Dr. King was told . . . in Montgomery . . . he was pushing too hard . . . going too fast . . . expecting too much . . . I wish we had been enslaved . . . at the same rate we are being set . . . free . . . It would be . . . an entirely different story . . . I wish the battleships . . . had sailed down the Mississippi River . . . when Emmett Till was lynched . . . at the same speed they sped to Cuba . . . during the missile crisis . . . I wish food . . . had been airlifted . . . to the sharecroppers in Tennessee . . . when they were pushed off the land . . . for exer-

cising their right to vote . . . at the same speed . . . it was air-
lifted . . . to West Berlin . . . at the ending of World War II . . . But
I'm only a colored poet . . . and my wishes . . . no matter which
star I choose . . . do not come true . . . But I'm also a writer . . .
and I know . . . that the Europeans aren't the only ones . . . who
keep time . . . some of the time is going . . . to be my time . . .
too . . .

Life teaches us not to regret . . . not to spend too much time on
what might have been . . . It is neither emotionally . . . nor intel-
lectually possible . . . for me to dwell on might-have-been . . . I
have a great love of history and antiques . . . the past is there to
instruct us . . . I am socially retarded . . . so I hold on . . . to old
friends . . . I like to be surrounded . . . by that which is warm and
familiar . . . yet I'm sorry . . . I never met Lorraine Hansberry . . . I
vividly understand that a writer is not the book she made . . . any
more than a child is the print of his parents . . . Many of us are
personally paranoid . . . generally uncommunicative . . . and basi-
cally unnice . . . just like most people . . . But I think Lorraine
must have been one . . . of those wonderful humans who . . . see-
ing both sides of the dilemma . . . and all sides of the coin . . . still
called "Heads" . . . when she tossed . . . And in her gamble . . .
never came up snake eyes . . . It's not that she wrote . . . beauti-
fully . . . and truthfully . . . though she did . . . It's not just that she
anticipated . . . our people and their reactions . . . though she
did . . . She also . . . when reading through . . . and between the
lines . . . possessed that quality of courage . . . to say what had to
be said . . . to those who needed to hear it . . . If writers are vision-
ary . . . her ministry was successful . . . She made it . . . possible
for all of us . . . to look . . . a little . . . deeper.

Hands: For Mother's Day ▪

I think hands must be very important . . . Hands: plait hair . . .
knead bread . . . spank bottoms . . . wring in anguish . . . shake
the air in exasperation . . . wipe tears, sweat, and pain from
faces . . . are at the end of arms which hold . . . Yes hands . . . Let's
start with the hands . . .

My grandmother washed on Mondays . . . every Monday . . . If
you were a visiting grandchild or a resident daughter . . . every
Monday morning at 6:00 A.M. . . . mostly in the dark . . . fre-
quently in the cold . . . certainly alone . . . you heard her on the
back porch starting to hum . . . as Black Christian ladies are prone
to do . . . at threshold . . . some plea to higher beings for forgive-
ness and the power to forgive . . .

I saw a photograph once of the mother of Emmett Till . . . a slight,
brown woman with pillbox hat . . . white gloves . . . eyes dark
beyond pain . . . incomprehensibly looking at a world that never
intended to see her son be a man . . . That same look is created
each year . . . without the hat and gloves, for mother seals are not
chic . . . at the Arctic Circle . . . That same look is in vogue in
Atlanta, Cincinnati, Buffalo . . . for much the same reason . . .
During one brief moment, for one passing wrinkle in time, Nancy
Reagan wore that look . . . sharing a bond, as yet unconsum-
mated . . . with Betty Shabazz, Jacqueline Kennedy, Coretta King,
Ethel Kennedy . . . The wives and mothers are not so radically
different . . . It is the hands of the women which massage the
balm . . . the ointments . . . the lotions into the bodies for bur-
ial . . . It is our hands which: cover the eyes of small children . . .
soothe the longing of the brothers . . . make the beds . . . set the
tables . . . wipe away our own grief . . . to give comfort to those
beyond comfort . . .

I yield from women whose hands are Black and rough . . . The
women who produced me are in defiance of Porcelana and Jergens

lotion . . . are ignorant of Madge's need to soak their fingernails in Palmolive dishwashing liquid . . . My women look at cracked . . . jagged fingernails that will never be adequately disguised by Revlon's new spring reds . . . We of the unacceptably strong take pride in the strength of our hands . . .

Some people think a quilt is a blanket stretched across a Lincoln bed . . . or from frames on a wall . . . a quaint museum piece to be purchased on Bloomingdale's 30-day same-as-cash plan . . . Quilts are our mosaics . . . **Michelle-Angelo's** contribution to beauty . . . We weave a quilt with dry, rough hands . . . Quilts are the way our lives are lived . . . We survive on patches . . . scraps . . . the leftovers from a materially richer culture . . . the throwaways from those with emotional options . . . We do the far more difficult job of taking that which nobody wants and not only loving it . . . not only seeing its worth . . . but making it lovable . . . and intrinsically worthwhile . . .

Though trite . . . it's nonetheless true . . . that a little knowledge is a dangerous thing . . . Perhaps pitiful thing would be more accurate . . . though that too is not profound . . . The more we experience the human drama . . . the more we are to understand . . . that whatever is not quite well about us will also not quite go away . . .

Sometimes . . . when it's something like Mother's Day . . . you really do wish you were smart enough to make the pain stop . . . to make the little hurts quit throbbing . . . to share with Star Trek's Spock the ability to touch your fingertips to the temples and make all the dumb . . . ugly . . . sad things of this world ease from memory . . . It's not at all that we fail to forgive others for the hurts we have received . . . we cannot forgive ourselves for the hurts we have meted . . . So . . . of course . . . we use our hands to push away rather than to pull closer . . .

We look . . . in vain . . . for an image of mothers . . . for an analogy for families . . . for a reason to continue . . . We live . . . mostly because we don't know any better . . . as best we can . . . Some of us are lucky . . . we learn to like ourselves . . . to forgive ourselves . . . to care about others . . . Some of us . . . on special occasions . . . watch the ladies in the purple velvet house slippers with the long black dresses come in from Sunday worship and we realize **man** never stood up to catch and kill prey . . . **man** never reared up on his hind legs to free his front parts to hold weapons . . . WOMAN stood to free her hands . . . to hold her young . . . to embrace her sons and lovers . . . WOMAN stood to applaud and cheer a delicate mate who needs her approval . . . WOMAN stood to wipe the tears and sweat . . . to touch the eyes and lips . . . that woman stood to free the arms which hold the hands . . . which hold.

This Is Not for John Lennon

(and this is not a poem)

Not more than we can bear . . . more than we should have to . . .
Those of us lacking the grace to kill ourselves take it in the gut . . .
from a gun or gossip . . . what's the difference . . . Anything in the
name of the Lord . . . or Freud . . . and don't forget the book con-
tracts and possible made-for-TV-movies starring that cute little
buttoned-down guy who you recently saw making some sort of
deal with a game show host . . . It's bad form to point out that
Jesus didn't wear no shoes nor carry any guns and wasn't even
known to have a choice on the presidential preference poll
(though His father was quoted a lot) . . . He has been seen how-
ever a lot at football games cheering the Catholic teams on to vic-
tory . . . let us all be born just one more time . . . we may yet get
it . . . right . . .

Something's wrong and this is not a poem . . . the main difference
being that you didn't think it was . . . Unlike those who profess to
be caring and Christian I didn't fool you . . . it's not about John
Lennon either . . . he's dead . . . And the man who killed him is
cutting a deal . . . with doctors whose only operations are with
lawyers over how to split the money and the 15 minutes of fame
Andy Warhol so solemnly promised . . . What a pitiful country this
is . . . Our beloved mayor who prefers capital punishment to Jesus
as a foolish belief all of a sudden defends the violence of New York
by saying, "But golly gee fellows there is violence in England
too" . . . Yes indeedy folks it's not the gun but the man . . . Maybe
the New Right is finally right about something . . . Let's ban the
men . . . Let's make them justify their existence and their right to
survival . . . Let us set up a board . . . a bureaucracy even . . .
where each one must come in and fill out in triplicate the reasons
why he should be allowed to live . . . All potential suicides need
not bother to apply . . . They can save us all grief by killing them
real selves instead of they play selves . . . Strange isn't it if you try
to live by getting a job or creating one there is no help . . . If you

307

try to die by drugs or pills or slicing your wrists you become very
very significant . . . No . . . Not more than we can bear . . . more
than we ought to . . .

But those who ride the night winds must learn to love the stars . . .
those who live on the edge must get used to the cuts . . . We are
told if we live in glass houses to neither throw nor stow the
stones . . . We are warned of bric-a-brac that easily breaks . . . IF
YOU BREAK IT YOU BOUGHT IT . . . the store sign says . . . sci-
ence being such a tenuous commodity we can only half believe for
every action there is an equal and opposite reaction . . . But if
Newton was as correct about apples as the snake we are at the
beginning not the end . . . Those who have nothing to offer take
something away . . . Don't cry for John Lennon cry for our-
selves . . . He was an astronaut of inner space . . . He celebrated
happiness . . . soothed the lonely . . . braced the weary . . . gave
word to the deaf . . . vision to the insensitive . . . sang a long low
note when he reached the edge of this universe and saw the Black-
ness . . . Poetry . . . like photography . . . functions best not only
in the available light but in the timeliness of the subject . . . There
are always those painters who think the only proper subjects are
those who can rent the galleries . . . Others know we who cut
stone must envision cathedrals . . . I don't believe you know some-
one just because you like what they do for a living . . . or the prod-
uct of it . . . You don't feel you know David Rockefeller and you all
like money . . . or what it can buy . . . You don't feel you know or
want to know Jerry Falwell and you all want to go to heaven . . . or
so you say . . . No this is not about John Lennon . . . He only wrote
and sang some songs . . . So did Chuck Willis . . . Johnny Ace . . .
Sam Cooke . . . Otis Redding . . . The blood on city streets and
backcountry roads isn't new . . . but now we can call this game
exactly what it is . . . This isn't about somebody who killed . . .
either . . . It's always a nut though isn't it . . . cashew . . .
peanut . . . walnut . . . pistachio . . . yeah . . . a real pissedaschio
nut . . . But take comfort music lovers . . . Reagan supports gun
control . . . ling freaks . . . And those who ride the night winds do

learn to love the stars . . . even while crying in the darkness . . . The whole may be greater than the sum of its parts . . . we'll never know now . . . one part is missing. No this is not about John Lennon . . . It's about us . . . And the night winds . . . Anybody want a ticket to ride?

Mirrors ▪

(for Billie Jean King)

The face in the window . . . is not the face in the mirror . . . Mirrors aren't for windows . . . they would block the light . . . Mirrors are for bedroom walls . . . or closet doors . . . Windows show who we hope to be . . . Mirrors reflect who we are . . . Mirrors . . . like religious fervors . . . are private . . . and actually uninteresting to those not involved . . . Windows open up . . . bring a fresh view . . . windows make us vulnerable

The French teach us in love . . . there is always one who kisses . . . and one who offers . . . the cheek . . . There is many a slip . . . 'twixt the cup and the lip . . . that's the reason . . . napkins were born . . . In love . . . there is always the hurt . . . and the hurter . . . even when the hurter doesn't want . . . to hurt . . . the hurtee selfishly strikes

    Lips . . . like brownish gray gulls infested by contact with polluted waters circling a new jersey garbage heap . . . flap in anticipation
    Lips . . . like an old pot-bellied unshaven voyeur with the grease of his speciality packed under his dirty ragged fingernails . . . move with the glee of getting a good lick in
    Lips . . . like a blind man describing an elephant by touch . . . give inadequate information

There are things . . . that we know . . . yet don't want to see . . . NOT THINGS . . . like abused children . . . that is public pain . . . and light must be focused . . . to bring the healing heat . . . NOT THINGS . . . like battered wives . . . that is public policy . . . if we allow silence to cover the cries . . . NOR THINGS . . . like the emotionally troubled . . . only Dick and Jane . . . or Ozzie and Harriet . . . are always smiling . . . NOT THINGS . . . like people in wheelchairs . . . who need sidewalk access . . . NOR THINGS . . . like the unsighted . . . who need braille in public elevators . . .

BUT THINGS . . . like love . . . and promises made after midnight . . . the rituals and responsibilities of courtship . . . have no place . . . in the court yard . . . are not a part of the public see . . . Pillow Talk is only a movie starring Doris Day or a song by Sylvia . . . something delightful if you're lucky . . . or necessary if you're needy . . . but always private . . . since you're human

The hands of children break . . . drinking glasses . . . dinner plates . . . wooden buses . . . dolls with long blond hair . . . Lego structures . . . down . . . While playing blind man's bluff . . . flower heads and beds suffer little gym-toed carelessness . . . When playing kickball . . . baseball . . . football . . . soccer . . . windows unshuttered shatter . . . it's only natural . . . they are children . . . Childish adults want to break mirrors . . . want to shatter lives . . . While eating and playing paraphernalia are easily replaced . . . toys forgotten . . . flowers regrown . . . windows quickly repaired . . . sometimes with a scolding/sometimes with a shrug . . . mirrors broken . . . promise seven years . . . bad luck . . . Like Humpty Dumpty . . . lives . . . once exposed to great heights . . . seem destined . . . for great falls . . . and are seldom properly repaired

Some people choose heroes . . . because they kiss a horse . . . and ride . . . alone . . . into the sunset . . . Some choose a hero . . . because he robbed the rich . . . and gave to the poor . . . Some want to emulate lives . . . that discovered cures for exotic diseases . . . or made a lot of money off foolish endeavors . . .
One of my heroes . . . is a tennis player . . . who has the courage of her game . . . and her life . . . "It Was A Mistake" for sure . . . if courtship turns to courts . . . if letters written to share a feeling come back . . . to testify against you . . . "It Was A Mistake" to choose the myopic . . . selfish . . . greedy as a repository of a feeling . . . "It Was A Mistake" to want that which does not want you but what you can do . . . but It Cannot Be A Mistake to have cared . . . It Cannot Be An Error to have tried . . . It Cannot Be Incorrect to have loved

It is illogical to spit . . . upon a face you once kissed
It is mean . . . to blacken eyes . . . which once beheld you
It is wrong . . . to punish the best . . . within

One of my heroes embraced . . . Medusa . . . but the mirror will
not break . . . it only shattered . . . The window did not crack . . . it
only opened . . . I am not ashamed . . . only sad . . . not for my
hero . . . but for those who fail to see . . . the true championship . . . match

Linkage ▪
(for Phillis Wheatley)

What would a little girl think . . . boarding a big . . . at least to
her . . . ship . . . setting sail on a big . . . to everybody . . .
ocean . . . Perhaps seeing her first . . . iceberg . . . or whale . . . or
shark . . . Watching the blue water kiss . . . the blue sky . . . and
blow white clouds . . . to the horizon . . . My mother . . . caused
awe . . . in me for blowing . . . smoke rings . . . What would a little
girl think . . . leaving Senegal . . . for that which had no name . . .
and when one was obtained . . . no place for her . . .

You see them now . . . though they were always . . . there . . . the
children of Hester Prynne . . . walking the streets . . . needing a
place . . . to eat . . . sleep . . . Be . . . warm . . . loved . . . alone . . .
together . . . complete . . . The block . . . that little Black girls . . .
stood upon . . . is the same block . . . they now walk . . . with little
white boys and girls . . . selling themselves . . . to the adequate . . .
bidder . . .

Hagar was a little Black girl . . . chosen by Sarah and Abraham . . .
looked like a breeder . . . they said . . . Phillis . . . a little Black
girl . . . chosen by Wheatley . . . looked intelligent . . . make a cute
pet . . . for the children . . . Old men . . . sweat curling round their
collars . . . choose a body and act . . . on the wait . . . through the
tunnel to Jersey . . . Looked like fun . . . they say . . . Family mem-
bers . . . and family friends . . . inhale to intoxication . . . the
allure of the youths . . . destroying in conception . . . that which
has never been . . . born . . .

Eyes . . . they say . . . are the mirror . . . of the soul . . . a reflec-
tion . . . of the spirit . . . an informer . . . to reality . . . What do
you see . . . if you are a little Black girl . . . standing on a stage . . .
waiting to be purchased . . . Is there kindness . . . concern . . .
compassion . . . in the faces examining you . . . Do your eyes
show . . . or other eyes acknowledge . . . that you . . . dusky . . .

naked of clothes and tongue . . . stripped of the protection of Gods . . . and countrymen . . . are Human . . . Do you see those who purchase . . . or those who sold . . . Do you see those who grab at you . . . or those who refused to shield you . . . Are you grateful to be bought . . . or sold . . . What would you think . . . of a people . . . who allowed . . . nay encouraged . . . abetted . . . regaled . . . in your chains . . . Hands . . . that handle heavy objects . . . develop callouses . . . Feet in shoes too tight . . . develop corns . . . Minds that cannot comprehend . . . like lovers separated too long . . . develop an affinity for what is . . . and an indifference . . . if not hostility . . . to that which has been denied . . . Little white boys . . . stalking Park Avenue . . . little white girls . . . on the Minnesota Strip . . . are also slaves . . . to the uncaring . . . of a nation . . .

It cannot be unusual . . . that the gene remembers . . . It divides . . . and redivides . . . and subdivides . . . again and again and again . . . to make the eyes brown . . . the fingers long . . . the hair coarse . . . the nose broad . . . the pigment Black . . . the mind intelligent . . . It cannot be unusual . . . that one gene . . . from all the billions upon billions . . . remembered clitorectomies . . . infibulations . . . women beaten . . . children hungry . . . garbage heaping . . . open sewers . . . men laughing . . . at it all . . . It cannot be unusual . . . that the dark . . . dusky . . . murky world . . . of druggery . . . drums . . . witch doctors . . . incantations . . . MAGIC . . . was willingly shed . . . for the Enlightenment . . . At least man . . . was considered rational . . . At least books . . . dispensed knowledge . . . At least God . . . though still angry and jealous . . . was reachable through prayer and action . . . if those are not redundant . . . terms . . . We cannot be surprised that young Phillis chose poetry . . . as others choose prostitution . . . to express her dismay . . .

The critics . . . from a safe seat in the balcony . . . disdain her performance . . . reject her reality . . . ignore her truths . . . How could she . . . they ask . . . thank God she was brought . . . and bought . . . in this Land . . . How dare she . . . they decried . . . cheer George Washington his victory . . . Why couldn't she . . . they want to know . . . be more like . . . more like . . . more like . . . The record sticks . . . Phillis was her own precedent . . . her own image . . . her only ancestor . . . She wasn't like Harriet Tubman because she is Tubman . . . with Pen . . . rather than body . . . Leading herself . . . and therefore her people . . . from bondage . . . not like Sojourner Truth . . . she was Truth . . . using words on paper . . . to make the case . . . that slavery is people . . . and wrong to do . . . We know nothing of the Life . . . we who judge others . . . of the conditions . . . we create . . . and expect others to live with . . . or beyond . . . broken spirits . . . broken hearts . . . misplaced love . . . fruitless endeavor . . . Women . . . are considered complete . . . when they marry . . . We have done . . . it is considered . . . our duty . . . when we safely deliver a person from the bondage of Father . . . to the bondage of duty . . . and husband . . . from house slaves who read and write . . . to housewives who have time for neither . . . We are happy . . . when their own race is chosen . . . their own class reaffirmed . . . their own desire submerged . . . into food . . . dishes . . . laundry . . . babies . . . no dreams this week thank you I haven't the time . . . Like overripe fruit in an orchard embraced by frost . . . the will to live turns rotten . . . feckless . . . feculent . . .

What is a woman . . . to think . . . when all she hears . . . are words that exclude her . . . all she feels . . . are emotions that deceive . . . What do the children think . . . in their evening quest . . . of those who from platform and pulpit . . . deride their condition . . . yet purchase their service . . . What must life be . . . to any young captive . . . of its time . . . Do we send them back . . . home to the remembered horrors . . . Do we allow them their else-wheres . . . to parade their talents . . . Do we pretend that all is well . . . that Ends . . .

Charles White ■

The art of Charles White is like making love
in the early evening
after the cabs have stopped
to pick you up and the doorman said
"Good evening ma'am. Pleasant weather we're having"

The images of Charles White remind me
of eating cotton candy at the zoo on a rainy day
and the candy not melting and all the other kids wondering
why

I remember once when I was little
before I smoked too many cigarettes
entering the church picnic sack race
I never expected to win just thought it would be fun
I came in second and drank at least a gallon
of lemonade then wandered off
to an old rope swing

Of all the losses of modern life the swing
in the back yard is my special regret
one dreams going back and forth of time and space
stopping bowing to one's sheer magnificence
pumping higher and higher space blurs time
and the world stops spinning while I in my swing
give a curtsey correctly
my pigtails in place and my bangs cut
just right

"But why aren't the artists the politicians" she asked
"because they're too nice" was the reply
"too logical too compassionate"
which not understanding I took to mean "sexy"—at least

that's how come and passionate were used in the novels
Johnetta and I used to sneak and read

And in the grown up world I think I understand
that passion is politics that being is beauty
and we are all in some measure responsible
for the life we live and the world
we live in

Some of us take the air, the land, the sun
and misuse our spirits   others of us have earned
our right to be called men and women

Charles White and his art were introduced to me
through magazines and books—that's why I love them

Charles White and his art were shared with me through
love and concern—that's why I value those

Charles White and his art live in my heart and the heart
of our people—that's why I think
love is worthwhile

The Drum ▪

(for Martin Luther King, Jr.)

The drums . . . Pa-Rum . . . the rat-tat-tat . . . of drums . . .
The Pied Piper . . . after leading the rats . . . to death . . . took
the children . . . to dreams . . . Pa-Rum Pa-Rum . . .

The big bass drums . . . the kettles roar . . . the sound of
animal flesh . . . resounding against the wood . . . Pa-Rum
Pa-Rum . . .

Kunta Kinte was making a drum . . . when he was
captured . . . Pa-Rum . . .
Thoreau listened . . . to a different drum . . . rat-tat-tat-Pa-
Rum . . .
King said just say . . . I was a Drum Major . . . for peace . . .
Pa-Rum Pa-Rum . . . rat-tat-tat Pa-Rum . . .

Drums of triumph . . . Drums of pain . . . Drums of life . . .
Funeral drums . . . Marching drums . . . Drums that call . . .
Pa-Rum Pa-Rum . . . the Drums that call . . . rat-tat-tat-tat . . .
the Drums are calling . . . Pa-Rum Pa-Rum . . . rat-tat-tat Pa-
Rum . . .

A Poem on the Assassination ◼
of Robert F. Kennedy

Trees are never felled . . . in summer . . . Not when the fruit . . .
is yet to be borne . . . Never before the promise . . . is fulfilled. . .
Not when their cooling shade . . . has yet to comfort . . .

Yet there are those . . . unheeding of nature . . . indifferent to
ecology . . . ignorant of need . . . who . . . with ax and sharpened
saw . . . would . . . in boots . . . step forth damaging . . .

Not the tree . . . for it falls . . . But those who would . . . in
summer's heat . . . or winter's cold . . . contemplate . . . the
beauty . . .

Eagles ▪

(a poem for Lisa)

Eagles are a majestic species . . . living in the thin searing air . . .
building
nests on precipitous ledges . . .
    they are endangered . . . but unafraid . . .

An eagle's nest is an inverted dimple . . . made of ready smiles . . .
unbleached
saris . . . available arms . . . and clean soap smells . . .
    to withstand all . . . elements . . .

Nestled in the chocolate chaos . . . destined to become:
        roller skaters
        submarine eaters
        telephone talkers
        people
    are improperly imprinted ducklings . . .

Eagles perched . . . on those precipitous ledges . . . insist upon
teaching . . .
    the young . . . to fly . . .

Flying Underground ▪
(for the children of Atlanta)

Every time the earth moves . . . it's me . . . and all my friends . . .
flying underground . . . Off to a soccer game . . . or basketball
showdown . . . sometimes stickball . . . baseball . . . wicket . . . Sweat
falls from clouds . . . crowded 'neath the sun . . . cheering us . . .
Sweat climbs up . . . to morning grass . . . when we run too
fast . . . Always running . . . always fun . . . flying underground . . .
I can make the earth move . . . flying underground . . .

I work . . . Saturday afternoons . . . and sometimes after school . . .
Going to the store . . . for Mrs. Millie Worthington . . . Everybody
knows her . . . with her legs swollen . . . 'bout to burst . . . Most
times Chink . . . Mr. Chink Mama says . . . but everybody calls
him Chink . . . gives me a dime . . . to get his snuff . . . or some
chewing tobacco . . . Always go to Hunter Street . . . or to the Col-
iseum . . . when a show's in town . . . Do groceries . . . bags . . .
peanuts/popcorn/ice cold pop! . . . Never gonna do dope . . . but
maybe run a number . . . Walking . . . running . . . I get tired . . .
Been cold . . . but not too much . . . Never been . . . really hungry . . .
Just get tired . . . a lot . . .

Teacher says I do . . . real good . . . in school . . . I like to read
books . . . where things happen . . . if I was Tom . . . Sawyer I'd get
that fence . . . painted . . . I draw pictures . . . with lots of sun and
clouds . . . Like to play I do . . . a lot . . . and I talk . . . in class . . .

I cried once . . . I don't know why . . . I can't remember now . . .
Mrs. Evans held my hand . . . Nothing holds me now . . . They
opened up a spot . . . and put me underground . . . Don't cry
Mama . . . look for me . . . I'm flying . . .

Her Cruising Car ▪

A Portrait of Two Small Town Girls

There is nothing . . . that can be said . . . that can frighten me . . .
anymore . . . Sadden me . . . perhaps . . . disgust me . . . certainly . . .
but not make me afraid . . . It has been said . . . Learn What You
Fear . . . Then Make Love To It . . . dance with it . . . put it on
your dresser . . . and kiss it good . . . night . . . Say it . . . over and
over . . . until in the darkest hour . . . from the deepest sleep . . .
you can be awakened . . . to say Yes . . .

She never learned . . . no matter how often people tried . . . that it
was hers . . . the fear and the Life . . . the glory of the gamble . . .
It was her quarter . . . she had to pick the machine . . . She never
understood . . . simple duty . . . knowing only to give all of
herself . . . or none . . . There was no balance . . . to her trian-
gle . . . though three points . . . are the strongest mathematical fig-
ures . . . no tingle . . . when struck . . . no joy . . . in her song . . .
no comfort in her chair . . . war/always war . . . with whom she
was . . . who she wanted to be . . . and what they wanted . . . of
her . . .

One reason I think . . . I am qualified . . . to run the world . . .
though my appointment is not imminent . . . is when I get . . .
what I want . . . I am happy . . . It is surprising to me . . . how few
people are . . . When they win . . . like Richard Nixon or John
McEnroe . . . they are unhappy . . . when they lose . . . impossible . . .
One reason I think . . . I have neither ulcers nor nail biting habits . . .
is I know to be careful . . . of what I want . . . I just may get
it . . .

She was never taught . . . that everything is earned . . . that New-
ton was right . . . for every action there is an equal and opposite
reaction . . . Interest is obtained . . . only on Savings . . . Personal-
ity is developed . . . only on risk . . . What is sought . . . must first

be given . . . We please others . . . by only allowing them access . . . to that part of ourselves which is public . . . If familiarity breeds contempt . . . use breeds hatred . . .

Turtles . . . the kind you find in pet stores . . . the kind Darwin met on Galápagos . . . grow to fit the environment . . . There are . . . probably . . . some genetic limits . . . but a small turtle . . . in a small bowl . . . will not outgrow . . . her home . . . Flowers . . . will rise . . . proportionate more to the size . . . of the pot . . . than the relationship of sun . . . to rain . . . Humans seldom deviate . . . If she hadn't been a small town girl . . . with a mind and heart molded absolutely . . . to fit the environment . . . she might have developed . . . a real skill . . . a real desire . . . to discover herself . . . and her gifts . . . As it was . . . as it is . . . she simply got used . . . and used to using . . .

She was never a loner . . . never made . . . to understand that life . . . in fact . . . is a solitary journey . . . that only *one* . . . was going to St. Ives . . . that no one held her bag . . . while the old woman traveled to Skookum . . . that the Little Red Hen and the Engine That Could . . . did it themselves . . . She was . . . let's face it . . . the leader of the pack . . . the top of the heap . . . cheerleader extraordinaire . . . She was very popular . . . sought after by all the right people . . . for her jokes . . . her parties . . . her parents' car . . . The telephone was invented . . . just for her . . . She set up the friendships . . . the going steadys . . . the class officers . . . yearbook staff . . . Who's-In-Who's-Out . . . through the witch wire . . . Nothing could happen . . . without her input . . . She actually thought . . . it was important . . . who went with whom . . . to the junior prom . . . But somebody had to pick up the fallen streamers . . . sweep the now scarred dance floor . . . turn out the lights before they could go home . . .

We were born . . . in the same year . . . our mothers delivered . . . by the same doctor . . . of the same city . . . in the same hospital . . . We were little chubby girls in pink . . . passing cigarettes at the lawn parties . . . My mother made me play . . . with her . . . and hers . . . with me . . . We didn't really mind . . . we shared the same friends . . . hers . . . and the same ideas . . . mine . . . Maybe I became . . . too accustomed . . . to the sameness . . . It was certainly easier . . . for me to shed . . . her friends . . . than she to shed . . . my notions . . . Our mothers belonged . . . to the same clubs . . . Our fathers tracked . . . the same night devils . . . They all had the same expectations . . . from . . . of . . . at . . . or to . . . us . . . I liked to brood . . . she didn't . . . She liked to laugh . . . I didn't . . . I thought I was ugly . . . she didn't . . .

Pots are taught not to call kettles Black . . . people who live in glass houses . . . don't throw stones . . . small town girls learn early . . . or not at all . . . that they can make a life . . . or abort the promise . . . One of us tried . . . one of us didn't have to . . . To each . . . according to her birth . . . from each according to her ability . . . Which is bastardized Marx . . . but legitimate bourgeoisie . . . She was never caring . . . She never learned to see . . . beyond her own windshield . . . that there were other people on the sidewalk . . . other cars . . . on the road . . . She drank . . . too much . . . for too long . . . Maybe in the back of her mind . . . or heart . . . or closet . . . there was a sign saying: There-Is-More-Than-This . . . but she wouldn't pull it out . . . put it up . . . or even acknowledge that some things . . . many things . . . were missing . . . I accept . . . if not embrace . . . the pain . . . the sign on my car says: I Brake For Gnomes . . . the one in my heart reads: Error In Process—Please Send Chocolate . . .

Into the rising sun . . . or setting years . . . accustomed to the scattered friends littering the road . . . she drives on . . . with the confidence of small town drivers who know every wayfall . . . toward the smaller minds . . . around the once hopeful lovers . . . into the illusion of what it is . . . to be a woman . . . through the delusion that trip necessitates . . . never once slowing . . . to ask Did I Hurt You . . . May I Love You . . . Can I/May I Please Give . . . You A Lift . . . With the surety . . . of one who never had to walk . . . she accelerates . . . toward boredom . . . secure in the understanding . . . that everybody knows her . . . and would be unlikely to ticket . . . her cruising car . . . She was my friend . . . more than a sister . . . really . . . a part of the mirror . . . against which I adjust . . . my makeup . . . I have no directions . . . but here is a sign . . . Thomas Wolfe was wrong . . . Maybe it will be read . . .

The Cyclops in the Ocean ▪

Moving slowly . . . against time . . . patiently majestic . . . the
cyclops . . . in the ocean . . . meets no Ulysses . . .

Through the night . . . he sighs . . . throbbing against the
shore . . . declaring . . . for the adventure . . .

A wall of gray . . . gathered by a slow touch . . . slash and
slither . . . through the waiting screens . . . separating into nod-
ules . . . making my panes . . . accept the touch . . .

Not content . . . to watch my frightened gaze . . . he clamors
beneath the sash . . . dancing on my sill . . .

Certain to die . . . when the sun . . . returns . . .

Harvest ■

(for Rosa Parks)

There is an old story . . . I learned in church . . . one eve-
ning . . . about a preacher . . . and his deacon . . . fishing . . .
It seems that every time . . . the good brother got a bite . . . the
fish would scamper . . . away . . . and the deacon . . . would
curse . . . The preacher . . . probably feeling . . . his profession
demanded . . . a response . . . said to the deacon Brother . . .
should you curse like that . . . with me here . . . over some
fish . . . And the deacon agreed . . . They fished on . . . the
deacon losing more fish . . . when finally a big big one . . . got
away . . . The deacon remembered his vow . . . looked at his
empty pole . . . reminded himself of the vow . . . looked at his
empty pole . . . sucked in his breath . . . turned to the
preacher . . . and remarked Reverend . . . Something Needs To
Be Said . . .

I guess everybody wants . . . to be special . . . and pretty . . . the
boys . . . just want to be strong . . . or fast . . . all the same
things . . . children want . . . everywhere . . . It was ordinary . . . as
far as I can see . . . my childhood . . . but . . . well . . . I don't
know . . . much . . . about psychology . . . We had a lot of
pride . . . growing up . . . in Tuskegee . . . You could easily see . . .
what our people could do . . . if somebody set a mind . . . to it . . .
Father was a carpenter . . . Mama taught school . . . I got
married . . . at nineteen . . .

You always felt . . . you should do something . . . It just wasn't
right . . . what they did to Negroes . . . and why Negroes . . . let it
happen . . . Colored people couldn't vote . . . couldn't use the
bathroom in public places . . . couldn't go to the same library they
paid taxes for . . . had to sit on the back of the buses . . . couldn't
live places . . . work places . . . go to movies . . . amusement
parks . . . Nothing . . . if you were colored . . . Just signs . . .
always signs . . . saying No . . . No . . . No . . .

My husband is a fine man . . . a fighting man . . . When we were young . . . belonging to the N double A C P was radical . . . dangerous . . . People got killed . . . run out of town . . . beaten and burned out . . . just for belonging . . . My husband belonged . . . and I belonged . . . In 1943 . . . during the war . . . Double Victory was just as important . . . one thing without the other was not good . . . enough . . . I was elected Secretary . . . of the Montgomery branch . . . I am proud . . . of that . . . Many people just think History . . . just fell on my shoulders . . . or at my feet . . . 1 december 1955 . . . but that's not true . . .

Sometimes it seemed it was never going . . . to stop . . . That same driver . . . who had me arrested . . . had put me off a bus . . . from Maxwell Air Base . . . where I had worked . . . or maybe they all . . . look the same . . . I wasn't looking . . . for anything . . . That Colvin girl had been arrested . . . and nobody did anything . . . I didn't think . . . they would do anything . . . when the driver told us . . . it was four of us . . . to move . . . Three people moved . . . I didn't . . . I couldn't . . . it was just so . . . wrong . . . Nobody offered to go . . . with me . . . A neighbor . . . on the same bus . . . didn't even tell . . . my husband . . . what had happened . . . I just thought . . . we should let them know . . . *I* should let them know . . . it wasn't right . . . You have to realize . . . I was forty years old . . . all my life . . . all I'd seen . . . were signs . . . that everything was getting worse . . .

The press people came . . . around after . . . we won . . . I had to reenact . . . everything . . . I was on the aisle . . . the man by the window . . . got up . . . I don't fault him . . . for getting up . . . he was just doing . . . what he was told . . . Across the aisle were two women . . . they got up . . . too . . . There was a lot of violence . . . physical and verbal . . . I kinda thought . . . something might happen . . . to me . . . I just didn't . . . couldn't . . . get up . . .

They always tell us one . . . person doesn't make any difference . . . but it seems to me . . . something . . . should be done . . . In all these years . . . it's strange . . . but maybe not . . . nobody asks . . . about my life . . . If I have children . . . why I moved to Detroit . . . what I think . . . about what we tried . . . to do . . . somehow . . . you want to say things . . . are better . . . somehow . . . they are . . . not in many ways . . . People . . . older people . . . are afraid . . . younger people . . . are too . . . I really don't know . . . where it will end . . . Our people . . . can break . . . your heart . . . so can other . . . people . . . I just think . . . it makes a difference . . . what one person does . . . young people forget that . . . what one person does . . . makes a difference . . .

The deacon . . . of course . . . wanted to curse . . . because the fish got . . . away . . . perhaps there is something . . . other to be done . . . about the people we lose . . . We always talk . . . about how everyone was Black . . . before it was fashionable . . . overlooking the reality . . . that were that true . . . Black would have been fashionable . . . before it was . . . and might have stayed in vogue . . . longer than it did . . . Something needs to be said . . . about Rosa Parks . . . other than her feet . . . were tired . . . Lots of people . . . on that bus . . . and many before . . . and since . . . had tired feet . . . lots of people . . . still do . . . they just don't know . . . where to plant them . . .

Reflections/On a Golden Anniversary ▪

You never know . . . when you meet . . . Is it at introduction . . .
with polite handshakes and an exchange of names . . . Or is it with
eyes . . . that ask can you . . . will you . . . maybe . . . love me

It seems sometimes that I always wanted . . . to be grown . . . and
warm . . . and free . . . and loved . . . yet you never know . . . until
it stops . . . that you were . . . Until the dolls . . . that some called
children . . . had children . . . you think of as dolls . . . and you
remember Yes . . . maybe I was grown . . . up perhaps . . . wider for
sure . . . more patient . . . less tolerant . . . who knows what . . .
exactly . . . until it stops

Love is more than stopping that ache . . . It's paying those bills . . .
cooking that food . . . cleaning this house . . . answering when
someone says Mama . . . and hoping it's a child . . . who calls

Did we meet when we were only a dream . . . of each other . . . Or
did we meet with the cries . . . of labor . . . or fever . . . or no work
this week

Do we know . . . because of the change of names . . . each
other . . . Or do we know . . . because of an exchange of
glances . . . that each is a bridge . . . free standing . . . stretched
between the good years and the bad

It's hard to remember . . . when we met . . . I am constantly being
introduced . . . to a you . . . I never knew . . . I offer you the
same . . .

Hello

Love: Is a Human Condition ■

An amoeba is lucky it's so small . . . else its narcissism would lead
to war . . . since self-love seems so frequently to lead to self-
righteousness . . .

I suppose a case could be made . . . that there are more amoebas
than people . . . that they comprise the physical majority . . . and
therefore the moral right . . . But luckily amoebas rarely make
television appeals to higher Gods . . . and baser instincts . . . so
one must ask if the ability to reproduce oneself efficiently has any-
thing to do with love . . .

The night loves the stars as they play about the Darkness . . . the
day loves the light caressing the sun . . . We love . . . those who
do . . . because we live in a world requiring light and Darkness . . .
partnership and solitude . . . sameness and difference . . . the
familiar and the unknown . . . We love because it's the only true
adventure . . .

I'm glad I'm not an amoeba . . . there must be more to all our lives
than ourselves . . . and our ability to do more of the same . . .

Sky Diving ■

I hang on the edge
    of this universe
    singing off-key
    talking too loud
    embracing myself
    to cushion the fall

I shall tumble
    into deep space
    never in this form
    or with this feeling
    to return to earth

    It is not tragic

I will spiral
    through that Black hole
    losing skin   limbs
      internal organs
    searing
    my naked soul

Landing
    in the next galaxy
    with only my essence
    embracing myself
    as

I dream of you

A Journey ▪

It's a journey . . . that I propose . . . I am not the guide . . . nor technical assistant . . . I will be your fellow passenger . . .

Though the rail has been ridden . . . winter clouds cover . . . autumn's exuberant quilt . . . we must provide our own guide-posts . . .

I have heard . . . from previous visitors . . . the road washes out sometimes . . . and passengers are compelled . . . to continue groping . . . or turn back . . . I am not afraid . . .

I am not afraid . . . of rough spots . . . or lonely times . . . I don't fear . . . the success of this endeavor . . . I am Ra . . . in a space . . . not to be discovered . . . but invented . . .

I promise you nothing . . . I accept your promise . . . of the same we are simply riding . . . a wave . . . that may carry . . . or crash . . .

It's a journey . . . and I want . . . to go . . .

Resignation ▪

I love you
>   because the Earth turns round the sun
>   because the North wind blows north
>>   sometimes
>   because the Pope is Catholic
>>   and most Rabbis Jewish
>   because winters flow into springs
>>   and the air clears after a storm
>   because only my love for you
>>   despite the charms of gravity
>>   keeps me from falling off this Earth
>>   into another dimension

I love you
>   because it is the natural order of things

I love you
>   like the habit I picked up in college
>>   of sleeping through lectures
>>   or saying I'm sorry
>>   when I get stopped for speeding
>   because I drink a glass of water
>>   in the morning
>>   and chain-smoke cigarettes
>>   all through the day
>   because I take my coffee Black
>>   and my milk with chocolate
>   because you keep my feet warm
>>   though my life a mess

I love you
>   because I don't want it
>>   any other way

I am helpless
>   in my love for you

334

It makes me so happy
    to hear you call my name
I am amazed you can resist
    locking me in an echo chamber
    where your voice reverberates
    through the four walls
    sending me into spasmatic ecstasy
I love you
    because it's been so good
    for so long
    that if I didn't love you
    I'd have to be born again
    and that is not a theological statement
I am pitiful in my love for you

The Dells tell me Love
    is so simple
    the thought though of you
    sends indescribably delicious multitudinous
    thrills throughout and through-in my body
I love you
    because no two snowflakes are alike
    and it is possible
    if you stand tippy-toe
    to walk between the raindrops
I love you
    because I am afraid of the dark
      and can't sleep in the light
    because I rub my eyes
      when I wake up in the morning
      and find you there
    because you with all your magic powers were
      determined that
I should love you
    because there was nothing for you but that
I would love you

I love you
> because you made me
> > want to love you
> more than I love my privacy
> > my freedom   my commitments
> > and responsibilities

I love you 'cause I changed my life
> to love you
> > because you saw me one friday
> > afternoon and decided that I would

love you
I love you I love you I love you

I Wrote a Good Omelet ▪

I wrote a good omelet . . . and ate a hot poem . . .
after loving you

Buttoned my car . . . and drove my coat home . . . in the
   rain . . .
after loving you

I goed on red . . . and stopped on green . . . floating
   somewhere in between . . .
being here and being there . . .
after loving you

I rolled my bed . . . turned down my hair . . . slightly confused
   but . . . I don't care . . .
Laid out my teeth . . . and gargled my gown . . . then I
   stood . . . and laid me down . . .
to sleep . . .
after loving you

Three/Quarters Time ■

Dance with me . . . dance with me . . . we are the song . . . we
are the music . . . Dance with me . . .

Waltz me . . . twirl me . . . do-si-do please . . . peppermint twist
me . . . philly
Squeeze

Cha cha cha . . . tango . . . two step too . . .
Cakewalk . . . charleston . . . bougaloo . . .

Dance with me . . . dance with me . . . all night long . . .
We are the music . . . we are the song . . .

Cancers ▪
(not necessarily a love poem)

Cancers are a serious condition . . . attacking internal organs
   . . . eating
them away . . . or clumping lumps . . . together . . .

The blood vessels carry . . . cancerous cells . . . to all body parts
   . . . cruising
would be the term . . . but this is not necessarily a love poem . . .

Cancer is caused . . . by . . .
     the air we breathe
     the food we eat
     the water we drink
Indices are unusually high . . . in cities that have baseball teams
   . . . or people . . .

     Coffee . . . milk . . . saccharine
     cigarettes . . . sun . . . and birth control
       devices . . .
are among the chief offenders . . .
     Monthly phenomena stopped . . . internally . . . will
       only lead . . .
     to shock syndrome . . .
What indeed . . . porcelana . . . does a woman . . . want . . .
Cancers are . . .
     the new plague
     the modern black death
     all that is unknown
       yet

I have a cancer . . . in my heart . . . I'm told . . . on
   knowledgeable authority . . .
it is not possible

For the heart we have . . .

       cardiac arrest . . . and outright attacks . . .

       holes in valves . . . and valve stoppage . . .

       constricted vessels . . . and nefarious air

          bubbles . . .

But then . . . my doctor never saw you . . . and doesn't believe . . .
in the zodiac . . .

A Word for Me . . . Also ■

Vowels . . . are a part of the English language . . . There are five in the alphabet . . . though only one . . . between lovers . . .

My father . . . you must understand . . . was Human . . . My mother . . . a larva . . . and while I concede most Celestial Beings . . . have taken the bodies of the majority . . . I chose differently . . . No one understands me . . . at all . . . except the clouds . . . and grasses . . . and waters cresting . . . against the Heavens . . .

I just don't know . . . what to do . . . with myself . . . I have forgotten the names . . . I feared being called . . . I have rested the burdens . . . of my will . . . I inhale the illogic . . . of the moment . . . exuding inert emotions . . . I am still . . . beside you . . . happily confused . . .

Words . . . are the foundation of thought . . . Many people think they think . . . but cannot put it . . . into words . . . My grandmother thought . . . she could drive a car . . . too . . . though she couldn't do Reverse . . . There is a word for me . . . also . . .

I Am She

(for Nancy)

I am she . . . making rainbows . . . in coffee cups . . . watching fish jump . . . after midnight . . . in my dreams . . .

On the stove . . . left front burner . . . is the stew . . . already chewed . . . certain to burn . . . as I dream . . . of waves . . . of nothingness . . .

Floating to shore . . . riding a low moon . . . on a slow cloud . . . I am she . . . who writes . . . the poems . . .

The Room With the Tapestry Rug

And when she was lonely . . . she would go into the room . . . where all who lived . . . knew her well . . .

Her hands would touch . . . her lips . . . silently moving . . . would punctuate the talk . . . with a smile . . . or a frown . . . an occasional "Oh My" . . .

If it was cold . . . she would wrap herself . . . in the natted blue sweater . . . knitted by a grandmother . . . so many years ago . . . If warm . . . the windows were opened . . . to allow the wind . . . to partake of their pleasure . . .

Holidays were never sad . . . seasons in fact . . . unchanging . . . Family and friends . . . lovers and longings . . . rested . . . waited . . . never to betray . . . never to leave her . . .

Her books . . . her secret life . . . in the room with the tapestry rug . . .

Wild Flowers

We are like a field . . . of wild flowers . . . unpollinated . . . swaying against the wind . . .

Dew sparkling . . . buds bursting . . . we await the drying day . . . Let's not gain . . . the notice of the woman . . . with the large straw basket . . .

Autumn will come . . . anyway . . . Let us continue . . . our dance . . . beneath the sun . . .

Love Thoughts ▪

Planes fly patterns . . . rather than land . . . on icy runways . . .
        I ran a pattern . . . around you . . .

Captains cut their engines . . . to passively ride storm waves . . .
        You put me . . . on hold . . .

        Only clear skies . . . and still waters . . .
        Can support engines of displacement

Aretha said it best . . . in Lady Soul . . . Ain't No Way . . . (for
  me to love you) . . .
        If you don't . . . let me . . .

You Were Gone ▪

You were gone
    like a fly lighting
    on that wall
    with a spider in the corner
You were gone
    like last week's paycheck
    for this week's bills
You were gone
    like the years between
    twenty-five and thirty
    as if somehow
You never existed
    and if it wouldn't be
    for the gray hairs
    I'd never know that
You had come

A Song for New-Ark ■

When I write I like to write . . . in total silence . . . Maybe total . . .
silence . . . is not quite accurate . . . I like to listen to the notes
breezing by my head . . . the grunting of the rainbow . . . as she
bends . . . on her journey from Saturn . . . to harvest the
melody . . .

There is no laughter . . . in the city . . . no joy . . . in the sheer
delight . . . of living . . . City sounds . . . are the cracking of ice in
glasses . . . or hearts in despair . . . The burglar alarms . . . or
boredom . . . warning of illicit entry . . . The fire bells
proclaiming . . . yet another home . . . or job . . . or dream . . . has
deserted the will . . . to continue . . . The cries . . . of all the lonely
people . . . for a drum . . . a tom-tom . . . some cymbal . . .
some/body . . . to sing for . . .

I never saw old/jersey . . . or old/ark . . . Old/ark was a forest . . .
felled for concrete . . . and asphalt . . . and bridges to Manhat-
tan . . . Earth acres that once held families . . . of deer . . . fox . . .
chipmunks . . . hawks . . . forest creatures . . . and their predators . . .
now corral business . . . men and women . . . artists . . . and intel-
lectuals . . . People . . . and their predators . . . under a banner of
neon . . . graying the honest Black . . . cradling the stars above . . .
and the earth below . . . turning to dust . . . white shirts . . . lace
curtains at the front window . . . automobiles lovingly polished . . .
Dreams . . . encountering racist resistance . . . New-Ark knows
too much pain . . . sees too many people who aren't special . . .
watches the buses daily . . . the churches on Sunday . . . the bars
after midnight . . . disgorge the unyoung . . . unable . . . unquali-
fied . . . unto the unaccepting . . . streets . . . I lived . . . one sum-
mer . . . in New-Ark . . . New-Jersey . . . on Belleville Avenue . . .
Every evening . . . when the rats left the river . . . to visit the cen-
tral ward . . . Anthony Imperiali . . . and his boys . . . would chunk
bullets . . . at the fleeing mammals . . . refusing to recognize . . .
the obvious . . . family . . . ties . . . I napped . . . to the rat-tat-

tat . . . rat-tat-tat . . . wondering why . . . we have yet to learn . . . rat-tat-tats . . . don't even impress . . . rats . . .

When I write I want to write . . . in rhythm . . . regularizing the moontides . . . to the heart/beats . . . of the twinkling stars . . . sending an S.O.S. . . . to day trippers . . . urging them to turn back . . . toward the Darkness . . . to ride the night winds . . . to tomorrow . . . I wish I understood . . . bird . . . Birds in the city talk . . . a city language . . . They always seem . . . unlike humans . . . to have something . . . useful . . . to say . . . Other birds . . . like Black americans . . . a century or so ago . . . answer back . . . with song . . . I wish I could be a melody . . . like a damp . . . gray . . . feline fog . . . staccatoing . . . stealthily . . . over the city . . .

Occasional Poems

1991–1998

Poem of Angela Yvonne Davis ■

(October 16, 1970)

i move on feeling and have learned to distrust those who
    don't
i move in time and space determined by time and space
    feeling
that all is natural and i am
a part of it and "how could you?" they ask you had everything
but the men who killed the children in birmingham aren't on
the most wanted list and the men who killed schwerner,
    chaney
and Goodman aren't on the most wanted list and the list of
    names
unlisted could and probably would include most of our
    "finest
Leaders" who are WANTED in my estimation for at least
    serious
questioning so we made a list and listed it

"but you had everything," they said and i asked
    "quakers?" and i asked
"jews?" and i asked "being sent from home?" my mother
    told me the world
would one day speak my name then she recently suggested
    angela Yvonne
why don't you take up sports like your brother and i sais "i
    don't run
as well as he" but they told me over and over again "you
    can have them
all at your feet" though i knew they were at my feet when
    i was born
and the heavens opened up sending the same streak of
    lightning through
my mother as through new york when i was arrested

and i saw my sisters and brothers and i heard them tell the
   young
racists "you can't march with us" and i thought i can't
   march at all
and i looked at the woman whose face was kissed by night
   as she said
"angela you shall be free" and i thought i won't be free
   even if i'm set
loose, the game is set the tragedy written my part is
   captive
i thought of betty shabazz and the voices who must have
   said "aren't you
sort of glad it's over?" with that stupidity that fails to
   notice
it will never be over for some of us and our children and
   our
grandchildren.   betty can no more forget that staccato than i
   the pain
in jonathan's face or the love in george's letters.   and i
   remember
the letter where i asked "why do't you write Beverly
   axelrod and become
rich and famous" and his complete reply

i remember water and sky and paris and wanting someone
   to be mine
a german? but the world is in love with germans so why
   not? though
i being the youngest daughter of Africa and the sun was
   rejected
and all the while them saying "isn't she beautiful?" and
   she being i
thinking "aren't you sick" and i remember wanting to give
   myself but

nothing being big enough to take me and searching for the
    right way
to live and seeing the answer understanding the right way
    to die
though death is as distasteful as the second cigarette in the
    morning
and don't you understand? i value my life so surely all
    others must value
theirs and that's the weakness the weak use against us.
    they so
casually make decisions like who's going to live and who's
going to
starve to death and who will be happy or not and they
    never know
what their life means since theirs lacks meaning and they
    never
have to try to understand what someone else's life could mean
those guards and policemen who so casually take the only
    possession
worth possessing and dispense with it like an empty r.c.
    cola bottle
never understanding the vitality of its contents

and the white boys and girls came with their little erections
    and i
learned to see but not show feeling and i learned to talk
    while not
screaming though i would scream if anyone understands
    that language
and i would reach if there were a substance and Black
    people say
i went communist and i only and always thought i went
    and Black people
say "why howard johnson's" but i could think of no other
    place and Black
people ask "why didn't i shoot it out?" when i thought i

had. and they say
they have no responsibility and i knew they would not rest
    until my
body was brought out in tiny flabby pieces

the list is long and our basic Christianity teaches us to
    sacrifice
the good to the evil and if the blood is type O positive
    maybe they
will be satisfied but white people are like any other gods
    with an insatiable
appetite and as long as we sacrifice our delicate to their
    coarse we will sacrifice
i mean i started with a clear head cause i felt i should and
    feeling
is much more than mere emotion though that is not to be
    sacrificed
and through it all i was looking for this woman angela
    yvonne
and i wanted to be harriet tubman who was the first
    WANTED Black woman
and i wanted to bring myself and us out of the fear and
    into the Dark
but my helpers trapped me and this i have learned of
    love—it is harder
to be loved than to love and the responsibilities of letting
    yourself
be loved are too great and perhaps i shall never love again
cause i would rather need than allow, and what i'm saying
    is
i had five hours of freedom when i recognized my lovers
    had decided
and i was free in my mind to say—whatever you do you
    will not know
what you have done

we walked that october afternoon among the lights and
    smells of autumn
people and i tried so to hold on. and as i turned 51st street
    and eighth
and saw, i knew there was nothing more to say so i thought
and i entered the elevator touching the insides as a woman
    is touched
i looked into the carpet as we were expelled
and entered the key
which would both open and close me
and i thought to them all
to myself just make it easy
on yourself

A Poem ∎

for langston hughes

diamonds are mined . . . oil is discovered
gold is found . . . but thoughts are uncovered

wool is sheared . . . silk is spun
weaving is hard . . . but words are fun

highways span . . . bridges connect
country roads ramble . . . but i suspect

   if i took a rainbow ride
   i could be there by your side

metaphor has its point of view
allusion and illusion . . . too

meter . . . verse . . . classical . . . free
poems are what you do to me

let's look at this one more time
since i've put this rap to rhyme

   when i take my rainbow ride
   you'll be right there at my side

hey bop hey bop hey re re bop

But Since You Finally Asked ▪

(A Poem Commemorating the 10th Anniversary of the
Slave Memorial at Mount Vernon)

No one asked us . . . what we thought of Jamestown . . . in
1619 . . . they didn't even say . . . "Welcome" . . . "You're Home" . . .
or even a pitiful . . . "I'm Sorry . . . But We Just Can't Make It . . .
Without You" . . . No . . . No one said a word . . . They just snatched
our drums . . . separated us by language and gender . . . and put us
on blocks . . . where our beauty . . . like our dignity . . . was
ignored

No one said a word . . . in 1776 . . . to us about Freedom . . . The
rebels wouldn't pretend . . . the British lied . . . We kept to a
space . . . where we owned our souls . . . since we understood . . .
another century would pass . . . before we owned our bodies . . .
But we raised our voices . . . in a mighty cry . . . to the Heavens
above . . . for the strength to endure

No one says . . . "What I like about your people" . . . then ticks off
the wonder of the wonderful things . . . we've given . . . Our song
to God, Our strength to the Earth . . . Our unfailing belief in for-
giveness . . . I know what I like about us . . . is that we let no one
turn us around . . . not then . . . not now . . . we plant our feet . . .
on higher ground . . . I like who we were . . . and who we are . . .
and since someone has asked . . . let me say: I am proud to be a
Black American . . . I am proud that my people labored hon-
estly . . . with forbearance and dignity . . . I am proud that we
believe . . . as no other people do . . . that all are equal in His
sight . . . We didn't write a constitution . . . we live one . . . We
didn't say "We the People" . . . we are one . . . We didn't have to
add . . . as an after-thought . . . "Under God" . . . We turn our
faces to the rising sun . . . knowing . . . a New Day . . . is
always . . . beginning

Stardate Number 18628.190* ◾

This is not a poem . . . this is hot chocolate at the beginning of Spring . . . topped with hand whipped double cream . . . a splash of brandy to give it sass . . . and just a little cinnamon to give it class . . . This is not a poem

This is a summer quilt . . . log cabin pattern . . . see the corner piece . . . that was grandmother's wedding dress . . . that was grandpappa's favorite Sunday tie . . . that white strip there . . . is the baby who died . . . Mommy had pneumonia so that red flannel shows the healing . . . This does not hang from museum walls . . . nor will it sell for thousands . . . This is here to keep me warm

This is not a sonnet . . . though it will sing . . . Precious Lord . . . take my hand . . . Amazing Grace . . . how sweet the sound . . . Go down, Moses . . . Way down to the past . . . Way up to the future . . . It will swell with the voice of Marian Anderson . . . lilt on the arias of Leontyne . . . dance on the trilling of Battle . . . do the dirty dirty with Bessie . . . moan with Dinah Washington . . . rock and roll through the Sixties . . . rap its way into the Nineties . . . and go on out into Space with Etta James saying At Last . . . No, this is not a sonnet . . . but the truth of the beauty that the only authentic voice of Planet Earth comes from the black soil . . . tilled and mined . . . by the Daughters of the Diaspora

This is a rocking chair . . . rock me gently in the bosom of Abraham . . . This is a bus seat: No, I'm not going to move today . . . This is a porch . . . where they sat spitting at fireflies . . . telling young Alex the story of The African . . . This is a hook rug . . . to cover a dirt floor . . . This is an iron pot . . . with the left over vegetables . . . making a slow cooking soup . . . This is pork . . . simmering chitterlings . . . surprising everybody with our ability to make a way . . . out of no way . . . This is not rest when we are weary . . . nor comfort when we are sad . . . It is laughter . . . when we are in pain . . . It is

"N'mind" when we are confused . . . It is "Keep climbing, chile" when the road takes the unfair turn . . . It is "Don't let nobody turn you round" . . . when our way is dark . . . It is the faith of our Mothers . . . who plaited our hair . . . put Vaseline on our faces . . . polished our run down shoes . . . patched our dresses . . . wore sweaters so that we could wear coats . . . who welcomed us and our children . . . when we were left alone to rear them . . . who said "Get your education . . . and nobody can put you back"

This is not a poem . . . No . . . It is a celebration of the road we have traveled . . . It is a prayer . . . for the roads yet to come . . . This is an explosion . . . The original Big Bang . . . that makes the world a hopeful . . . loving place

This is the Black woman . . . in all our trouble and glory . . . in all our past history and future forbearance . . . in all that ever made love a possibility .This is about us . . .
  bleached and natural . . . braided and straightened hair . . .
  made up . . . or . . . beaten up faces . . .
  tall . . . short . . . stately . . . bent . . .
  CC Riders . . . junkies . . . whores . . .
  wives . . . mothers . . . grandmothers . . . aunts
  working in the home or outside . . .
  working in the system or outside . . .
  working praying working to survive . . .
  giving pride . . . giving succor . . . giving voice . . . giving
  encouragement . . . giving whatever . . . we can give

This is a flag . . . that we placed over Peter Salem and Peter Poor . . . the 54th Regiment from Massachusetts . . . All the men and women lynched in the name of rape . . . Emmett Till . . . Medgar Evers . . . Malcolm X . . . Martin Luther King, Jr. . . . . This a banner we fly for Respect . . . Dignity . . . the Assumption of Integrity . . . for a future generation to rally around

This is about us . . . Celebrating ourselves . . . And a well deserved honor it is . . . Light the candles, Essence . . . This is a rocket . . . Let's ride

Brother Brother Brother ▪

(the Isley Brothers of Lincoln Heights)

You see . . . I Know the Isley Brothers. Know where they come from. Know the high school they went to. Remember when they moved to Blue Ash. Knew their little brother Vernon who used to do a mad and wonderful itch. And who remembers the itch? But Vernon would stand on stage and reach around and swizzle his hips and the amateur night audience would be on their feet though Rudolph and O'Kelly were probably the beneficiaries of that energy but . . . you see . . . I know them

You see . . . We all come from Lincoln Heights which is an independent Black city just outside Cincinnati and we mostly say we are from Cincinnati because nobody knows Lincoln Heights but back in the old days when white people would periodically go crazy and need/want/have to kill somebody Black lots of Black people moved from the river front into the West End and when they could if they could out of the West End and into the Valley and in the Valley . . . you see . . . land was ten cents an acre which is not a lot today but from folks walking away from slavery and folks running from crazy folks who wanted to/needed to/were definitely going to/kill them ten cents meant the difference between life and death . . . But

You see . . . it's like everything else so Black folks moved way out there and the Erie Canal was suppose to go from Cleveland down what ultimately became I-75 to connect the Lake to the River and if that had happened instead of it not happening then all the Black folks who scraped together a nickel or so so that they could get a little piece of land would have had worthless condemned land but the canal did not happen though Lincoln Heights did

And then wars and stuff started happening and General Electric where progress is the most important product wanted to have a lot of land but they didn't want to have to pay for it so they split the land and called it Evendale and what was left on the hill was Lincoln Heights and I'm sure I don't have to say which is Black and which is white but I bet you can guess . . . So

You see . . . The Valley Homes were built for folks to work in the GE plant not to mention folks needing some place to live and other folks not wanting to live near them though the Valley Homes were good enough for us which considering the alternative they were but that doesn't make it right but it was definitely O.K. because Lincoln Heights had great athletes who would have been famous if they had been allowed to go to desegregated schools so that Virgil Thompson went to West Virginia State but nobody much cared about talented boys from a small Black town that was incorporated and he came back

You see . . . we had singers too and Pookey Smith could really sing and everybody loved to hear him at Christmas or any other time but Pookey and his brother didn't have a mother like Mrs. Isley who was determined that her boys were going to get out not because she didn't like Lincoln Heights or even the Valley Homes but she knew if she could get them out then the talents they had would have a chance to grow and that's more or less when they moved to Blue Ash and Vernon was run over by a car and all of Lincoln Heights wanted to see them become rich and famous since we already knew they were talented and beautiful. But Ernie came along and we all were happy though nobody does the itch anymore since that's what Vernon did . . . And we all remembered.

You see . . . When they started perfecting SHOUT and Mrs. Isley said she was taking her boys to New York and Elaine said she was going with Rudolph and Ronald used to date my sister but she had to go on to college and the Isleys know because . . . you see . . . they are from Lincoln Heights that they had to take care of each other and they have done that . . . We all mourned when O'Kelly now called Kelly died because he was such a good friend to all of us and none of them ever forgot where they came from and how much love all of Lincoln Heights still sends out to all of them and just recently

You See . . . I was home and it was Mother's Day at church and their Grandmother wanted to sing a tribute and she was still doing that Isley *SHOUT* at 92 and a lot of other people did that Isley *SHOUT* like the Beatles and Joey Dee and stuff but it was the Isley *SHOUT* that was our thing and other than the Beatles they have sold the most records . . . and Lincoln Heights

You see . . . Always knew they were special and that's why we know Brother Brother Brother may be an album title but it is a way of life with these powerful, wonderful sons of Lincoln Heights who are Brother to us all . . . don'cha know

Afterword
Some Poems Are More Useful Than Others

My second visit to the African continent was at the invitation of the USIA. I was excited to return to Africa and this time I was taking my son and Debbie Russell, who had worked for me off and on since I had taught her at Livingston College. I was always teasing Debbie about having her passport which she had not had ready when *Soul!* took us to London to film the dialogue with James Baldwin. For sure, that was a different time because Debbie borrowed the passport of a friend under the auspices of "all colored people look alike." "But, Nikki," she said. "What if they know it's not me?" "Well, then," I comforted her, "you'll go to jail and we'll have to go to London without you." But I honestly didn't think they would care and they really never noticed the difference. When we got back my first question was: Going to get your passport? And she scurried on down to the main post office. When Africa came up she was ready. Her mother wasn't so sure, so she traveled over from Newark to have a talk with me. She wanted to be assured that I would bring Debbie back. "Whatever else would I do?", I wanted to know. But as it turned out her mother was quite prescient as I had not an inconsiderable number of good offers if I would let Debbie marry. If Debbie had played tennis she would remind you of Serena. Not that tall but that same African-American butt that is so interesting to people who are used to looking at flat behinds. Some just wanted to know if they could keep her overnight and others were more honorable. But I kept my vow to Mrs. Russell and not only brought Debbie back but made sure she was chaperoned while there. I got quite a few good gifts trying to win my favor but I definitely played hard ball. No. I have promised her mother.

In trying to get ready I put a big map of Africa up on the playroom wall. I colored in all the countries we were to visit. Since I am, shamefully, language poor I was only being invited to the English speaking countries: Ghana, Nigeria, Botswana, Lesotho, Swaziland, Uganda, Tanzania and Kenya. This was before you could travel directly to Africa so we had a stopover in Paris. Change planes and on to Liberia. Stop over briefly in Liberia then on to Ghana. Disembark in Ghana. Since I wanted Thomas to not only know the geography but where he was going we went over our routine and route many times. "What are we going to do to get to Africa?" I would innocently ask. "First we say 'Where is that Debbie? If she doesn't come right away we're going to leave her," Thomas would reply. "Then we go downstairs and I say: Taxi! Then we say Kennedy Airport." And I would cheer him on. "That's wonderful! What next?" "Then we get on the plane and go to sleep," he'd say. Then looking accusingly at me he would invariably add: "You always do." Which is true. Flying so petrifies me that if I don't go to sleep I fear I'd be screaming in the aisles. There were people who refused to fly after 9-11-01 but not me. Friends said to me after the events "Aren't you afraid to fly after all that's happened?" I had to say nothing has changed for me. I was afraid to fly way before anything like the unimaginable happened and I'm afraid now. I figure I'm lucky to have always been scared. Not only has nothing changed, I'm not angry with anyone because of my own fears. Sort of a different way of looking at fear but at least I can smile when I see brown people on the plane. "Mommy works hard," I explain which sounds a whole lot better than Mommy is scared shitless. "What happens next?" "We wake up in Paris! And we get good food." I've never been a fan of airplane or airport food. And after all those people got sick on United back in the 1970's I refuse to eat anything at all. Plus mostly I am asleep. I can sleep from coast to almost coast. If I wake up its usually within the hour of landing and I have been known to drink a Coke. But I try to lull myself back to dreamland because landing is as dangerous as take-off and I really don't want to start screaming. "In Paris we change airports then off to Africa!" I am reward prone and at that he gets hugs and kisses. This is really good for a not quite first grader. "Where will we land?" "Mommy, we land in Monrovia, Liberia.

Named for President Monroe and started by slaves." I am so proud I could burst. "Do we get off the plane?" "No. We stay on until take-off. Then the plane flies to Ghana. We get off at Accra. Ghana was started by a nice man who went to school in the United States." Still pretty good for a kid. "And where do we go?" "To our hotel." I am so pleased. I think he really understands this visit and will get lots out of it.

The day comes and Debbie is on time. We go downstairs and Thomas hails the taxi. Out to the airport. On to the plane. A beautiful, sunny day in Paris. Out to the airport. On to Liberia. The plane lands and I ask my darling, precocious son "Where are we?" "Monrovia, Liberia named for President Monroe and founded by slaves!" I am telling myself what a great job I have done. People around us are smiling, so pleased are they at the young mother and her wonderfully informed son. The plane takes off and we are watching the green of Africa. We land in Ghana. Deplane. Head off for the hotel. Get checked in. Shower. And go down to have afternoon tea. We are sitting there on the terrace relaxing. Thomas is looking a bit puzzled. Then he pops the question: "Mommy, why are these people speaking Spanish?" My goodness! After all we have been through my son thinks he's somewhere in Spanish Harlem. Nevermind all the lessons. Nevermind all the recitations. He hasn't got a clue in the world where we are. My spirits fall. Debbie tries to reassure me. But I know. I have failed. All the people who said he is too young to go to Africa are right. All the people who said it was a waste of time and money, that he would never remember anything are right. All those people who told me I was wrong are right. My shoulders were down on my knees and my spirit was even lower. I recovered though. I told myself we are here and there's nothing else to be done. I explained they were not speaking Spanish but Twi. Thomas looked at me like I was playing a joke. We went on to my readings and our touring. We flew to Lagos, Nigeria where we had a wonderful visit. Everyone was very nice and everyone was especially nice to Thomas. There was an especial appreciation that I had brought my son with me because it seemed to indicate some level of trust.

We were on our way to the BLS countries, Botswana, Lesotho and Swaziland. The plane we were suppose to be on got commandeered by the military which happened a lot in those days so instead of our non-stop to Johannesburg we had to take what amounted to a local. The plane made a couple of stops then we took off for Zaire. As we were landing Thomas asked: "Where are we, now?" It had been a long day and we still had some hours flying before we reached the place where we would change planes. "We're landing in Zaire, Thomas," I answered rather absentmindedly. "Where is that, Mommy? Where *are* we?" he demanded. It dawned on me that there was no way he could know Zaire which had recently changed its name. "Thomas, we're landing in the Congo," I explained. "The Congo!" he said excitedly. "Mommy you were born here! We must be in Africa." He was beaming. And so was I. I was never so happy that I had written a poem than I was at that very moment. "Yes, Thomas. We're in Africa. I was born in the Congo . . ."

NIKKI GIOVANNI

July 2003

Notes to the Poems

Black Feeling Black Talk

Black Feeling Black Talk was privately printed in 1968 and distributed by Giovanni herself. Because she feared rejection, as she stated in an interview published in *Ingenue* in February 1973, Giovanni did not submit the collection to a publisher; instead, with money borrowed from family and friends, she had it printed and distributed it herself: "I decided to take my poetry to the people, and if they rejected it, that would be that." In fact, some 2,000 copies of this volume were sold during its first year, an extraordinary figure for a privately printed *and* privately distributed book of poetry.

"Detroit Conference of Unity and Art (For HRB)"
The Detroit Conference of Unity and Art was held in late May 1967.

HRB:H. Rap Brown, now Jamil Abdullah Al-Amin (1943–). Civil Rights activist who became the chairman of SNCC (Student Nonviolent Coordinating Committee) after Stokely Carmichael left to join the Black Panthers. Al-Amin was recently convicted of killing a Fulton County (Georgia) sheriff's deputy and sentenced to life in prison. Giovanni considers the charges absurd. See the title poem of *Quilting the Black-Eyed Pea*.

L. 15: "Malcolm": Malcolm X, later Al Hajj Malik Al-Shabazz (1925–65).

"On Hearing 'The Girl with the Flaxen Hair'"
"The Girl with the Flaxen Hair" (*La Fille aux cheveux de lin*) is a piano composition by Claude Debussy (1862–1918), published in 1910 in Book 1 of his *Préludes*.

This is a very early poem, dating to 1965; the second or third poem Giovanni wrote, it was rejected by *The Atlantic Monthly*.

"Poem (For TW)"

TW: Thelma Watson, Giovanni's French teacher at Fisk University. The teacher and her student often speculated about the possibility that they were kinswomen because Ms. Watson had the same family name as Giovanni's maternal grandparents.

"Poem (For BMC No. 1)"

BMC: Blanche McConnell Cowan was the dean of women at Fisk University when Giovanni returned there in 1964. Cowan purged the file on Giovanni that had been generated by the former dean, Ann Cheatam, and became an important friend and mentor both during Giovanni's years at Fisk and after. Cowan died in 1986.

L. 6: "no sun from Venice": *No Sun in Venice* is a 1957 album released by the Modern Jazz Quartet.

L. 7: "green cricket with a pink umbrella": Blanche Cowan was a member of the African American sorority Alpha Kappa Alpha, whose colors are green and pink.

"Our Detroit Conference (For Don L. Lee)"

Don L. Lee, now Haki R. Madhabuti (1942–), is a Chicago poet and founder of Third World Press who was an important leader in the Black Arts movement. Giovanni met him at the Detroit Conference of Unity and Art in May 1967.

L. 2: "Digest": The *Negro Digest,* which was relaunched in the 1960s by Johnson Publications. Under the editorship of Hoyt Fuller (1923–81), *Negro Digest* (renamed *Black World* in 1970) played a central role in helping shape the Black Arts movement. Both Giovanni and Lee were regular contributors.

"Poem (For Dudley Randall)"

Dudley Randall (1914–2000) was a poet and the founder of Broadside Press (1963), which published the work of many young poets of the Black Arts movement. Broadside distributed Giovanni's *Black Judgement* and published her *Re: Creation.*

"Poem (For BMC No. 2)"

BMC: Blanche McConnell Cowan; see note to "Poem (For BMC No. 1)."

L. 7: "barefoot boy": An allusion to "Barefoot Boy with Cheeks of Tan" by John Greenleaf Whittier (1807–92).

L. 8: "John Henry": John Henry was born a slave in the 1840s or 1850s. The legend that grew up around his work as a steel driver for the railroads during Reconstruction is expressed in the many versions of the song "John Henry, Steel Driving Man."

L. 9: "camel with a cold nose": A reference to the folk story about a man whose camel begged to be allowed to stick just his cold nose in the tent at night; the next morning, of course, the entire camel was in the tent and the man was outside in the cold.

"Personae Poem (For Sylvia Henderson)"

Sylvia Henderson: In the summer of 1967, Giovanni organized Cincinnati's first Black Arts Festival, held in the West End, where she did volunteer social work. As a part of the festival, she adapted Virginia Hamilton's novel *Zeely* to the stage. Sylvia Henderson had the title role in the play, directed by Giovanni and performed at a synagogue in Avondale, a Cincinnati neighborhood. Giovanni selected the West End as the location for the three-day festival because she volunteered there, her mother was a social worker there, and her father had grown up and was widely respected there; Giovanni knew, in other words, that she could get widespread participation and support in the West End, at that time a neighborhood of project housing. The conservative director of the neighborhood YWCA was unwilling to let Giovanni and her colleagues use the Y's stage for the production. Many of the people with whom Giovanni worked also worked for or with a social work agency in Avondale called Seven Hills, and one of them offered the use of the synagogue's stage.

"Poem (For PCH)"

PCH: Perri Harper. The response to the Black Arts Festival and to Giovanni's production of *Zeely* (see preceding note) was overwhelmingly positive. The success of the play demonstrated the potential for an ongoing black theater in Cincinnati. Giovanni suggested to Charles Sells, the director of Seven Hills (see preceding note), that he hire a director for the theater group she had organized. He agreed to do so if she could find someone. She contacted John Oliver Killens, with whom she had studied at Fisk, and he eventually recommended Perri Harper. Harper had worked for a number of years with small theaters in Greenwich Village, where she lived with the jazz pianist Bill Evans. Possibly because of problems in her relationship with Evans, Harper accepted the position in Cincinnati. Charles Holman, another social worker involved in the theater group, helped win grant money and donations, and Harper directed a series of plays; within three or four years, this group was incorporated into the Cincinnati Playhouse, which had previously had an all-white board of directors, all white actors, and all-white play selections.

Ll. 7 ff.: Perhaps an allusion to the fact that Harper, who had been hired through Giovanni's efforts, later refused to provide a letter of recommendation for her application to graduate school.

"Poem (For BMC No. 3)"

BMC: Blanche McConnell Cowan; see note to "Poem (For BMC No. 1)," page 370.

"A Historical Footnote to Consider Only When All Else Fails (For Barbara Crosby)"

Barbara Crosby: Several years older than Giovanni, Crosby was originally a friend of Gary Giovanni, the poet's sister. Crosby graduated from Cincinnati's prestigious Walnut Hills High School and Fisk University. She was active in the Civil Rights movement and was a member of SNCC (Student Nonviolent Coordinating Committee). As a participant in the International Village Movement, she had also spent a good deal of time in Europe. She was a social worker with Seven Hills (see note to "Personae Poem," page 371), and she and Giovanni shared an apartment in Cincinnati during the summer of 1967.

"The True Import of Present Dialogue, Black vs. Negro (For Peppe, Who Will Ultimately Judge Our Efforts)"

"Black vs. Negro": Naming has always had enormous importance to Black Americans because of its connection to identity and power. Africans brought to this country and sold into slavery were stripped of their names and forced to take the names given them by their new masters. In the 1960s special attention was focused on this issue. Those involved in the Black Power and Black Arts movements drew significant distinctions between the terms "Negro," "nigger," and "Black." Sarah Webster Fabio wrote a definitive essay on this topic for *Negro Digest*, in which she offered the following analysis:

> Scratch a Negro and you will find a nigger and a potential black man; scratch a black man and you may find a nigger and the remnants of a Negro. Negro is a psychological, sociological, and economical fabrication to justify the status quo in America. Nigger is the tension created by a black man's attempt to accommodate himself to become a Negro in order to survive in a racist country. Black is the selfhood and soul of anyone with one drop of black blood, in America, who does not deny himself.
>
> The black community has always known—and it is becoming apparent to the world—that America wants Negroes and niggers but not black people.

> James Baldwin makes reference to the observation that "the Negro-in-America is a form of insanity which overtakes white men." The Negro is a pathology: Baldwin has also said that there is "no Negro, finally, who has not had to make his own precarious adjustment to the 'nigger' who surrounds him and to the 'nigger' in himself." Being black, then, is a reaffirmation of selfhood; it is a meaningful antidote to white racism; it is a move toward deniggerizing the world population of non-white people and of humanizing the white people. ("Who Speaks Negro? What Is Black?" *Negro Digest*, Sept.–Oct. 1968.)

Peppe: Family nickname for Giovanni's nephew, Christopher Black (1959–).

L. 2: "Can you kill": Giovanni stated that she wrote this poem because "it bugged me to always hear talk of going out to die for our rights. . . . That's not the hardest thing to do. It's harder to go out and kill for your rights. I wrote the poem as a protest against that attitude" (Peter Bailey, "Nikki Giovanni: 'I Am Black, Female, Polite . . .'" *Ebony,* February 1972, p. 50).

"A Short Essay of Affirmation Explaining Why (With Apologies to the Federal Bureau of Investigation)"

This poem was written in July 1967, when Giovanni was living in Cincinnati. Often referred to as a "hot summer," the summer of 1967 witnessed race riots and racial disturbances across the country. The most serious occurred in Newark, New Jersey, and Detroit, Michigan, but there were outbreaks in dozens of other cities, including Cincinnati. Giovanni shared an apartment with Barbara Crosby (see note to "A Historical Footnote," page 372), who was as well-known to left-wingers in Cincinnati as Giovanni was to Black nationalists; as a consequence, their telephone was wiretapped. Giovanni herself was at her parents' home in Lincoln Heights when the riot broke out in Cincinnati.

L. 1: "Honkies": white people.

L. 48: "Miss Hoover": A reference to the then director of the Federal Bureau of Investigation, J. Edgar Hoover (1895–1972), whose abuse of his powers, especially in matters regarding Black people, has been widely documented.

"Poem (No Name No. 3)"

L. 3: "Anne Frank": Anne Frank (1929–45) gained international attention when her diaries were published after her death. Between 1942 and 1944, during World War II, when Jews were being rounded up and sent to "work camps," Anne Frank and her family hid in a secret annex of the building housing her father's business in Amsterdam. Anne wrote in her diary during these two years. In 1944 the family was arrested and deported; Anne eventually was sent to Bergen-Belsen concentration camp, where she died the following year.

L. 11: "Malcolm": Malcolm X, later Al Hajj Malik Al-Shabazz (1925–65).

L. 12: "LeRoi": LeRoi Jones, now Amiri Baraka (1934–), poet, playwright, and social activist. He was arrested during the 1967 Newark riots and charged with illegal possession of weapons and resisting arrest. Although he was later convicted and sentenced to a three-year jail term, the conviction was reversed on appeal.

L. 13: "Rap": H. Rap Brown (1943–), now Jamil Abdullah Al-Amin. "Strapped a harness" probably refers to the fact that Brown was on probation and thereby rendered relatively powerless. See note to "Detroit Conference of Unity and Art," page 369.

L. 14: "Stokely's teeth": Stokely Carmichael, later Kwame Ture (1941–1998). Carmichael became the chairperson of SNCC (the Student Nonviolent Coordinating Committee) in May 1966 and took the organization in a more radical direction just a month later, when he announced the advent of Black Power. In 1967 he left SNCC to join the Black Panther Party. Giovanni's figure (a toothless panther) suggests that Carmichael has been made harmless.

"Wilmington Delaware"

When Giovanni entered the University of Pennsylvania's School of Social Work, she lived in Wilmington, where housing was cheaper than in Philadelphia. Part of her graduate study entailed working at the People's Settlement House in Wilmington, where she continued even after she had dropped out of graduate school. This poem, written during the eight or nine months she lived in Wilmington, is a scathing satire on both the city and its personification, the man who directed the People's Settlement.

L. 16: "Due-pontee": A reference to the du Pont family, whose money helped fund the settlements and much else in the state of Delaware. Founded in 1802 as an explosives company, Du Pont subsequently focused on chemicals and energy, and it is the corporation behind well-known brands such as Teflon, Lycra, and

Dacron. Today it is ranked the seventieth largest U.S. industrial-service corporation, with revenues in 2002 of $24 billion.

L. 26: "nourishment at the 'Y'": When Giovanni lived in Wilmington, the YMCA was a networking hub for Black businessmen and professionals. The double entendre, like the many orthographic jokes, marks the poem as a youthful composition.

L. 30: "East side of town": In the late 1960s the east side of Wilmington, which had originally been populated by white people, had become predominantly Black; the same was true of the People's Settlement and Christiana Settlement Houses, which were both on the east side.

Ll. 42–43: "party more . . . Asphalt is bad": Possibly a reference to the marches and demonstrations which were used by those in both the Civil Rights and the Black Power movements but which would have been anathema to someone like Wilmington, whose dancing is still a "shuffle," regardless of its "militancy."

Ll. 56–57: "replaced jello . . . jellied gas (a Due-pontee specialty; housewise)": A reference to napalm, a jellied gas produced by the Du Pont Corporation and used extensively in the Vietnam War.

"Letter to a Bourgeois Friend Whom Once I Loved (And Maybe Still Do If Love Is Valid)"

Written in July 1967.

L. 12: "Johnson": Lyndon B. Johnson (1908–73), thirty-sixth President of the United States (1963–69).

L. 13: "Detroit": The summer of 1967 was witness to race riots all over the United States. One of the worst started in Detroit on July 22 and lasted for several days. President Johnson ordered 4,700 federal troops into Detroit. In all some forty-three people were killed, thirty-three of them Black (see Charles M. Christian, *Black Saga: The African American Experience,* 1995).

L. 18: "Rap": H. Rap Brown, now Jamil Abdullah Al-Amin (1943–). See note to "Detroit Conference of Unity and Art," page 369.

"Love Poem (For Real)"

Ll. 10–11: "go back/to half": The poem was written in December 1968, just weeks before Richard M. Nixon (1913–94) was inaugurated the thirty-seventh President of the United States (1969–74). Nineteen sixty-eight was a devastating year in American history—both Martin Luther King, Jr., and Robert F. Kennedy were assassinated, in April and June, respectively.

L. 13: "johnson": Lyndon B. Johnson (1908–73), thirty-sixth President of the United States (1963–69).

L. 22: "cabinet": A reference to Nixon's choices for his cabinet.

L. 23: "no dick": A phrase used frequently by Giovanni and others to refer to President Nixon.

L. 28: "united quakers": Nixon's religious background was Quaker.

L. 28: "crackers": White people.

L. 38: "honkies": White people.

Ll. 39–41: "riderless horses . . . eternal flame": Most likely a reference to the funeral of John F. Kennedy (1917–63), thirty-fifth President of the United States (1961–63), and the eternal flame that marks his grave.

"For an Intellectual Audience"

In an interview Giovanni told me that she has always associated the made-up word *moile* with Dr. Seuss's *Horton Hears a Who.* In that story, the "whos" live in an elephant's ear. Because they want the elephant to know they are there, they all agree to shout at the same time—and, except for one little who, they do. Only when that little who also shouts does Horton hear them. The whos live in a little ball, and Giovanni said she thought of the little ball as a *moile.*

Black Judgement

Black Judgement was originally published in 1968, just a few months after *Black Feeling Black Talk.* Giovanni invested the money she had made from the sales of *Black Feeling Black Talk* in professional cover art and high-quality printing for her second self-published volume; the cover included photographs of LeRoi Jones, Rap Brown, Ron Karenga, and Charles Kenyatta. She also experimented with the appearance of the poems on the page: they are alternately justified on the left side and the right side. Of the twenty-seven poems originally constituting this volume, twenty-six were written in 1968; many reflect the poet's responses to the devastating public events of that year: the assassination of Martin Luther King, Jr., in April; the assassination of Robert F. Kennedy in June; and the election of Richard M. Nixon as the thirty-seventh president in November.

Within six months of its publication, *Black Judgement* had sold 6,000 copies, a phenomenal figure. Containing what Margaret Walker called Giovanni's "signature poem"—"Nikki-Rosa"—the volume signaled to the literary world that a new, serious writer had emerged.

The original publication of *Black Judgement* included the following lines on its title page:

> Sometimes we find we have nothing to give
> but love
> which is a poem
> which I give
> For the Black Revolution

"The Dance Committee (Concerning Jean-Léon Destiné)"

During her stint at the People's Settlement House in Wilmington, Giovanni organized a Black Arts Festival to which she invited—and succeeded in bringing—the distinguished Haitian dancer and choreographer Jean-Léon Destiné (1925–).

L. 2: "Fanon": Frantz Fanon (1925–61), a West Indian philosopher and psychoanalyst who argued that the victims of oppression (especially of colonialism and racism) should and would eventually turn to violence and that the violence would be redemptive. His work influenced many groups in the 1960s, including members of the Black Panthers. His most influential works were *Black Skin, White Masks* (1952) and *The Wretched of the Earth* (1961).

L. 13: "double V": A verbal play on the campaign spearheaded by the Black press during World War II; "Double V" meant "victory at home and victory abroad."

L. 18: "wouldn't be in the Black community": The dance troupe performed in a white high school rather than at the People's Settlement House, which was in the Black community.

L. 19: "Black French": Haiti (home of Destiné) was originally a French colony.

"Of Liberation"

L. 12: "3/5 of a man": The U.S. Constitution originally defined a male slave as three fifths of a man.

Ll. 35–36: "The last bastion . . . mind": In her public readings, Giovanni attributes this statement to the historian Lerone Bennett, Jr., author of *Before the Mayflower* and other works.

L. 91: "The Red Black and Green": Especially during the 1960s, Black Nationalists began sporting these colors as a symbol of Blackness and Black solidarity. The origin of these colors, however, dates back to Marcus Garvey's United Negro Improvement Association (UNIA), which was founded in 1914 and promoted the unification of African peoples throughout the Diaspora. The UNIA's flag was red, black, and green.

L. 97: "Professor Neal": Larry Neal (1937–1981), poet, dramatist, and essayist, was a central figure in the Black Arts movement.

"Poem for Black Boys (With Special Love to James)"

This is the only poem in the volume not written during 1968 (its date of composition was April 2, 1967).

L. 5: "Mau Mau": The Mau Mau movement in Kenya led a revolt against British rule and eventually helped bring about Kenyan independence in 1963.

L.7: "Rap Brown": H. Rap Brown, now Jamil Abdullah Al-Amin (1943–). See note to "Detroit Conference of Unity and Art," page 369.

L. 31: "any nickel bag": A reference to a bag of marijuana.

"Concerning One Responsible Negro with Too Much Power"

This poem was written on April 3, 1968, just one day before the assassination of Martin Luther King, Jr. The National Guard was moved into Wilmington, where Giovanni was living, on April 3, which led her (in retrospect) to believe that the federal government knew King would be assassinated the next day; Wilmington was key to the flow of traffic up and down the East Coast. Giovanni herself managed to get out of the city just before all traffic was stopped in the wake of King's assassination.

The poem seems to be about the individual described in "Wilmington Delaware." See note to that poem on page 375.

"Reflections on April 4, 1968"

Written just one day after King's assassination, this poem considers it "an act of war," the only response to which can be the destruction of white America. The prose form reinforces the devastating impact of this event on the poet.

Stanza 2: "President johnson": A reference to Lyndon B. Johnson (1908–73), thirty-sixth President of the United States (1963–69).

Stanza 2: "distinction between us and negroes": See note to "The True Import of Present Dialogue" on page 373.

Stanza 4: "the warriors in the streets": Following King's assassination, riots broke out in more than one hundred cities across the country.

Stanza 5: "statements from Dallas": A reference to the site of the assassination of John F. Kennedy (1917–63), thirty-fifth President of the United States, on November 22, 1963.

Stanza 6: "Johnson's footprints": A reference to the fact that Lyndon B. Johnson (1908–73) succeeded to the presidency because of the assassination of John Kennedy; Johnson was Kennedy's vice president (1961–63).

Stanza 7: "Zeus has wrestled the Black Madonna": In Greek mythology, Zeus was the chief Olympian god. Here he is represented as having been defeated by Black Christianity. The Shrine of the Black Madonna, a Black church originally established in Detroit, has an eighteen-foot sculpture of a Black Madonna.

Stanza 7: "nadinolia gods": Nadinolia is a product advertised to lighten skin color.

Stanza 7: "fire this time": A reference to James Baldwin's best-selling *The Fire Next Time,* published in 1963. Baldwin (1924–87) insisted that if Black Americans did not gain their essential liberties, there would be a revolution of fire, which would destroy the country.

"The Funeral of Martin Luther King, Jr."

Martin Luther King, Jr. (1929–68) was assassinated in Memphis, Tennessee, on April 4, 1968. His funeral in Atlanta, Georgia, was on April 9, 1968.

"A Litany for Peppe"

Peppe was a childhood nickname for the poet's nephew, Christopher Black (1959–).

Line 8: "Blessed be": Allusion to Christ's beatitudes. See Matthew 5:1–11.

Line 13: See note to "Wilmington Delaware" on page 375.

Ll. 19–20: "Blessed is . . . earth": An inversion of Christ's beatitudes. See Matthew 5:1–11.

"Nikki-Rosa"

"Nikki-Rosa" was the nickname given to the poet when she was a child by her sister, Gary. The poem, described by Margaret Walker as Giovanni's signature poem, was written on April 12, 1968.

L. 3: "Woodlawn": A suburb of Cincinnati in which Giovanni and her family lived briefly before they moved to nearby Wyoming.

Ll. 15–18: "Hollydale . . . stock": Hollydale is a subdivision outside Cincinnati that was created for Black people. Giovanni's father was one of many who pooled their money to buy the land. They intended to use the land as collateral for the loans to build houses. But because they were Black, they could not find banks to lend them the money. Eventually the homes in Hollydale would be built, but the poet's father, like many others, was unable to keep his money tied up for so long. He sold his stock and used the proceeds as a down payment on a house in Lincoln Heights.

"The Great Pax Whitie"

L. 1: See John 1:1–5.

L. 8: "peace be still": These are the words spoken by Jesus when he calmed the waters of the Sea of Galilee; see Mark 4:39. The biblical story is also the basis of the gospel song, "Peace, Be Still," by James Cleveland. On her award-winning album *Truth Is on Its Way*, Giovanni reads this poem to the accompaniment of the song, performed by the New York Community Choir.

L. 18: "Lot's wife . . . Morton company": For the account of Lot's wife being turned into a pillar of salt, see Genesis 19:1–26.

L. 24: "our Black Madonna": A reference to the eighteen-foot sculpture in the Shrine of the Black Madonna in Detroit.

Ll. 28–34: In Mark's version of the story, when Jesus is brought before the high priests for interrogation, Peter is present. When asked directly about his knowledge of Jesus, Peter denies any association with him. See Mark 14:53–72. In Matthew 16:18, Jesus says to Peter, "Thou art Peter, and upon this rock I will build my church," a statement which in the Greek involves a play on words (*petros* means "little rock"). The interpretation of this statement has sharply divided Christians; Giovanni makes reference to the interpretation of the Roman Catholic Church.

L. 37: "Carthaginians": Carthage was an ancient city of North Africa on the Bay of Tunis. Despite having one of the greatest military leaders of the ancient world—Hannibal—the city was ultimately defeated by Roman forces.

L. 38: "great appian way": The most famous of the Roman roads, the Appian Way connected Rome to Greece and the East.

L. 39: "the Moors": A nomadic people of North Africa, the Moors, who became Muslims, established kingdoms throughout Spain. During the Middle Ages, Christian rulers attempted to conquer Moorish strongholds. The last Moorish city was Granada, which was conquered by Ferdinand and Isabella in 1492, and most of the Moors were driven out of Spain.

L. 53: "great emancipator": Abraham Lincoln (1809–65), sixteenth President of the United States (1861–65).

L. 55: "making the world safe for democracy": From Woodrow Wilson's April 2, 1917, address to Congress, in which he sought a declaration of war.

L. 58: "barbecued six million": A reference to Hitler's genocidal attack on the Jews.

L. 60: "38th parallel": A reference to the division of Korea, at the end of World War II, at the Thirty-eighth Parallel into the Soviet-occupied North and the U.S. occupied South. The Korean War resulted when North Korea crossed this line and invaded South Korea.

L. 63: "champagne was shipped out of the East": Giovanni told me in an interview that she intended this as a reference to the defeat of the French in 1954 in the French Indochina War.

Ll. 64–65: "kosher pork . . . Africa": Giovanni stated in an interview with me that this line compares the Zionists in Israel to pigs.

Ll. 71–72: "great white prince . . . texas": John F. Kennedy (1917–63), thirty-fifth President of the United States.

Ll. 73–74: "Black shining prince . . . cathedral": Malcolm X, later Al Hajj Malik Al-Shabazz (1925–65), was assassinated on February 21, 1965, at the Audubon Ballroom in New York City. A charismatic Black Nationalist leader, he was suspended from the Black Muslim movement and subsequently founded the Organization of Afro-American Unity. He was gunned down by three Black Muslims who were eventually convicted, but controversy about his assassination continues. Thomas à Becket (1118–70) was Archbishop of Canterbury. King Henry II of England and Becket were friends when then Archbishop Theobald died; Henry appointed Becket to the post in hopes of strengthening his own position vis-à-vis the Church. But Becket did not automatically support the king; their relationship deteriorated steadily. In a standoff about the power of the state over the Church, King Henry became infuriated with Becket and apparently spoke words to the effect that he wished someone would rid him of the archbishop. Four knights hoping to gain favor with Henry went to Canterbury and killed Becket on the altar of the cathedral, in the midst of a service. Not only did the knights fail in their attempt to court Henry's favor but the king himself, some four years later, made a penitential walk through Canterbury and spent the night in Becket's crypt.

L. 75: "our nigger in memphis": Martin Luther King, Jr. (1929–68), who was assassinated in Memphis, Tennessee, on April 4, 1968.

"Knoxville, Tennessee"
Giovanni and her sister usually spent their summers with their maternal grandparents, Louvenia and John Brown Watson, in Knoxville.

"Records"
U.S. Senator Robert F. Kennedy (1925–68), a presidential candidate, was shot in Los Angeles on June 5, 1968, and died on June 6. This poem was written on June 6, the day before Giovanni's twenty-fifth birthday.

L. 5: "johnson": President Lyndon B. Johnson (1908–73), thirty-sixth President of the United States (1963–69).

L. 13: "family": The Kennedy family.

L. 17: "bobby": Senator Robert F. Kennedy.

"Adulthood (For Claudia)"
Claudia Anderson was a friend in Cincinnati with whom Giovanni worked at Walgreens.

Ll. 2–4: "indianapolis . . . my aunt": Giovanni often visited one of her aunts, Agnes Chapman, who lived in Indianapolis, a short distance from Cincinnati.

L. 36: "hammarskjöld": Dag Hammarskjöld (1905–61), secretary-general of the United Nations (1953–61). He was killed on his way to the Congo when his plane crashed in northern Rhodesia (now Zambia).

L. 37: "lumumba": Patrice Lumumba (1925–61) was the first prime minister of the Republic of the Congo (now Zaire). A charismatic leader of the independence movement in the Congo, Lumumba had radical anticolonialist politics that eventually led to a split in the Congo's first national political party, Mouvement National Congolais, which he founded in 1958. He was killed in January 1961; both his death and unsuccessful attempts to cover up the truth about it outraged activists throughout the world. The possible role played by the Belgian or the U.S. government in his death is still uncertain.

L. 38: "diem": Ngo Dinh Diem (1901–63), president (1955–63) of South Vietnam, murdered in a military coup which was covertly backed by the United States on November 1, 1963.

L. 39: "kennedy": John F. Kennedy (1917–63), thirty-fifth President of the United States, was assassinated on November 22, 1963, in Dallas, Texas.

L. 40: "malcolm": Malcolm X, later Al Hajj Malik Al-Shabazz (1925–65), was assassinated on February 21, 1965, at the Audubon Ballroom in New York City. A charismatic Black Nationalist leader, he was suspended from the Nation of Islam and subsequently founded the Organization of Afro-American Unity. He was gunned down by three Black Muslims who were eventually convicted, but controversy about his assassination—for example, the possible role in it of the federal government—continues.

L. 41: "evers": Medgar Wiley Evers (1925–63), Civil Rights activist and Mississippi field secretary for the National Association for the Advancement of Colored People (NAACP), was murdered in the doorway of his home in Jackson, Mississippi, on June 12, 1963, by the white supremacist Byron de la Beckwith. Beckwith stood trial twice, in 1963 and 1964, but not until 1994 was he convicted of the crime.

L. 42: "schwerner, chaney and goodman": Michael Schwerner (1940–64), James E. Chaney (1943–64), and Andrew Goodman

(1943–64) were three Civil Rights activists who worked in Black voter registration in Mississippi and were murdered by members of the Ku Klux Klan, with the complicity of law enforcement officers. After a massive search, including 200 naval personnel, their bodies were found buried not far from Philadelphia, Mississippi. Despite the fact that everyone—including the Federal Bureau of Investigation—knew who the killers were, it was three years before Neshoba County Sheriff Lawrence Rainey, Chief Deputy Sheriff Cecil Price, and five others were convicted on federal charges of violating the civil rights of the three. No state charges were ever filed.

L. 43: "liuzzo": Viola Gregg Liuzzo (1925–65), a medical lab technician, mother, and activist from Michigan. She was killed in an automobile on the Selma Highway on March 26, 1965, because a car with members of the Ku Klux Klan saw her, a white woman, in the same automobile as a black man. The four KKK members were arrested, and one agreed to testify against the other three, but they were all acquitted of murder. Eventually, through orders from President Johnson, they were convicted on federal charges of conspiring to deprive Liuzzo of her civil rights. Viola Liuzzo is the only white woman honored at the Civil Rights Memorial in Montgomery, Alabama.

L. 44: "stokely": Stokely Carmichael, later Kwame Ture (1941–98), Civil Rights activist, chair of the Student Nonviolent Coordinating Committee (1966–67), and "prime minister" of the Black Panthers. Carmichael is credited with creating the slogan "Black Power." He moved to Guinea in 1968, and in 1973 he became a citizen of Uganda.

L. 45: "le roi": LeRoi Jones, now Amiri Baraka (1934–). See note to "Poem (No Name No. 3)," page 374.

L. 46: "rap": H. Rap Brown, now Jamil Abdullah Al-Amin (1943–). See note to "Detroit Conference of Unity and Art," page 369.

L. 47: "pollard, thompson and cooper": Three SNCC workers on their way to California who were killed in Texas.

L. 48: "king": Martin Luther King, Jr. (1929–68).

L. 49: "kennedy": Robert F. Kennedy (1925–68).

"From a Logical Point of View"

L. 12: "dream deferred": See Langston Hughes's poem "Harlem," the famous first line of which is "What happens to a dream deferred?"

"Dreams"

L. 6: "raelet": The Raelettes (originally known as the Cookies) were a female backup trio for the singer Ray Charles.

L. 7: "dr o wn d in my youn tears": "Drown in My Own Tears" was one of Ray Charles's big hits.

L. 8: "tal kin bout": Another Ray Charles hit, "Talking About You."

L. 9: "marjorie hendricks": Marjorie Hendricks was the gritty-voiced lead singer of the Raelettes.

L. 12: "baaaaaby nightandday": Words from another big Ray Charles hit, "The Night Time Is the Right Time."

L. 19: "sweet inspiration": The Sweet Inspirations were background singers for Atlantic Records. The lead singer was Cissy Houston (mother of Whitney); the others were Estelle Brown, Sylvia Shemwell, and Myrna Smith. The Sweet Inspirations, who sang background vocals for many of Aretha Franklin's hits, sang three-part harmony, unlike the Raelettes, who sang the blues.

"Revolutionary Music"

This poem, which is both about and constructed from the names of musical groups, themes, and songs, asserts the political implications of much popular music recorded by Black musicians during the 1960s. It was cited by Stephen Henderson as an excellent example of "the use of tonal memory as poetic structure" in Black poetry. By "tonal memory," he means "the practice . . . of forcing the reader to incorporate into the structure of the poem his memory of a specific song, or passage of a song, or even of a specific delivery technique. Without this specific memory the poem cannot be properly realized." See Stephen Henderson, *Understanding the New Black Poetry: Black Speech and Black Music as Poetic References* (New York: William Morrow, 1973), pp. 53–54.

Ll. 1–2: "sly/and the family stone": Sly and the Family Stone was an important musical group in the late 1960s; they brought together gospel, rhythm and blues, and rock.

L. 4: "dancing to the music": "Dance to the Music" was the first major hit by Sly and the Family Stone.

L. 5: "james brown": James Brown (1933–), the Godfather of Soul, inventor of funk, and quite likely the most important contributor to and influence on soul music.

Ll. 11–14: "although you happy . . . taking you on": This line is from "Money Won't Change You," a big hit for James Brown that later was covered by Aretha Franklin.

L. 19: "good god! ugh!": Words from James Brown's "I Can't Stand Myself (When You Touch Me)."

L. 21: "i got the feeling baby": Another James Brown hit, "I've Got the Feeling."

L. 23: "martha and the vandellas dancing in the street": Martha and the Vandellas, one of the most important girl groups of the 1960s, were a gritty and soulful alternative to their chief rivals, the Supremes. The group originated in Detroit in 1962 and was anchored by Martha Reeves, the lead singer. "Dancin' in the Streets" was perhaps their biggest hit. In an interview, Giovanni stated that she and other young Black revolutionaries understood the song to be a coded reference to the Detroit riots.

L. 24: "shorty long . . . at that junction": Frederick "Shorty" Long, born in Birmingham, Alabama, was a musician and recording artist who signed with Motown in 1963. He cowrote (with Eddie Holland) and performed "Function at the Junction," which eventually became a classic and which carries a strong political message.

Ll. 26–27: "aretha said they better/think": Aretha Franklin (1942–), the undisputed "Queen of Soul." "Think" was a hit single with significant political overtones; it was recorded on the album *Aretha Now,* released in 1968.

L. 29: "ain't no way to love you": "Ain't No Way," which was written by Aretha Franklin's sister, Carolyn, was recorded on the album *Lady Soul*, released in 1968.

L. 31: "the o'jays": Taking their name from the radio DJ Eddie O'Jay, the O'Jays had more than fifty hit singles during their forty-year career.

L. 34: "mighty mighty impressions": The Impressions were a Chicago group led by Curtis Mayfield; the original group also included Jerry Butler, whose lead vocals helped make "For Your Precious Love" a huge hit and launched Butler's solo career. Among their many hits was the 1968 "We're a Winner," one of the earliest R & B celebrations of Black pride.

L. 40: "temptations": The Temptations, a five-member group, were the most successful of Motown's male vocal groups.

L. 41: "supremes": The Supremes, eventually a three-member group, were the most successful of Motown's female vocal groups.

L. 42: "delfonics": A male trio, the Delfonics were one of the first groups to exhibit the smooth and soulful style that eventually became known as the "Philly sound."

L. 43: "miracles": The Miracles, a male vocal group led by the singer and songwriter Smokey Robinson, helped define the Motown sound.

L. 44: "intruders": The Intruders were a male vocal group from Philadelphia who signed with Kenny Gamble and Leon Huff's record company, Philadelphia International Records. They were innovators in the Philly sound.

L. 45: "beatles": Contrary to the suggestion of these lines, Giovanni is actually an admirer of the music of the Beatles (witness her poem "This Is Not for John Lennon," page 307).

L. 45: "animals": A British male quintet, the Animals were one of the most important of the British R & B groups of the 1960s.

L. 46: "young rascals": A white, male rock band, the Young Rascals had a penchant for playing Black soul music, sometimes dubbed "blue-eyed soul."

L. 49: "sam cooke": Sam Cooke (1931–64) was a popular and influential singer who emerged in the 1950s as a gospel star and then began recording popular songs, including the megahits "You Send Me" and "Wonderful World." His influence on soul music as well as on many of its best-known performers cannot be overstated. "A Change Is Gonna Come," recorded in February 1964, was his last great ballad. Controversy still surrounds his violent death.

"Beautiful Black Men (With compliments and apologies to all not mentioned by name)"

L. 9: "running numbers": The numbers was a popular illegal gambling game played in Black communities all over the country, similar to (and largely replaced by) state lotteries. A numbers runner (analogous to a bookie) collected and paid off bets made each day.

L. 10: "hogs": Cadillac automobiles.

L. 11: "walking their dogs": "Walking the Dog" was a dance popularized by Rufus Thomas, a DJ in Memphis and father of Carla Thomas, who recorded the smash hit "Gee Whiz (Look at His Eyes)."

L. 15: "jerry butler": The performer and composer Jerry "the Iceman" Butler started his career as a member of the Impressions and subsequently had many hit songs as a soloist.

L.15: "Wilson pickett": Wilson Pickett was unrivaled in the sheer energy he brought to a number of hits in the 1960s, including "In the Midnight Hour" and "Mustang Sally."

L. 15: "the impressions": The Impressions were a Chicago group led by Curtis Mayfield; the original group also included Jerry Butler, whose lead vocals helped make "For Your Precious Love" a huge hit and launched Butler's solo career.

L. 16: "temptations": The Temptations, a five-member group, were the most successful of Motown's male vocal groups.

L. 16: "mighty mighty sly": Sly and the Family Stone was an important group in the late 1960s; they brought together gospel, rhythm and blues, and rock.

L. 20: "new breed men": New Breed was a store in Harlem in the 1960s.

L. 20: "breed alls": Overalls made of leather, suede, or velvet, popular in the late 1960s.

"Ugly Honkies, or The Election Game and How to Win It"

The first portion of the poem (lines 1–149) was written on August 8, 1968, and the postelection lines (150–58) were written on November 18.

L. 5: "lyndon": Lyndon B. Johnson (1908–73), thirty-sixth President of the United States (1963–69).

L. 6: "ike": Dwight D. Eisenhower (1890–1969), thirty-fourth President of the United States (1953–61).

L. 6: "nixon": Richard M. Nixon (1913–94), vice president under Eisenhower (1953–61) and thirty-seventh President of the United States (1969–74).

L. 6: "hhh": Hubert H. Humphrey (1911–78), vice president to Lyndon B. Johnson (1965–69), and the Democratic presidential candidate in 1968. He narrowly lost the 1968 election to Richard Nixon.

L. 6: "wallace": George C. Wallace (1919–98), governor of Alabama for multiple terms. Wallace was an open segregationist who attempted to block integration of public schools in the 1960s. He was an Independent presidential candidate in the 1968 election, in which he received roughly 13 percent of the vote and carried five Southern states.

L. 6: "maddox": Lester Maddox (1915–2003), governor of Georgia from 1967 to 1971 and lieutenant governor from 1971 to 1975. Before he entered politics Maddox gained notoriety for closing down his Atlanta restaurant (1964) rather than desegregate it. He unsuccessfully sought the 1968 Democratic presidential nomination.

L. 16: "daley": Richard J. Daley (1902–76), Democratic mayor of Chicago from 1955 to 1976. Daley brought national attention to himself during the 1968 Democratic Convention in Chicago by allowing city police to use violence against demonstrators protesting the Vietnam War.

L. 17: "booing senator ribicoff": At the 1968 Democratic Convention in Chicago, Senator Abraham Ribicoff (1910–98) nominated George McGovern (1922–) to be the party's presidential candidate. In his nomination speech, Ribicoff referred to the "Gestapo tactics on the streets of Chicago," which provoked a torrent of expletives from Daley. Ribicoff was Secretary of Health, Education, and Welfare under President John F. Kennedy and served as a U.S. senator from Connecticut from 1963 to 1981.

L. 21: "julian bond": Julian Bond (1940–) served four terms in the Georgia House of Representatives (1967–74) and six terms in the Georgia Senate (1975–87). He was first elected to a one-year term in 1965, but the House refused to seat him because of his opposition to the Vietnam War. He was again elected in 1966 to fill his own vacant seat, and the House again voted against seating him. After he won a third election, to a two-year term, in November 1966, the U.S. Supreme Court ruled unanimously that the Georgia House had violated Bond's rights. Bond had been one of the founding members of SNCC (Student Nonviolent Coordinating Committee) and subsequently editor of the protest newspaper *The Atlanta Inquirer*. He is currently chairman of the NAACP (National Association for the Advancement of Colored People).

L. 24: "life": *Life* magazine.

L. 24: "muskie and huskie humphrey": Edmund Muskie (1914–96) was a U.S. senator from Maine (1958–80). He was the Democratic running mate of Hubert H. Humphrey (see page 391) in the 1968 presidential election.

L. 30: "john and bobby": John F. Kennedy (1917–63) and Robert F. Kennedy (1925–68), both assassinated.

L. 31: "evers and king": Medgar Wiley Evers (1925–63) and Martin Luther King, Jr. (1929–68). See note to "Adulthood," page 384.

L. 32: "caroline": Caroline Kennedy Schlossberg (1957–), daughter of President John F. Kennedy and Jacqueline Bouvier Kennedy. An attorney and writer, she is today president of the Kennedy Library Foundation.

L. 34: "arthur miller": Arthur A. Miller (1915–), award-winning playwright, author of *Death of a Salesman*. Miller in fact attended the 1968 Democratic National Convention in Chicago as the delegate from Roxbury.

Ll. 46–47: "and hhh says . . . wrong": The 1968 presidential candidate Hubert H. Humphrey refused to denounce Chicago's Mayor Daley for his deployment of the police during the convention.

L. 55: "politics of '64": The 1964 Democratic ticket was President Lyndon B. Johnson and Hubert H. Humphrey. Johnson had succeeded to the presidency after the assassination of John F. Kennedy in 1963; because he was the sitting president, his election in 1964 was virtually guaranteed, and he enjoyed a landslide victory over Barry M. Goldwater, the Republican candidate.

Ll. 56–62: "the deal . . . chicago": Giovanni's argument is that the leaders of the Republican and Democratic political parties conspired together, agreeing that Johnson would be allowed to win the presidency in 1964 in return for which Nixon would be allowed to win the 1968 election. The 1968 Democratic Convention produced a candidate (Humphrey) less likely to win than, for example, Robert F. Kennedy might have been had he not been assassinated. Like many intellectuals of the 1960s, Giovanni was convinced that national events were orchestrated through the conspiracies of a few powerful figures.

L. 56: "the bird": An allusion to President Johnson's wife, "Lady Bird" Johnson.

L. 58: "dallas": An allusion to Kennedy's assassination in Dallas, Texas.

L. 60: "los angeles": An allusion to the assassination of the presidential hopeful Robert F. Kennedy in June 1968, in Los Angeles.

L. 61: "tricky dick": Nickname for Richard M. Nixon (1913–94), thirty-seventh President of the United States (1969–74), who was forced to resign early in his second term.

L. 62: "chicago": Site of the 1968 Democratic Convention.

L. 66: "second reconstruction": Just as the first Reconstruction, following the Civil War, was largely a failure and was followed by increasing violence against Blacks in the South and the erosion of their civil liberties, Giovanni sees the events leading to the election of Nixon as tied to the erosion of gains made during the Civil Rights movement.

L. 77: "gregory or cleaver": An allusion to the comedian and activist Dick Gregory (1932–), who ran for president in 1968, and to Eldridge Cleaver (1935–98), Black militant minister of information for the Black Panthers; Cleaver was wounded in a Panther shoot-out with police in 1968, jumped bail, and fled to Algeria.

L. 81: "nixon-agnew": Spiro T. Agnew (1918–96), Richard Nixon's running mate in the 1968 presidential election. Formerly the governor of Maryland, Agnew served as vice president from 1969 to 1973, when he resigned after being fined for income tax evasion.

Ll. 87–88: "about nigeria . . . on'": An allusion to the thirty-month civil war in Nigeria, also known as the Biafran War (1967–70), which cost an estimated one million lives, most of them lost to starvation.

L. 119: "mccarthy": Eugene J. McCarthy (1916–) was a candidate for the 1968 Democratic presidential nomination. He announced his candidacy in 1967 on an antiwar platform, challenging President Johnson and his policies. McCarthy's campaign success in New Hampshire (in March 1968) helped draw Robert F. Kennedy into the race and influenced President Johnson's decision not to seek reelection. McCarthy was a U.S. representative from Minnesota from 1949 to 1959 and a U.S. Senator from 1959 to 1971. After he lost the presidential nomination, he finished his term in the Senate and returned to university teaching.

L. 124: "the assassination of one": A reference to Robert F. Kennedy.

L. 128: "teddy": A reference to Senator Edward M. Kennedy (1932–), brother of John F. Kennedy and Robert F. Kennedy, and a member of the U.S. Senate since 1962.

L. 150: "wallace": George C. Wallace, who ran as an Independent in the 1968 presidential election; see note to line 6 on page 391.

"Cultural Awareness"

L. 17: "maulana": Maulana Karenga, a Black Nationalist, first instituted the celebration of Kwanza (Swahili for "first fruits") in 1966.

L. 17: "elijah": Elijah Muhammad (1897–1975), longtime leader (1933–75) of the Nation of Islam.

L. 17: "el shabbaz": Malcolm X, later Al Hajj Malik Al-Shabazz (1925–65), was assassinated on February 21, 1965, at the Audubon Ballroom in New York City.

L. 23: "zig-zag papers": Used to roll marijuana.

"For Saundra"

L. 21: "no-Dick": Richard M. Nixon (1913–94), thirty-seventh President of the United States (1969–74).

"For a Poet I Know"

L. 14: "aretha": Aretha Franklin (1942–), "Queen of Soul."

L. 15: "james brown's is humphrey": James Brown (1933–), "Godfather of Soul," was an important supporter of Hubert H. Humphrey and his presidential campaign.

L. 16: "columbia": This poem was written in January 1968, when Giovanni was enrolled in Columbia University.

L. 29: "joe goncalves": Dingane Joe Goncalves, founder of *Journal of Black Poetry.*

L. 30: "carolyn rodgers": Carolyn M. Rodgers (1945–), Chicago-born poet associated with the Black Arts movement.

L. 31: "hoyt fuller": Hoyt Fuller (1927–81), journalist, educator, and editor of *Black World* (formerly *Negro Digest*), an important publication during the 1960s and early 1970s.

L. 32: "jet poem": A reference to *Jet* magazine.

"For Teresa"

Teresa Elliott was a close friend of Giovanni's mother.

L. 24: "peppe": The poet's nephew, Christopher Black (1959–).

L. 26: "gary": The poet's sister, Gary Ann (1940–).

"My Poem"

L. 3: "wrote a poem": A reference to "The True Import of Present Dialogue, Black vs. Negro," page 19.

Re: Creation

Re: Creation was published in 1970 by Broadside Press. It is composed of forty-two poems (including the poem of dedication), which were written between May 1969 and July 1970, that is, during the last few months of Giovanni's pregnancy and the first year of her son's life.

"For Tommy"

In the original edition, this poem was under the heading "Dedication." Thomas Watson Giovanni, the poet's only child, was born August 31, 1969.

"Two Poems From Barbados"

These two poems were written in June 1969 and July 1969, respectively.

"For Harold Logan (Murdered by 'persons unknown' cause he wanted to own a Black club on Broadway)"

Harold Logan, together with the rhythm and blues singer Lloyd Price, acquired in the 1960s the old Birdland jazz club, just north of Fifty-second Street on Broadway. Although Logan and Price dubbed the club the Turntable (also the name of their recording company), it continued to be remembered affectionately as Birdland. It was, of course, closed on Sundays, and the intrepid Giovanni decided it would be a great place to have a book party to promote *Black Judgement*. She approached Logan, who let her use it with the proviso that she bring in at least a hundred people; if she failed to do so, she would have to pay him $500. Logan was rumored to be connected to the mob, which gave Giovanni added incentive to advertise her event and fill the house. Ironically, she did such effective publicity that people were lined up for over a block to get in. The offices of *The New York Times* overlooked this line, and a reporter got interested in where all those people were going on a Sunday afternoon. A photograph and story were featured in the *Times* on Monday, which boosted Giovanni's sales even more.

Logan was, in fact, brutally murdered inside the club, and Price distanced himself as much as possible; he moved to Africa and involved himself in nonmusical ventures through most of the 1970s. After he returned to the United States in the early 1980s, Price's career took on new life, and he continues to perform at concerts and festivals.

"No Reservations (for Art Jones)"
Art Jones was a prisoner who wrote Giovanni a letter.

"For Gwendolyn Brooks"
This poem was written for *To Gwen With Love: An Anthology Dedicated to Gwendolyn Brooks,* which was published in 1971 by Johnson Publishing Company. In the anthology, the poem has the subtitle "a 'note of love.'"

"Poem for Aretha"
L. 55: "billie holiday's life": Billie Holiday (1915–59), influential but tragic jazz singer whose life was marked by financial difficulties, attachments to abusive men, and addiction to drugs.

L. 56: "dinah washington's death": Dinah Washington (1924–63), singer and pianist whose range included blues, gospel, rhythm and blues, and pop. She died of an accidental overdose of sleeping pills.

L. 67: "johnny ace": John Marshall Alexander, Jr., a.k.a. Johnny Ace (1929–54), popular rhythm and blues singer whose premature, bizarre death sustained his reputation long after he had died. Franklin covered several songs he had written, including "Never Let Me Go" and "My Song."

L. 67 "lil green": Lil Green (1919–54), Chicago blues singer who achieved a successful touring and recording career. One of her big hits was "Romance in the Dark," which Franklin recorded as "In the Dark."

Ll. 69–70: "'i say a little prayer' . . . anymore": Dionne Warwick (1940–), pop singer whose string of hits from her collaboration with Burt Bacharach and Hal David earned her multiple Grammys. "I Say a Little Prayer" was a Bacharach-David composition for Warwick that Franklin later recorded as well.

L. 71: "money won't change you": This song was initially a James Brown hit.

L. 72: "james can't sing 'respect'": "Respect," written by Otis Redding, was one of Franklin's biggest hits, if not her signature song. Although she had a hit with her cover of James Brown's "Money Can't Change You," Brown could not similarly record "Respect."

L. 73: "ray charles from marlboro country": In the 1960s, Ray Charles moved away from R & B into country and western music, recording, for example, "Your Cheatin' Heart" in 1962.

L. 75: "nancy wilson": Nancy Wilson (1937–) jazz and pop singer.

L. 77: "dionne": Dionne Warwick; see note to line 69.

L. 81: "you make me/feel": One of Franklin's big hits was "(You Make Me Feel Like) A Natural Woman," first released on her 1968 album, Lady Soul. The song was written by Carole King and Jerry Wexler.

L. 81: "the blazers": Dyke & the Blazers, a little remembered R & B group led by Dyke Christian (1943–71); they had a huge hit with "Let a Woman Be a Woman—Let a Man Be a Man."

Ll. 83–85: "when my soul . . . claim it": Another line from Franklin's "(You Make Me Feel Like) A Natural Woman."

L. 85: "joplin said 'maybe'": Janis Joplin (1943–70), blues and rock and roll star who died of an accidental drug overdose. She had a hit song entitled "Maybe."

Ll. 87–89: "when humphrey . . . james brown": Franklin declined to help with Hubert Humphrey's presidential campaign, but James Brown agreed to do so.

L. 90: "otis": Otis Redding (1941–67), one of the greatest soul singers and writers of all time, was killed in an airplane crash in Madison, Wisconsin. Although some people aboard survived the crash, Redding and four members of his backup group, the Bar-Kays, were killed; Giovanni has stated her belief that the crash was not an accident. Redding wrote "Respect," which Franklin recorded in the spring of 1967 (he died on December 10 of that year).

Ll. 91–92: "the impressions . . . 'moving/on up'": The Impressions were a Chicago group led by Curtis Mayfield; the original group also included Jerry Butler, whose lead vocals helped make "For Your Precious Love" a huge hit and launched Butler's solo career. The quoted line is from their hit song, "We're a Winner."

L. 98: "temptations say . . . 'think about it'": The Temptations, a five-member group, were the most successful of Motown's male vocal groups.

"Revolutionary Dreams"

Ll. 12–15: "natural/dreams . . . natural": This poem makes use of Aretha Franklin's 1968 hit song, "(You Make Me Feel Like) A Natural Woman."

"Walking Down Park"

L. 1: "park": Park Avenue in New York City.

L. 2: "amsterdam": Amsterdam Avenue in New York City.

L. 3: "columbus": Columbus Avenue in New York City.

L. 18: "central park": Central Park in New York City.

L. 30: "time's squares": A play on Times Square, also in New York City.

"Kidnap Poem"

L. 6 "jones beach": Jones Beach State Park in Wantagh, Long Island.

L. 7: "coney island": Coney Island is an amusement park and beach spot in Brooklyn, New York.

L. 16: "red Black green": Especially during the 1960s, Black

Nationalists began sporting these colors as a symbol of Blackness and Black solidarity. The origin of the colors, however, dates back to Marcus Garvey's United Negro Improvement Association (UNIA), which was founded in 1914 and promoted the unification of all African peoples throughout the Diaspora. The UNIA's flag was red, black, and green.

"The Genie in the Jar (For Nina Simone)"

Nina Simone (1933–2003), "High Priestess of Soul," musician, singer, and political diva. Giovanni dedicated two poems to Simone, with whom she enjoyed a brief friendship; the other is "Poem (For Nina)," page 175.

"The Lion In Daniel's Den (for Paul Robeson, Sr.)"

Paul Robeson (1898–1976) was an activist, athlete, singer, and actor. The son of a runaway slave and an abolitionist Quaker, Robeson won a four-year academic scholarship to Rutgers University, where he excelled in both athletics and academics: he won fifteen varsity letters in sports, was initiated into Phi Beta Kappa in his junior year, and graduated as valedictorian. Despite having been named twice to the All-American Football Team, he was not inducted into the College Football Hall of Fame until 1995, nearly two decades after his death. He attended Columbia Law School and practiced law briefly but then turned to theater and music. He played many lead roles on the stage for which he won international acclaim, and he starred in a number of films. His outspokenness about injustice and inequality eventually led to charges of being a Communist brought against him by the House Un-American Activities Committee, which grievously harmed his career. In 1950 the United States revoked his passport, and he struggled for eight years to regain it so as to be able to travel abroad, essential to his work. At the time this poem was written (1970), both Robeson and his son, Paul Robeson, Jr., were alive; hence the designation "Sr."

The poem combines two biblical stories, the conversion of Paul on the road to Damascus and the testing of Daniel's faith through his being cast into the den of lions.

Ll. 1–2: "on the road . . . christians": Before his conversion, Saul was opposed to Christianity and did what he could to help eradicate it. He was chasing Jewish Christians who had fled to Damascus when he experienced his conversion. See Acts 9.

L. 8: "I Am Paul": Paul was born into a Hellenistic Jewish family and given the Hebrew name Saul as well as the name Paul; he was a Roman citizen. Although his embrace of Christ's teachings and divinity did not in his own mind conflict with his Jewish faith, he is traditionally identified as Saul before the conversion and Paul after.

L. 13: "red black and green songs": Especially during the 1960s, Black Nationalists began sporting these colors as a symbol of Blackness and Black solidarity. The origin of the colors, however, dates back to Marcus Garvey's United Negro Improvement Association (UNIA), which was founded in 1914 and promoted the unification of all African peoples throughout the Diaspora. The UNIA's flag was red, black, and green.

"For A Lady of Pleasure Now Retired"

L. 23: "louvenia smiled": A reference to Giovanni's maternal grandmother, Emma Louvenia Watson (1898–1967).

"2nd Rapp"

L. 2: "rap": H. Rap Brown, now Jamil Abdullah Al-Amin (1943–). See note to "Detroit Conference of Unity and Art," page 369. Rap Brown went underground in 1970, the year this poem was published, because he had been charged with violating the terms of his bail and two of his friends had been killed in a suspicious explosion. He was arrested in 1971 after being wounded by police, stood trial in 1972, and began serving a prison sentence in 1973.

"Poem For Unwed Mothers (to be sung to "The Old F.U. Spirit")"

Giovanni was herself, of course, "an unwed mother," which subjected her to far more criticism than a "single mother" would receive today; she was, in fact, one of the first public figures who insisted on her right to control her life as she wished. She is certainly one of the women who changed the language we use to describe mothers who are unattached to their children's fathers.

"Ego Tripping (there may be a reason why)"

L. 12: "nefertiti": Nefertiti was one of the most celebrated of the ancient Egyptians, despite the fact that relatively little is known about her. She was the wife of King Akhenaten (1353–1336 BC) and with him raised six daughters. When one of the daughters died, the parents' mourning was depicted in wall paintings. Nefertiti disappeared from the court after her daughter's death. Her name means "the beautiful woman has come."

L. 24: "hannibal": Hannibal (c. 247–c. 183 BC) was a Carthaginian general and the leader of the march across the Alps. He was a precocious child, reputed to have begun at the age of nine following his father on campaigns.

"A Poem/Because It Came As A Surprise To Me"

L. 2: "saul": St. Paul. Paul was born into a Hellenistic Jewish family and given the Hebrew name Saul as well as the name Paul; he was a Roman citizen. Although his embrace of Christ's teachings and divinity did not in his own mind conflict with his Jewish faith, he is traditionally identified as Saul before the conversion and as Paul after.

"Oppression"

L. 4: "mme. walker": Madame C. J. Walker (1867–1919), the first African American millionaire, made her fortune through hair-straightening and beauty products.

L. 7: "APA to GDI": Alpha Phi Alpha Fraternity, Inc., a Black Greek fraternity originally founded at Cornell University, and "Goddamn Independent," the slang term for students in historically Black colleges and universities who do not join a sorority or fraternity. Although Giovanni eventually became an honorary member of Delta Sigma Theta, Incorporated, she was a GDI as an undergraduate.

L. 9: "howard university": The first African American sorority, Alpha Kappa Alpha, was founded at Howard University in 1908. There is fierce if good-natured competition between the AKAs and the Deltas, of which Giovanni is an honorary member.

L. 13: "diana ross leaving the supremes": Diana Ross (1944–) was the lead performer of the Supremes, Motown's biggest female group. In 1967 the Supremes were renamed Diana Ross and the Supremes by Barry Gordy, head of Motown; in 1970 Ross left the group for a solo career.

"Toy Poem"

L. 4: "loving rawls": Lou Rawls (1935–), blues and rhythm and blues singer popular in the 1960s and 1970s.

L. 5: "st. jacques": Raymond St. Jacques (1930–90) was a stage and film actor who supported himself with menial jobs between acting opportunities. His big break was in the off-Broadway production of Jean Genet's *The Blacks*. His film credits include *Black Like Me* (1964), *The Pawnbroker* (1965), *Cotton Comes to Harlem* (1970), and *Glory* (1989), in which he played Frederick Douglass but received no screen credit.

L. 22: "i wanna take you higher": "I Want to Take You Higher" is the title of a song by Sly and the Family Stone.

"Poem For Flora"

Flora Alexander was a close friend of Giovanni's parents.

L. 6: "nebuchadnezzar": Nebuchadnezzar is the common misspelling of Nebuchadrezzar, king of Babylon from 605 to 562 B.C.E. He is credited with rebuilding Babylon—including the hanging gardens—as a wonder of the ancient world.

L. 9: "shadrach, meshach, and abednego": In the Bible the three young friends of Daniel who were deported with him to Babylon by Nebuchadrezzar. They were cast into the fiery furnace, from which they emerged unscathed. See Daniel 3.

L. 15: "Sheba": The unnamed (in the Bible) Queen of Sheba, ruler of the Sabeans, who were located in southwest Arabia, roughly where Yemen is today. She visited Solomon, the king of

Israel, and gave him many treasures. Tradition has it that she was African and that her relationship with Solomon resulted in a son who was the founder of the royal house of Ethiopia. See 1 Kings 10:1–13 and 2 Chronicles 9:1–12.

"Poem For My Nephew (Brother C. B. Soul)"

When he was young, Giovanni's nephew, Christopher Black, would sign his drawings "Brother C. B. Soul."

"Yeah . . . But . . ."

L. 3: "diana": Diana Ross (1944–), who had left the Supremes for a solo career in 1970, the year this poem was written.

L. 5: "dionne": Dionne Warwick (1940–), pop singer whose string of hits from her collaboration with Burt Bacharach and Hal David earned her multiple Grammys.

L. 5: "making way for": Most probably a reference to the album *Make Way for Dionne Warwick*, released in 1963.

L. 5: "just like me": From a line in Warwick's enormously successful "(They Long to Be) Close to You," which was included on *Make Way for Dionne Warwick* and recorded again for the 1972 album *Dionne*.

"Poem For A Lady Whose Voice I Like"

This poem was originally written for the singer and actress Lena Horne (1917–).

My House (1972)

With the exception of two poems ("Just a New York Poem" and "We"), written in 1970, all the poems in *My House* were composed between January 1971 and June 1972. In an interview Giovanni said that when she came to write this book she knew she wanted to do something different; she would not write any more "revolutionary" poems.

Between the publication of *Re: Creation* in 1970 and *My*

House in 1972, Giovanni traveled abroad for the first time, both to Europe and, more significant, to Africa. While she was in Africa, *Truth Is on Its Way* was released (July 1971) and became quite unexpectedly a huge success. The award-winning album presented Giovanni reading her poetry to the background of gospel music performed by the New York Community Choir. In July 1972, before *My House* was published, Giovanni read many of its poems to an audience of almost 1,100 people at Lincoln Center's Alice Tully Hall. Her audience had grown considerably, then, by the time *My House* was published, a fact that is reflected in its initial sales, which surpassed those of the earlier volumes.

The volume was divided into two parts: "The Rooms Inside," consisting of twenty-three poems on personal themes and arranged to follow the speaker's progress from childhood to adulthood; and "The Rooms Outside," consisting of thirteen poems on larger, more public themes, with the exception of the final, title poem.

"THE ROOMS INSIDE"

"Mothers"

L. 10: "burns avenue": Giovanni and her family lived on Burns Avenue in Wyoming, a suburb north of Cincinnati, from about the time she was in kindergarten until about the end of her third grade year.

L. 23: "samson myth": Samson's strength lay in his hair, which he told Delilah had never been cut. Delilah exploited his weakness with women both to cut his hair and to blind him. See Judges 13–16.

"A Poem for Carol (May She Always Wear Red Ribbons)"

L. 3: "lincoln heights": Lincoln Heights was the all-black suburb of Cincinnati where Giovanni and her family moved in 1948.

L. 4: "jackson street": Giovanni's parents first bought a house on Jackson Street in Lincoln Heights; later, they bought a home on Congress Street, just a few blocks from Jackson.

"Conversation"

This poem is clearly connected to the earlier "Alabama Poem" (see page 120), published in *Re: Creation*.

"Rituals"

L. 14: "*chandlers*": A chain store that sold inexpensive shoes.

"Poem for Stacia"

Stacia Murphy was an African American whom Giovanni met in Lagos, Nigeria. When Giovanni was unable to find a hotel room, Ms. Murphy let the poet stay with her.

"I Remember"

L. 11: "play *ohmeohmy*": "Oh Me Oh My (I'm a Fool for You Baby)" was an Aretha Franklin hit song included in her album *Young, Gifted, and Black*, released in January 1972.

"Just a New York Poem"

Ll. 7–8: "women/in love": A 1969 film version of the D.H. Lawrence novel.

Ll. 9–10: "The Spirit/In The Dark": The actual title of Aretha Franklin's 1970 album is *Spirit in the Dark*.

"The Wonder Woman (A New Dream—for Stevie Wonder)"

This poem looks back to "Dreams" (from *Black Judgement*, see page 67) and "Revolutionary Dreams" (from *Re: Creation*, see page 106).

Stevie Wonder had a female backup vocal group called Wonderlove, but Giovanni said she always thought of the group as the Wonderwomen.

L. 7: "sweet inspiration": The Sweet Inspirations were background singers for Atlantic Records. The lead singer was Cissy Houston (mother of Whitney); the others were Estelle Brown, Sylvia Shemwell, and Myrna Smith. The Sweet Inspirations, who did background vocals for many of Aretha Franklin's hits, sang three-part harmony. See the reference to being a "sweet inspiration" in the earlier poem "Dreams."

"Categories"

In an interview Giovanni stated that she originally wrote this poem for Edie Locke, who was editor in chief at *Mademoiselle* magazine the year Giovanni won one of its Women-of-the-Year Awards (1971). Giovanni said she thought the surprise some people expressed at her winning the award was attributable to their habit of thinking in categories.

"Straight Talk"

Straight Talk was the name of a women's television talk show in New York City in the early 1970s. It was hosted by Carol Jenkins.

Ll. 27–28: "the shadow/and the act": *Shadow and Act* is the title of a 1964 collection of essays by Ralph Ellison (1914–94).

L. 28: "essence": *Essence* magazine.

L. 28: "encore!": From 1972 to 1980, Giovanni was a regular columnist for the Black newsmagazine *Encore American & Worldwide News*.

L. 29: "the preceding . . . the letter E": This was a tag line used regularly by the children's television show *Sesame Street*.

Ll. 33–34: "enjoyed waiting on/the lord": "Why Can't I Wait on the Lord" is the title of a gospel song by Harrison Johnson. It is sung as the background to Giovanni's reading of "Straight Talk" on her album *Like A Ripple On A Pond*.

L. 38: "youth and truth are making love": A line from "Thank You (Falettinme Be Mice Elf Agin)," a 1969 hit single by Sly and The Family Stone.

L. 45: "spear o agnew association": Spiro T. Agnew (1918–96) served as vice president under Richard M. Nixon from 1969 to 1973, when he resigned after being fined for income tax evasion.

L. 46: "HEY! this is straight talk!": The television program *Straight Talk* ended with this line.

"Scrapbooks"

L. 9: *"green dolphin street"*: Title of a 1944 novel by Elizabeth Goudge.

L. 10: *"the sun is my undoing"*: Title of a 1944 novel by Marguerite Steen.

L. 19: *"jack and jill dance"*: Jack & Jill of America, Inc., a nonprofit African American family organization aimed at improving the growth and development of children, ages two to nineteen.

Ll. 32–34: "from the dean . . . fisk": Ann Cheatam, dean of women at Fisk University when Giovanni was a freshman, expelled her at the end of her first semester.

L. 37: "grandfather graduated": Giovanni's maternal grandfather, John Brown Watson (1887–1962), was a high school Latin teacher who graduated from Fisk in 1905.

L. 49: "miles davis record": Miles Davis (1926–91), trumpet player who had a tremendous influence on bebop and cool jazz.

L. 58: *"something cool"*: The title of a 1953 song and album recorded by the jazz singer June Christy (1925–90). Giovanni was a Christy fan during the 1960s and 1970s.

L. 59: *"tears on my pillow"*: A 1958 hit song that sold more than one million copies and ensured a career for Little Anthony and the Imperials.

"[Untitled] (For Margaret Danner)"

Margaret Danner (1915–82?), a Chicago poet, wrote Giovanni a letter expressing pride in Giovanni's work. One of the lines in the letter was "one ounce of truth benefits like a ripple in a pond." This line also provided the title for Giovanni's 1973 album, *Like A Ripple On A Pond*.

"My Tower (For Barb and Anthony)"

"Barb" is Giovanni's friend Barbara Crosby, who had a new son, Anthony.

L. 12: "black pearl of immeasurable worth": See Matthew 13:45–46.

L. 18: "harriet's route": Harriet Tubman (c. 1820–1913) was the most famous conductor on the Underground Railroad.

"Poem (For Nina)"

This is the second poem Giovanni wrote for Nina Simone (1933–2003), "High Priestess of Soul," musician, singer, and political diva. The other is "The Genie in the Jar," page 110.

L. 1: "in the castle of our skins": In the Castle of My Skin is the title of the 1953 autobiography by the Caribbean writer George Lamming (1927–).

"Africa I"

L. 1: "kola nut": Two kola trees bearing nuts are found in Africa; the kola nut is used to make medicines and beverages.

L. 9: "look ida": Ida E. Lewis (1935–), journalist, editor, and publisher. At the time this poem was written, Lewis was the editor of Encore American & Worldwide News and a good friend of Giovanni.

L. 17: "john brown": Giovanni's maternal grandfather, John Brown Watson (1887–1962).

L. 20: "accra": Accra, capital of Ghana and an important center in the gold and slave trade.

L. 25: "your mother": Africa.

"Africa II"

L. 4: "cape coast castle": Cape Coast Castle, on the coast of Ghana, was an important holding fort of the slave trade. Africans would be brought from the interior of the continent to places like Cape Coast Castle, where they would be placed in dungeons until enough had been gathered to fill the hold of a slave ship.

L. 5: "18th century clock": Evidence of the presence of a high-ranking British officer. See lines 13–15.

L. 20: "there are thousands": A reference to Africans intended to be shipped as slaves to the New World who died in the horrible conditions that prevailed at Cape Coast Castle (and other holding forts).

Ll. 22–23: "secret passageway . . . governor's quarters": African women awaiting transport in the dungeon were routinely subjected to rape by the British governor in charge.

L. 24: "roberta flack recorded a song": Roberta Flack (1940–), pop singer who had several number-one hits in the 1970s, including "The First Time Ever I Saw Your Face." While she was at one of the slave-holding forts on the African coast, she recorded a song (not commercially released).

L. 25: "les mccann": Les McCann (1935–), jazz pianist and singer who also visited a slave-holding fort on the African coast.

"They Clapped"

L. 9 "fanon": Frantz Fanon (1925–61), political philosopher, writer, and activist whose work on the effects of colonialism on Africa—especially *Black Skin, White Masks* and *The Wretched of the Earth*—were highly influential.

L. 9: "davenport": Giovanni does not recall whom she had in mind here, and I have been unable to identify a likely candidate.

L. 10: "j.h. clarke's lectures": John Henrik Clarke (1915–98) was an important educator and writer and a prominent figure in the pan-African movements of the 1960s and 1970s.

L. 11: "nkrumah": Kwame Nkrumah (1909–72), leader and later president of Ghana, the first sub-Saharan African country to gain independence.

L. 11: "nigeria in the war": A reference to the thirty-month civil war in Nigeria, also known as the Biafran War (1967–70), triggered by the Eastern Region's declaration of itself as a separate state, Biafra.

L. 20: "lagos": The former capital, largest city, and main port of Nigeria.

Ll. 26–27: "sly and the family/stone": Sly and the Family Stone was an important singing group in the late 1960s; they brought together gospel, rhythm and blues, and rock.

L. 30: "james brown": James Brown (1933–), a.k.a. the Godfather of Soul and Mr. Dynamite, inventor of funk, and the most important contributor to and influence on soul music.

"Poem (For Anna Hedgeman and Alfreda Duster)"

Anna Hedgeman (1899–1990) was an educator and Civil Rights activist. She was the only woman on the planning committee of the 1963 March on Washington. Giovanni met Hedgeman when she visited Fisk University and came to a history class in which Giovanni was enrolled. Giovanni subsequently ran into Hedgeman periodically in New York.

Alfreda Duster (1904–83), daughter of Ida B. Wells, was a civic leader and social worker in Chicago. On a visit to Chicago, Giovanni met her, but only once.

"Atrocities"

L. 1: "napalmed children": Newspaper and television images of children whose bodies were on fire from the napalm used so widely during the Vietnam War (1954–75) were common during the late 1960s and early 1970s.

L. 4: "one president": John F. Kennedy (1917–63), thirty-fifth President of the United States (1961–63), who was assassinated in Dallas, Texas, on November 22, 1963.

L. 4: "one nobel prize winner": Martin Luther King, Jr. (1929–68) received the Nobel Prize for Peace in 1964; he was assassinated in Memphis, Tennessee, on April 4, 1968.

L. 5: "one president's brother": U.S. Senator Robert F. Kennedy (1925–68), a presidential candidate, was shot in Los Angeles on June 5, 1968, and died the next day.

L. 5: "four to six white students": Probably a reference to the May 18, 1970, incident at Kent State University, when four student protesters were shot and killed by National Guardsmen.

Ll. 8–9: "c.i.a. . . . pull/the trigger on malcolm": Malcolm X, later Al Hajj Malik Al-Shabazz (1925–65), was assassinated on February 21, 1965, in the Audubon Ballroom in New York by gunmen associated with the Nation of Islam; many people (including Giovanni) believed that an agency of the federal government, such as the Central Intelligence Agency, had played a role in his death.

L. 10: "eight nurses in chicago": The 1966 massacre of eight student nurses from South Chicago Community Hospital climaxed a life of violence and a three-month killing spree for Richard Speck (1941–91). Evidence suggests that Speck had murdered four other people in the three months leading up to the July 10 massacre.

L. 11: "sixteen people at the university of texas": Charles Whitman's 1966 killing spree was perhaps the first time Americans realized that public spaces are not necessarily safe. On August 1, 1966, Whitman made his way to the top of the Texas Tower on the University of Texas campus and began shooting at the people below; in his ninety-six-minute siege, he killed sixteen people and wounded another thirty. Immediately before he stood atop the tower, Whitman had killed his mother, his wife, a receptionist, and two couples he encountered on the stairs.

L. 12: "the boston strangler": Although no one was ever officially identified as the Boston Strangler, the general public believed that Albert DeSalvo was that individual. During the period 1962–64, thirteen single women from the Boston area were sexually molested and strangled in their apartments; the public felt that these murders were the work of the same individual. Despite the fact that DeSalvo confessed to eleven "official" Strangler murders, controversy continues about whether he was the real murderer.

L. 13: "john coltrane": John Coltrane (1926–67) was a jazz saxophonist, composer, and innovator who died of liver failure. Although there is no evidence that his death was from anything other than natural causes, Giovanni said in an interview that her "paranoia" has always made her suspicious of the early deaths of so many musicians.

L. 14: "sonny liston": Charles "Sonny" Liston (1932–70), heavyweight boxing champion who was knocked out in 1964 in the seventh round by Cassius Clay and in a 1965 rematch in the first round, this time by Clay with the new name Muhammad Ali.

L. 14: "jimi hendrixs": Jimi Hendrix (1942–70), hugely successful rock star who died at age twenty-seven of an apparent drug overdose, but mystery still surrounds his death.

L. 14: "janis joplin": Janis Joplin (1943–70), blues and rock and roll star who died of an accidental drug overdose.

L. 15: "featherstone": Ralph Featherstone (19?–70), field secretary for the Student Nonviolent Coordinating Committee who was killed on March 9, 1970, in a car bombing intended for H. Rap Brown; the bombing occurred outside the Maryland courthouse where Brown was to stand trial.

L. 16: "che": Che Guevara (1928–67), Latin American guerrilla leader whose revolutionary theories became popular during the 1960s. Guevara was an important figure in Fidel Castro's 1959 revolution against Fulgencio Batista in Cuba. Guevara was shot to death by the Bolivian army in October 1967.

L. 17: "agnew": Spiro T. Agnew (1918–96), formerly governor of Maryland, served as vice president under Richard M. Nixon from 1969 to 1973, when he resigned after being fined for income tax evasion.

L. 20: "eugene robinson": According to Giovanni, Robinson was a police informant.

L. 21: "eldridge cleaver": Eldridge Cleaver (1935–98), militant minister of information for the Black Panthers. Cleaver was wounded in a Panther shoot-out with police in 1968, jumped bail, and fled to Algeria.

L. 22: "expel a martyr": An allusion to Huey Newton (1942–89) who with Bobby Seale formed the Black Panther Party for Self-Defense, later known simply as the Black Panther Party. While Newton was in prison on a murder conviction that was later overturned, Cleaver took over the Black Panther Party. Cleaver was more militant than Newton and gained influence over the East Coast branches of the Panthers, while Newton was always based on the West Coast.

L. 23: "The president": Richard M. Nixon (1913–94), thirty-seventh President of the United States (1969–74).

L. 24: "manson": Charles Manson (1934–) was convicted of

the 1969 murders of Sharon Tate and six other people. Although Manson did not commit the murders himself, his charismatic personality enabled him to convince others—his "Family"—to do so.

L. 26: "joe frazier": Joe Frazier (1944–), former heavyweight boxing champion. Frazier became heavyweight champion in 1970, in part, many thought, because of the absence of Muhammad Ali (1942–) from the boxing scene. Ali had been stripped of his title in 1967, when he refused to fight in the Vietnam War. His match with Frazier in March 1971 was his first fight after being stripped of the title, and Frazier won the fifteen-round match by unanimous decision. In two subsequent matches, Ali defeated Frazier.

"Nothing Makes Sense"

L. 36: "aretha": Aretha Franklin (1942–), the undisputed "Queen of Soul."

L. 41: "julian bond": Julian Bond (1940–) served four terms in the Georgia House of Representatives (1967–74) and six terms in the Georgia Senate (1975–87).

L. 41: "rap brown": H. Rap Brown, now Jamil Abdullah Al-Amin (1943–). Civil Rights activist who became the chairman of SNCC (Student Nonviolent Coordinating Committee) after Stokely Carmichael left that post.

L. 42: "nixon": Richard M. Nixon (1913–94), thirty-seventh President of the United States (1969–74).

L. 44: "our man on the moon": Neil Armstrong or Buzz Aldrin, the first men to walk on the moon.

"I Laughed When I Wrote It (Don't You Think It's Funny?)"

L. 2: "i guess negro": See note to "The True Import of Present Dialogue," page 373.

L. 11 "shorter than hoover": J. Edgar Hoover (1895–1972), director of the Federal Bureau of Investigation (1924–72), whose abuse of his powers, especially in matters regarding Black people, has been widely documented.

L. 14: "rap brown": H. Rap Brown, now Jamil Abdullah Al-Amin (1943–). Civil Rights activist who became chairman of

SNCC (Student Nonviolent Coordinating Committee) after Stokely Carmichael left that post.

L. 32: "interpol": The International Criminal Police Organization.

L. 46: "aretha franklin": Aretha Franklin (1942–), a.k.a. "Queen of Soul."

"On Seeing Black Journal and Watching Nine Negro Leaders 'Give Aid and Comfort to the Enemy' to Quote Richard Nixon"

Black Journal was a nationally syndicated black news program that began airing in 1968. In 1970 Tony Brown (1933–) became its executive producer and host and initiated numerous changes, including an emphasis on self-help, which generated criticism from many African Americans.

For the significance of the use of "Negro" in the title, see note to "The True Import of Present Dialogue," page 373.

President Richard M. Nixon accused antiwar protesters of "giving aid and comfort to the enemy."

L. 4: "steal away": The title of a well-known slave spiritual.

The Women and the Men

Published in 1975, this volume brought together many of the poems originally published in Re: Creation and nineteen new poems. Re: Creation, which had been published by Broadside Press, had a smaller distribution than Giovanni's other volumes, published by William Morrow. Many readers who had learned "Ego Tripping" from listening to the album Truth Is on Its Way did not discover a print version of the poem until its inclusion in The Women and the Men. The volume was originally divided into three sections: "The Women," "The Men," and "Some Places." These section divisions are not maintained in the present text, which provides only the poems new to The Women and the Men.

"The Women Gather (for Joe Strickland)"

Joe Strickland was a journalist murdered in Boston by a house burglar. His widow asked if Giovanni would write something for his funeral. Giovanni knew Strickland because he wrote for *Encore American & Worldwide News*, a magazine in which she was actively involved.

L. 18: "rooms facing east": Perhaps a reference to the prayer breakfasts held in the East Room of the White House by Richard Nixon during his presidency (1969–74).

"The Life I Led"

L. 22: "bombs not falling in cambodia": Cambodia, which in 1970 became the Khmer Republic, was a major battlefield in the Vietnam War (1954–75).

"The Way I Feel"

This poem provided the title for a poetry with jazz album Giovanni released in 1975.

L. 19: "roberta flack": Roberta Flack (1940–), pop singer who had several hits in the 1970s, including "The First Time Ever I Saw Your Face." Flack also wrote the liner notes for Giovanni's album *The Way I Feel*.

"The Laws of Motion (for Harlem Magic)"

Esquire magazine originally requested that Giovanni provide words/dialogue for a series of paintings by a young painter. *Harlem Magic* was the name of the exhibition.

Stanza 5: "Professor Micheau": Lewis Michaux.

"Always There Are the Children"

This poem was written for the United Nations' first World Food Conference in 1974, held in Rome.

Cotton Candy on a Rainy Day

Cotton Candy on a Rainy Day was published on October 25, 1978, and its sales were quite strong. By the time it appeared, Giovanni had moved with her young son back to Cincinnati to help care for her father, who had suffered a stroke. The volume was dedicated to him.

"Cotton Candy on a Rainy Day"

Giovanni frequently describes the incident that gave rise to this poem when she reads it in live performances: One rainy day before she had moved to New York, she took her nephew, Christopher, to the Cincinnati Zoo. When they tried to buy some cotton candy, the vendor did not want to sell it because the rain would make it melt. The image and the vendor's denial of life's mutability stayed with the poet.

L. 49: *"as sweet as you are"*: "Stay As Sweet As You Are," written by Harry Revel and Mack Gordon, was in the film *College Rhythm* and was recorded by Ruth Etting in 1934. It was later covered by Nat "King" Cole (1919–65).

L. 50: *"in my corner"*: "Stay in My Corner" was a 1969 hit single by the Dells.

L. 51: *"just a little bit longer"*: "Stay (Just a Little Bit Longer)" was a 1960 hit single by Maurice Williams and the Zodiacs; it was subsequently covered by artists such as the Four Seasons, the Hollies, and Chaka Khan.

L. 52: *"don't change baby baby don't change"*: "Don't Change Your Love" was a 1968 hit single by the Five Stairsteps.

"Introspection"

L. 11: "Ian Smith": Ian Douglas Smith (1919–), former prime minister of Southern Rhodesia (now Zimbabwe), fought against the forces of African nationalism and staunchly supported apartheid in South Africa.

"Forced Retirement"

L. 31: "Namath": Joe Namath (1943–), football phenomenon who played for the New York Jets and, for one season, for the Los Angeles Rams; he retired in 1977.

L. 31: "Ali": Muhammad Ali (1942–), heavyweight boxing champion (1964–67, 1974–78, 1978–79); he retired in December 1981.

"Boxes"

Ll. 26–27: "muhammad ali . . . leon spinks relieved him": Muhammad Ali (1942–) held the heavyweight boxing title three times: 1964–67, 1974–78, 1978–79; he lost his title to Leon Spinks (1953–) in February 1978 but regained it that November in their rematch.

"Poem"

L. 20: "the president of the united states": Jimmy Carter (1924–), thirty-ninth President of the United States (1977–81).

L. 21: "Faith not deeds": Carter was a born-again Christian.

L. 23: "larry flynt": Larry Flynt (1942–), head of the *Hustler Magazine* publishing company, was the victim of a 1978 assassination attempt that left him paralyzed.

L. 42: "nixon": Richard M. Nixon (1913–94), thirty-seventh President of the United States (1969–74).

L. 44: "humphrey's funeral": Hubert H. Humphrey (1911–78), thirty-eighth vice president (1965–69), was twice an unsuccessful presidential candidate, losing to Richard M. Nixon (in 1968) and then to Jimmy Carter (in 1976).

L. 45: "opened his house": Richard Nixon's birthplace in Yorba Linda, California.

L. 48: "anita bryant": Anita Bryant (1940–), singer, Miss America runner-up, and orange juice saleswoman whose antigay crusade in 1976–77 ultimately strengthened the gay rights movement and destroyed Bryant's marriage and career.

L. 49: "carter or nixon": See preceding notes.

Ll. 58–59: "city . . . garbage can": Perhaps a reference to the 1974 sanitation workers' strike in New York.

"Fascinations"

L. 31: "con edison after all went out": A reference to the black-out in New York on the July 13 and 14, 1977.

"The Beep Beep Poem"

Ll. 11–12: "understand . . . troopers": A reference to the May 18, 1970, incident at Kent State University in which four student protesters were shot and killed by National Guardsmen.

L. 27: "encore american and worldwide news": The Black newsmagazine *Encore American & Worldwide News,* to which Giovanni was a regular contributor.

"A Poem for Ed and Archie"

Ed ran a lecture series at the University of North Carolina, Chapel Hill, and Archie was his student assistant.

"Poem (for EMA)"

EMA are the initials of Elizabeth "Liz" M. Armstrong, a friend of the Giovanni family.

"Winter"

L. 8: "Father John's Medicine": A cough medicine, the principal ingredient of which is cod-liver oil, once very popular and still available.

"A Response (to the rock group Foreigner)"

Foreigner was formed in 1976 as a collaboration between musicians formerly associated with other groups, both British and American. Their first album, released in 1977 and titled *Foreigner,* sold over four million copies in the United States alone. One of the hit singles on the album was "Cold As Ice."

"Being and Nothingness (to quote a philosopher)"

Being and Nothingness is the title of the 1943 classic work on existentialism by Jean-Paul Sartre (1905–80).

"That Day"

Giovanni stated in an interview with me that this poem is written to the rhythm of a song by Johnny Taylor (1938–2000) entitled "Your Love Is Rated X."

Those Who Ride the Night Winds

Published in 1983, *Those Who Ride the Night Winds* marks Giovanni's innovation of a new "lineless" poetic form in which word groups are separated from each other by ellipses rather than line breaks. This new form retains the rhythmic effects essential to Giovanni's conscious use of the elements associated with an oral tradition; at the same time, it enables a more expansive treatment of subject matter than is generally possible in free verse. Giovanni has said that she developed this form to question the absolutism and complacency which she saw as characteristic of public discourse in the late 1970s and early 1980s. Of the twenty-nine poems composing *Night Winds*, twenty employ this lineless form, which she has continued to use extensively, while nine are written in the free verse characteristic of her earlier volumes.

The volume was originally divided into two sections: "Night Winds" and "Day Trippers"; "Love: Is a Human Condition" is the first poem of the latter section, which takes its name from the title of a hit single by the Beatles.

"Charting the Night Winds"

This poem constituted the preface of the original volume.

Stanza 4: "Telstar": Although Telstar was not the first communications satellite, it is undoubtedly the best known. It was launched on July 10, 1962, allowing live television from the United States to be received in France.

Stanza 5: "State to poison Socrates": The ancient philosopher Socrates (469–399 B.C.E.) was convicted of corrupting the morals of Athenian youth and espousing religious heresies; he refused all efforts to save his life and drank the fatal hemlock given him by the State. See Plato's *Apology*.

Stanza 5: "Copernicus to recant": Nicolaus Copernicus (1473–1543) is generally considered the founder of modern astronomy. He postulated that the earth rotates on its axis once a day, that it travels around the sun once yearly, and that the sun is the center of the universe. These ideas ran completely counter to the prevailing geocentric ideas of the Middle Ages. Copernicus did not recant; but he also had no interest in publishing his ideas because he was a perfectionist who thought he should test and retest his hypotheses. In fact, Copernicus died without knowing the repercussions of his work. Giovanni probably means Galileo Galilei (1564–1642), who subscribed to Copernicus's theory, ran afoul of the Inquisition, and was convicted of heresy. Not until 1992 did the Catholic Church, through Pope John Paul II, admit to error in its treatment of Galileo—but not to having been wrong.

Stanza 5: "McCarthy": Joseph R. McCarthy (1908–57), a U.S. senator from Wisconsin who gained notoriety for his witch hunting of suspected "Communists" from 1950 to 1954.

Stanza 5: "I am . . . many things": A line from Lewis Carroll's "The Walrus and the Carpenter" in *Through the Looking-Glass and What Alice Found There* (1872).

"Lorraine Hansberry: An Emotional View"

Lorraine Hansberry (1930–65) was a Chicago-born activist and playwright whose *A Raisin in the Sun* was the first play by an African American woman to be produced on Broadway.

Stanza 2: "sculpt David": The statue *David* is generally considered the greatest work of Michelangelo (1475–1564), the Italian sculptor, poet, and painter.

Stanza 2: "like Charles White": The African American artist Charles White (1918–79).

Stanza 4: "from 1619": The first African settlers—numbering

twenty—in North America arrived on August 20, 1619, in Jamestown, Virginia, where they were exchanged by the Dutch ship's captain for food.

Stanza 4: "Little Linda Brown": Linda Carol Brown (1943–) was born in Topeka, Kansas. When she reached school age, her father, Oliver Brown, tried to enroll her in the all-white Sumner School, the school closest to their home. His name became the name of the plaintiff in what was to be the landmark case *Brown vs. Board of Education,* which challenged the structure of segregation first legalized in 1896.

Stanza 4: "Dr. King": Martin Luther King, Jr. (1929–68).

Stanza 4: "in Montgomery": The Montgomery Bus Boycott (1955–56), which was sparked by Rosa Parks's refusal to move to the back of the bus provided the occasion for Dr. King's emergence as a Civil Rights leader. Because King was relatively new to Montgomery, having been appointed to the Dexter Avenue Baptist Church in 1954, he was considered by experienced members of the NAACP such as E. D. Nixon to be an ideal leader for the boycott (he had no history with the city's white citizens). King was named president of the Montgomery Improvement Association, the organizational force behind the boycott. The boycott was ultimately successful, although not until the case had gone all the way to the Supreme Court, which upheld a lower court's order for the city to desegregate its buses.

Stanza 4: "Emmett Till": Emmett Louis Till (1941–55). Till, a Chicago boy who was visiting relatives in Money, Mississippi, was violently murdered and his body mutilated by Roy Bryant and J. W. Milam. When Till's mother, Mamie Till Bradley, decided to publicize the photograph of Emmett's body and to hold an open-casket funeral because she wanted "the world to see" what had been done to her son, the world "saw" and was outraged. Till was not the first victim of white southern racism, but he was possibly the most widely recognized, and his death galvanized the Civil Rights movement. The Montgomery Bus Boycott, which began in just months after Till's death in August 1955, was in some ways one of the results of that death.

Stanza 4: "Cuba . . . during the missile crisis": The Cuban Missile Crisis of 1962. After the United States detected the construction of missile launching sites by the Soviet Union in Cuba, President Kennedy ordered a naval blockade to surround Cuba until the Soviets agreed to dismantle the sites.

Stanza 4: "airlifted . . . to West Berlin": During the 1948–49 Soviet land and water blockade of West Berlin, the United States and other Western powers airlifted supplies to the city.

"Hands: For Mother's Day"

Stanza 3: "the mother of Emmett Till": Mamie Till Bradley Mobley (1922–2003). See note to "Lorraine Hansberry," above.

Stanza 3: "Nancy Reagan": Nancy Davis Reagan (1921–), wife of Ronald Reagan (1911–), fortieth president of the United States (1981–89). Shortly after he took office, he was shot in an assassination attempt; he recovered quickly.

Stanza 3: "Betty Shabazz": Activist, nurse, and educator, Betty Shabazz (1936–97) was present when her husband, Malcolm X, was assassinated in the Audubon Ballroom in New York City.

Stanza 3: "Jacqueline Kennedy": Jacqueline Bouvier Kennedy Onassis (1929–94) was riding in the limousine with her husband, President John F. Kennedy (1917–63), when he was fatally shot. The images of his widow in a bloodstained pink suit and with her two small children at the funeral are indelibly etched in the memories of several generations of Americans.

Stanza 3: "Coretta King": Coretta Scott King (1929–), widow of Martin Luther King, Jr., has continued to carry out his mission since his death by assassination in 1968.

Stanza 3: "Ethel Kennedy": Ethel S. Kennedy (1928–), social activist and humanitarian, was widowed when her husband, the presidential hopeful Robert F. Kennedy (1925–68), was assassinated.

Stanza 7: "Star Trek's Spock": Spock, who has a Vulcan father and a human mother, was one of the most popular characters of the original *Star Trek* television series. He was played by Leonard Nimoy.

"This Is Not for John Lennon (and this is not a poem)"

Stanza 2: "it's not about John Lennon": John Lennon (1940–80), singer and songwriter who some would argue was the creative genius behind the Beatles, was shot and killed outside the Dakota Apartments in New York City.

Stanza 2: "the man who killed him": Mark David Chapman (1955–) came to New York from Hawaii with the chief aim of killing Lennon. After pleading guilty, he was sentenced to twenty years in prison.

Stanza 2: "Andy Warhol": American artist and filmmaker Andy Warhol (1928–87).

Stanza 2: "Our beloved mayor": Ed Koch (1924–) served three terms as mayor of New York (1979–89).

Stanza 3: "Newton": Sir Isaac Newton (1642–1727), mathematician and physicist, one of whose laws of motion—"for every action there is an equal and opposite reaction"—is quoted later in this stanza. Tradition has it that Newton's conception of the force of gravity was the result of his seeing an apple fall in his orchard.

Stanza 3: "David Rockefeller": David Rockefeller (1915–), son of John D. Rockefeller, Jr., former president and CEO of Chase Manhattan, now a philanthropist and supporter of the arts.

Stanza 3: "Jerry Falwell": Jerry Falwell (1933–), is a fundamentalist and evangelist who initiated the Moral Majority and founded what is today known as Liberty University in Lynchburg, Virginia.

Stanza 3: "Chuck Willis": Chuck Willis (1928–58) was a singer and songwriter most often associated with the Stroll, a dance popular during the 1950s. He had a number of hit singles, including a pop version of the old folk song "C. C. Rider." He died from peritonitis following surgery for bleeding ulcers.

Stanza 3: "Johnny Ace": John Marshall Alexander, Jr., a.k.a. Johnny Ace (1929–54), popular rhythm and blues singer whose premature, bizarre death (reputedly an accident when he was playing Russian roulette) sustained his reputation long after he died.

Stanza 3: "Sam Cooke": Sam Cooke (1931–64) was a popular

and influential singer who emerged in the 1950s as a gospel star and then began recording popular songs, including the megahits "You Send Me" and "Wonderful World." His influence on soul music as well as on many of its best-known performers cannot be overstated. "A Change Is Gonna Come," recorded in February 1964, was his last great ballad. Controversy still surrounds his violent death.

Stanza 3: "Otis Redding": Otis Redding (1941–67), one of the greatest soul singers and songwriters of all time, was killed in an airplane crash in Madison, Wisconsin. Although some people aboard survived the crash, Redding and four members of his backup group, the Bar-Kays, were killed; Giovanni has stated her belief that the crash was not an accident.

Stanza 3: "now we can call this game exactly what it is": Slight variation on a line from the hit song "Rock Steady," as written and recorded by Aretha Franklin. The original line is "Let's call this song exactly what it is."

Stanza 3: "Anybody want a ticket to ride?": "Ticket to Ride" was a 1965 hit by the Beatles.

"Mirrors (for Billie Jean King)"

The poem was occasioned by the 1981 palimony suit brought against the tennis star Billie Jean King (1943–) by her former secretary and lover, Marilyn Barnett.

Stanza 4: "only Dick and Jane": Dick and Jane was an illustrated book series used as standard school texts from which it is estimated more than eighty-five million people learned to read from the 1930s through the 1960s. The Dick and Jane texts presented a white, homogeneous, middle-class world in which nothing bad (and nothing exciting) ever happened.

Stanza 4: "Ozzie and Harriet": An ABC situation comedy that ran from 1952 to 1966, *The Adventures of Ozzie and Harriet* featured the real-life Nelson family. It was the television equivalent of the Dick and Jane primers.

Stanza 4: "Pillow Talk is only a movie . . . or a song by Sylvia": The 1959 movie *Pillow Talk* starred Doris Day and Rock Hudson.

The hit single "Pillow Talk" was released in 1973 by Sylvia Robinson under the name Sylvia. Robinson, who had appeared in the 1950s as one half of the Mickey and Sylvia duo, went on to create Sugarhill Records, which played a major role in introducing the world to rap music.

Stanza 5: "Like Humpty Dumpty": In the Mother Goose story, Humpty-Dumpty shatters when he falls—because he is an egg.

Stanza 6: "because he robbed . . . poor": The classic example is Robin Hood.

Stanza 6: "It Was A Mistake": When Barnett outed King through the palimony suit, King, who had kept her relationships with women private, initially acknowledged the relationship with Barnett but called it "a mistake." Not until 1998 did King publicly share her sexual preference, but she has since become an advocate for gay rights.

Stanza 8: "embraced . . . Medusa": In Greek mythology, Medusa was a beautiful young woman whose hair was her most remarkable asset. When she made the mistake of competing in beauty with Athena, the goddess transformed Medusa's hair into hissing serpents. Medusa became a monster so frightening to gaze upon that anyone who did was turned into stone.

"Linkage (for Phillis Wheatley)"

Phillis Wheatley (1753?–84) was born in the Gambia, West Africa. Because she was the first African American to publish a book, she is generally regarded as the founder of the African American literary tradition. A victim of the slave trade, she was brought from Africa to Boston, Massachusetts, when she was about seven years old. She was bought by John and Susanna Wheatley, who named her for the ship on which she had been transported. Although she was originally purchased to be a domestic worker, the Wheatleys recognized her aptitude for learning and allowed their daughter to tutor her.

Stanza 1: "leaving Senegal": During the transatlantic slave trade, the Senegambia region was an important source of slaves. It was subsequently colonized by the French and the British and evolved into two countries, modern-day Senegal and Gambia.

Stanza 2: "the children of Hester Prynne": Hester Prynne is the heroine of Nathaniel Hawthorne's *Scarlet Letter* (1850).

Stanza 2: "The block . . . stood upon": The auction block.

Stanza 3: "Hagar . . . Abraham": Hagar, an Egyptian servant, was given to Abraham by his wife, Sarah, to be his concubine because Sarah was unable to have children. Hagar had a son, Ishmael, but when Sarah miraculously became pregnant and herself had a son, Isaac, she expelled Hagar and Ishmael from the household. See Genesis 16:1–6 and Genesis 21:8–21.

Stanza 5: "clitorectomies . . . infibulations": Female circumcision is still practiced in a number of African countries.

Stanza 6: "How could she . . . in this Land": Wheatley has sometimes been criticized for seeming to fail to express outrage at the institution of slavery; the specific poem suggested here is "On Being Brought from Africa to America." The recovery of her letters has made clear that Wheatley did in fact denounce and decry slavery but that her poetry was written with an understanding of the prejudices and power of the white audience who would read it. Giovanni, of course, is offering a different perspective altogether.

Stanza 6: "cheer George Washington his victory": In her poem "To His Excellency General Washington."

Stanza 6: "Harriet Tubman": Harriet Tubman (c. 1820–1913) was the most famous conductor on the Underground Railroad.

Stanza 6: "Sojourner Truth": Sojourner Truth (1797–1883) escaped from slavery and became an important preacher, abolitionist, and activist for women's rights.

"Charles White"

The work of African American artist Charles White (1918–79) celebrates Black Americans.

L. 31: "Johnetta": Johnetta Fletcher, niece of the family friend Flora Alexander and a childhood friend of Giovanni.

"The Drum (for Martin Luther King, Jr.)"

Martin Luther King, Jr. (1929–68). See also the earlier poems "Reflections on April 4, 1968" (page 49) and "The Funeral of Martin Luther King, Jr." (page 51).

Stanza 1: "The Pied Piper": The legend of the Pied Piper of Hameln comes to us from the Grimm Brothers as well as from "The Pied Piper of Hamlin" by the poet Robert Browning (1812–89), where Hameln is anglicized to Hamlin.

Stanza 3: "Kunta Kinte": The central character in Alex Haley's *Roots* (1976). Haley (1921–92) learned as a child that his family history included an African ancestor named Kunta Kinte.

Stanza 3: "Thoreau listened": Henry David Thoreau (1817–62), American writer and activist. In his most famous work, *Walden* (1854), Thoreau wrote, "Why should we be in such desperate haste to succeed, and in such desperate enterprises? If a man does not keep pace with his companions, perhaps it is because he hears a different drummer."

Stanza 3: "King said just say": King preached a sermon entitled "The Drum Major Instinct" on February 4, 1968, just two months before he was assassinated. Excerpts from it were played during his funeral service. The famous section from which Giovanni is quoting reads as follows: "Yes, if you want to say that I was a drum major, say that I was a drum major for justice; say that I was a drum major for peace; I was a drum major for righteousness. And all of the other shallow things will not matter. I won't have money to leave behind. I won't have the fine and luxurious things of life to leave behind. But I just want to leave a committed life behind." (From *The Essential Writings and Speeches of Martin Luther King, Jr.*, ed. James Melvin Washington [San Francisco: HarperSanFrancisco, 1986], p. 267.

"A Poem on the Assassination of Robert F. Kennedy"

U.S. Senator Robert F. Kennedy (1925–68), a presidential candidate, was shot in Los Angeles on June 5, 1968, and died the next day. See also the earlier poem "Records" (page 60).

In an interview with me, Giovanni stated that her poem had

been influenced by a poem by the Nigerian poet J. P. Clark (1935–). Quite probably this is the title poem from his collection *Casualties: Poems 1966–68*, which focuses on the Nigerian-Biafran War.

"Eagles (a poem for Lisa)"

The poem is for the daughter of Giovanni's good friend Lillian Pierce Benbow, fifteenth national president (1971–75) of Delta Sigma Theta Sorority, Inc. Giovanni was inducted into the organization as an honorary member during Benbow's presidency.

"Flying Underground (for the children of Atlanta)"

This poem was occasioned by the Atlanta child murders of 1979–81.

Stanza 3: "if I was Tom . . . Sawyer": Title character of *The Adventures of Tom Sawyer*, first novel by Mark Twain (1835–1910). In the second chapter, Tom is facing the chore of whitewashing the picket fence around his yard.

Beginning in the summer of 1979, when the bodies of two African American boys were found, fear spread through the black community in Atlanta. Not until two years and twenty murders later was the Atlanta Child Murder case officially closed with the arrest of twenty-three-year-old Wayne Williams, also an African American.

"Her Cruising Car: A Portrait of Two Small Town Girls"

The "Two Small Town Girls" to which the title refers are Giovanni herself and Frankie Lennon in Knoxville, Tennessee.

Stanza 3: "like Richard Nixon": Richard M. Nixon (1913–94), thirty-seventh President of the United States (1969–74), was forced to resign in August 1974 after three articles of impeachment had been brought against him because of his participation in a massive cover-up of illegal activities, including wiretapping and corporate payoffs for political favors.

Stanza 3: "John McEnroe": John McEnroe (1959–), winner of seven grand slam tennis titles, is perhaps best remembered for the temper tantrums he threw during matches.

Stanza 4: "Newton": Sir Isaac Newton (1642–1727), mathematician and physicist, one of whose laws of motion is quoted here.

Stanza 5: "Darwin": Charles Darwin (1809–82), author of *On the Origin of Species* (1859).

Stanza 5: "Galápagos": Among the many places Darwin visited on his cruise of the South American coast and Australia (1831–36) aboard the H.M.S. *Beagle*.

Stanza 6: "going to St. Ives": A reference to the nursery rhyme "As I was going to St. Ives, I met a man with seven wives. Every wife had seven sacks, every sack had seven cats, every cat had seven kitts. Kitts, cats, sacks, wives, how many were going to St. Ives?"

Stanza 6: "traveled to Skookum": A reference to a children's story about a man who asks people along the way if they will keep his bag while he goes to Skookum; no one is willing, so he ultimately must carry the bag with him.

Stanza 6: "the Little Red Hen": A reference to the children's story of the Little Red Hen, who had to do all the work herself and could get no help from any of her friends.

Stanza 6: "the Engine That Could": The classic children's story by Watty Piper, first published in 1930, features a Little Blue Engine whose determination—"I think I can, I think I can"— enables it to climb impossible hills.

Stanza 7: "We were born . . . same hospital": Although Giovanni grew up in Cincinnati, she was born in Knoxville in Old Knoxville General Hospital. Her parents, Yolande and Gus, were good friends with Frankie's parents, Estelle and Dusty, who were, however, much more affluent than the Giovannis.

Stanza 9: "Thomas Wolfe was wrong": Perhaps a reference to the novel *You Can't Go Home Again* by Thomas Wolfe (1900–38).

"The Cyclops in the Ocean"
This poem was prompted by Tropical Storm Dennis in 1981, the first hurricane Giovanni experienced firsthand.

Stanza 1: "cyclops . . . meets no Ulysses": A reference to Ulysses' memorable encounter with the Cyclops in the *Odyssey*.

"Harvest (for Rosa Parks)"

Rosa Parks (1913–) is generally regarded as the mother of the modern Civil Rights movement because her refusal to move to the back of the bus on December 1, 1955, led to her arrest and sparked the Montgomery Bus Boycott. Dr. Martin Luther King, Jr., gained national recognition when he was asked to be the spokesperson for and leader of the boycott.

Stanza 2: "in Tuskegee": Mrs. Parks was born and spent her early childhood years in Tuskegee, Alabama.

Stanza 2: "married . . . at nineteen": Mrs. Parks married Raymond Parks, a barber, in 1932.

Stanza 3: "Colored people couldn't . . . No": These lines describe the realities of living in the segregated South.

Stanza 3: "My husband . . . belonged": Both Mrs. Parks and her husband, now deceased, became active members of the local chapter of the NAACP. Raymond Parks helped with the efforts in the 1930s to free the Scottsboro Boys.

In 1930 in Scottsboro, Alabama, nine black youths, ranging in age from thirteen to twenty-one, were accused of having raped two white girls on a freight train—despite the lack of medical evidence of rape. The first young man to be brought to trial was convicted, as were the others in subsequent trials. The young men had no legal counsel until the day of the first trial, when two lawyers volunteered. The Scottsboro case was appealed to the U.S. Supreme Court three different times between 1931 and 1937. In 1937, the Supreme Court reversed the earlier convictions of five of the young men, and by 1950 the others were free. Not until 1976 was the last one cleared, when Governor George C. Wallace signed the pardon for his having escaped while on parole in 1948.

Stanza 3: "Double Victory": "Victory at home and abroad" became a slogan among African Americans during World War II. It signified the fact that for Black Americans, who constantly struggled against the violence bred by racism, there was a war in the United States as much as one abroad.

Stanza 3: "I was elected Secretary": Mrs. Parks served as secretary to the local chapter of the NAACP from 1943 to 1956.

Stanza 4: "Maxwell Air Base": Maxwell Air Force Base, just outside Montgomery, Alabama, is the national center of airpower education.

Stanza 4: "That Colvin girl had been arrested": In March 1955, Claudette Colvin, a fifteen-year-old high school student, had been arrested for refusing to give her bus seat to a white passenger. E. D. Nixon, president of the local chapter of the NAACP, with whom Mrs. Parks worked closely, decided against organizing a formal boycott around the Colvin case, but the group's leaders were waiting for the "right" test case.

Stanza 4: "forty years old": In December 1955 Mrs. Parks was actually close to being forty-three (her birthday is February 4, 1913).

Stanza 6: "If I have children . . . why I moved to Detroit": Mrs. Parks has no children. After the boycott ended her role in it made it difficult for her to find work, and Raymond Parks was ill. In 1957 the couple moved with Mrs. Parks's mother to Detroit.

Stanza 7: "other than her feet . . . were tired": In the mythologizing of Mrs. Parks's role, the notion emerged that she refused to move because her feet were tired; Giovanni finds this idea especially irksome.

"Reflections/On a Golden Anniversary"

This poem was originally written for Max and Dorian Washington, parents of Giovanni's friend Nancy Pate.

"Resignation"

Giovanni said in an interview with me that the rhythm of this poem is that of "Love Is So Simple," a 1968 song by the Dells from their album *There Is*. See also the explicit reference to the song in lines 47–48.

"I Am She (For Nancy)"

Nancy is Nancy Pate, Giovanni's childhood friend from Knoxville.

"The Room With the Tapestry Rug"

In an interview with me, Giovanni stated that this poem was for and about Miss Alfredda Delaney, Giovanni's English teacher for three years at Austin High School in Knoxville.

"Love Thoughts"

L1. 7–9: "Aretha . . . let me": "Ain't No Way," which was written by Aretha Franklin's sister, Carolyn, was recorded on the album *Lady Soul,* released in 1968.

"A Song for New-Ark"

This poem was originally written for the twenty-fifth anniversary issue of *NewArk Magazine.*

Occasional Poems

Broadside: "Poem of Angela Yvonne Davis (October 16, 1970)"

Giovanni wrote this poem to be sold as a broadside to help raise money for Angela Y. Davis's legal fees. The poem was a part of the international "Free Angela" movement, which erupted shortly after Davis was arrested in New York in October 1970.

Angela Davis (1944–) first gained public attention when her membership in the Communist Party was revealed and used as a reason for dismissal from her faculty position in the philosophy department at UCLA. She drew increasing attention when she became more active with the Black Panthers and with prison inmates, especially George Jackson (1941–71) and the "Soledad Brothers" at Soledad Prison. After Jackson was killed by prison guards during an alleged escape attempt, his brother Jonathan took guns from Davis's home and went to the Marin County Courthouse, where his attempt to take hostages ended in his own death and the deaths of three other people. Davis had acquired the guns for self-protection after she received death threats; they were registered. Nonetheless, after the guns were traced to Davis, a federal warrant for her arrest was issued; she went underground before the warrant could be served. Despite the absence of evidence that Davis herself had committed any crime, the FBI placed her on its Ten Most Wanted list on August 18, 1970. She was found about two months later in New York and extradited to California, where she was charged with kidnapping, conspiracy, and murder, and put in jail without bail. She was eventually acquitted of all charges.

Giovanni was not actually to meet Angela Davis until 2001, at Toni Morrison's seventieth birthday party. But as Giovanni states in *Gemini*, "I fell completely and absolutely in love with the image and idea of an Angela Yvonne" (p. 71).

L. 8: "children in birmingham": A reference to the 1963 bombing of the Sixteenth Street Baptist Church in Birmingham, Alabama, in which four young children were killed and twenty-one people injured. Birmingham was Davis's hometown, and she knew the girls who were killed.

Ll. 10–12: "schwerner,/chaney/and Goodman": Michael Schwerner (1940–64), James E. Chaney (1943–64), and Andrew Goodman (1943–64) were Civil Rights activists who worked in Black voter registration in Mississippi and were murdered by members of the Ku Klux Klan, with the complicity of law enforcement officers. After a massive search, including 200 naval personnel, their bodies were found buried not far from Philadelphia, Mississippi. Despite the fact that everyone—including the Federal Bureau of Investigation—knew who the killers were, it was three years before Neshoba County Sheriff Lawrence Rainey, Chief Deputy Sheriff Cecil Price, and five others were convicted on federal charges of violating the civil rights of the three. No state charges were ever filed.

L. 44: "betty shabazz": Hajj Bahiyah Betty Shabazz (1936–97), educator and widow of Macolm X, later Al Hajj Malik Al-Shabazz (1925–65).

L. 50: "no more forget that staccato": Betty Shabazz witnessed her husband's assassination, which happened in view of a large audience at New York's Audubon Ballroom.

L. 52: "jonathan's face . . . george's letters": Jonathan and George Jackson.

Ll. 54–55: "Beverly/axelrod": Beverly Axelrod (1924–2002) was an activist and lawyer whose most famous clients were the Black Panther leader Eldridge Cleaver and Jerry Rubin, cofounder of the Youth International Party.

L. 57: "water and sky and paris": Possibly a reference to the fact that Davis had spent her junior year (as a student at Brandeis University) abroad, studying at the Sorbonne.

L. 59: "a german?": Possibly a reference to Davis's graduate study (1965–67) at the Johann Wolfgang von Goethe University in Frankfurt, Germany.

L. 97: "i went communist": Davis joined the Communist Party on June 22, 1968.

L. 99: "why howard johnson's": During her two months of hiding, Davis stayed at a Howard Johnson's motel in New York City.

L. 120: "harriet tubman": Harriet Tubman (c. 1820–1913) was the most famous conductor on the Underground Railroad. Her numerous forays into the slave states to help slaves escape made her indeed "the first/WANTED Black woman."

L. 124: "but my helpers trapped me": Davis's companion while she was hiding proved to be a police officer.

"A Poem for langston hughes"

This poem was originally written for USA Today, in which it was published August 29, 1991.

"But Since You Finally Asked (A Poem Commemorating the 10th Anniversary of the Slave Memorial at Mount Vernon)"

This poem was written in 1993.

Stanza 1: "Jamestown . . . in 1619": The first African settlers—numbering twenty—in North America arrived on August 20, 1619, in Jamestown, Virginia, where they were exchanged by the Dutch ship's captain for food.

"Stardate Number 18628.190"

This poem was originally published as "Light the Candles" in *Essence* magazine's twenty-fifth anniversary issue, May 1995.

Stanza 3: "Precious Lord . . . take my hand": Classic gospel song written in 1938 by Thomas A. Dorsey.

Stanza 3: "Amazing Grace": Well-known song written by a former slave ship captain.

Stanza 3: "Go down, Moses": Well-known slave spiritual.

Stanza 3: "Marion Anderson": Marian Anderson (1900–1993), a Philadelphia-born singer, the first African American to perform at the Metropolitan Opera. In 1939 she drew national attention when the Daughters of the American Revolution denied her request to sing in Constitution Hall—because she was Black. Eleanor Roosevelt, then wife of the U.S. president, resigned from the DAR in protest. Subsequently Marian Anderson sang in front of the Lincoln Memorial on Easter Sunday, to an audience of 75,000 people.

Stanza 3: "Leontyne": Leontyne Price (1927–) is an internationally recognized diva whose opera career blossomed in the 1950s.

Stanza 3: "Battle": Kathleen Battle (1948–) is a soprano who has appeared at most of the world's major opera houses.

Stanza 3: "Bessie": Bessie Smith (1894–37), "Empress of the Blues."

Stanza 3: "Dinah Washington": Dinah Washington (1924–63), one of the great blues singers.

Stanza 3: "Etta James saying At Last": Etta James (1938–) is a rhythm and blues singer whose career peaked in the 1950s and 1960s; one of her early albums is entitled *At Last.*

Stanza 4: "This is a bus seat": An allusion to Rosa Parks (1913–). See note to "Harvest," page 431.

Stanza 4: "telling young Alex": An allusion to Alex Haley (1921–92), who first heard of his African ancestors through storytelling sessions on long summer nights in Tennessee.

Stanza 6: "CC Riders": "C. C. Rider" is the title of an old folk song that was transformed into a blues song.

Stanza 7: "Peter Salem and Peter Poor": Giovanni means Peter Salem (1750?–1816) and Salem Poor (dates uncertain), both African American heroes in the Revolutionary War Battle of Bunker Hill. Peter Salem is credited with killing Major John Pitcairn. Salem Poor is credited with killing Lieutenant Colonel James Abercrombie; he was cited for heroism by some fourteen officers.

Stanza 7: "the 54th Regiment from Massachusetts": This all-Black Civil War regiment demonstrated unsurpassed courage in its unsuccessful assault on Confederate forces at Fort Wagner in 1863. The regiment is the subject of the 1989 film *Glory*.

Stanza 7: "Emmett Till": Emmett Louis Till (1941–55). See note to "Lorraine Hansberry," page 421.

Stanza 7: "Medgar Evers": Medgar Wiley Evers (1925–63), Civil Rights activist and Mississippi field secretary for the National Association for the Advancement of Colored People (NAACP), was murdered in the doorway of his home in Jackson, Mississippi, on June 12, 1963.

Stanza 7: "Malcolm X": Malcolm X, later Al Hajj Malik Al-Shabazz (1925–65), was assassinated on February 21, 1965, at the Audubon Ballroom in New York City.

Stanza 7: "Martin Luther King, Jr.": Martin Luther King, Jr. (1929–68) was assassinated in Memphis, Tennessee, on April 4, 1968.

"BROTHER BROTHER BROTHER (the Isley Brothers of Lincoln Heights)"

The Isley Brothers, whose father was a professional singer and mother was a pianist, began singing together in the 1950s. Initially there were four brothers: O'Kelly (1937–86), Rudolph (1939–), Ronald (1941–), and Vernon (?–1954), but the core of the group consisted of three after Vernon was killed in an automobile accident. In the mid-1960s, they were joined by their younger brothers Ernie and Marvin and their cousin Chris Jasper.

Stanza 2: "into the Valley": Suburban area north of Cincinnati.

Stanza 4: "progress is the most important product": Advertising slogan used by General Electric.

Stanza 7: "perfecting *SHOUT*": "Shout," a soul music single reflecting gospel roots, was released in 1959 and brought national attention to the group.

Stanza 8: "Joey Dee": Joey Dee and the Starlighters were a white rock and roll group that had two huge hits, "Peppermint Twist" and "Shout—Part 1."

Index of Titles

Index of First Lines

It's a journey, 333
it's funny that smells and sounds return, 169
It's intriguing to me that "bookmaker" is a gambling, 301
it's not the crutches we decry, 238
it's so hard to love, 31
it's so important to record, 60
It starts with a hand, 15
it's wednesday night baby, 114
it was good for the virgin mary, 122
it was very pleasant, 158
it wouldn't have been, 187
i used to dream militant, 106
i usta wonder who i'd be, 62
i've noticed i'm happier, 205
i wanta say just gotta say something, 70
i wanted to sing, 139
i want to take, 161
i want to write an image, 218
I was born in the congo, 125
i will be bitter, 254
i wish i could have been oppressed, 128
i wish i were, 133
I wrote a good omelet, 337
i wrote a poem, 253

like a will-o'-the-wisp in the night, 208
like my mother and her grandmother before, 199

Moving slowly, 326

Nigger, 19
No one asked us, 357
Not more than we can bear, 307

once a snowflake fell, 148
one day, 35